# Feed My Sheep

*by*

*Barry Stebbing*

## A Rainbow that Bridges the Lamb's Book & How Great Thou ART

*"He shall feed His flock like a shepherd; He shall gather the lambs with His arm, and carry them in His bosom...."*
Isaiah 40:11

*"The mediocre teacher tells.*
*The good teacher explains.*
*The superior teacher demonstrates.*
*The great teacher inspires. "*　　　William Arthur Ward

# Introduction

*Feed My Sheep* has been specially created for the homeschooling family and students working in an independent environment. Aspiring to be an artist from an early age makes me aware of the needs of young artists who find themselves in a sometimes isolated situation and with little direction in the arts. One of the main purposes of this book is to inspire! The goal is to make students excited about doing the assignments in this text and to encourage them to complete the book. Inspiration is not easy to instill in a student; however, it is free. There are many forms of inspiration, such as: God, quality music, and a teacher with enthusiasm. Placing these into your art curriculum will help to inspire the students.

After traveling the country and meeting many homeschooled children and their parents, several things seemed to be imperative for a basic art program: drawing, art appreciation, and painting.

There are over 100 drawing lessons in *Feed My Sheep*. Many other subjects will also be introduced to the students in this text: color, penmanship, art appreciation, rules and measurements, painting, academia, creativity, etc.; however, over half of the text will focus on drawing. The drawing program is extensive, covering many techniques and fundamentals that are important for students in this age range to learn (approximately 8 and up). Maintaining the child's joy and interest are of the utmost importance. That is why most of the lessons have been created to be as simple as possible.

Keeping the student's interest and enthusiasm in the lessons is our main desire. From teaching in the classroom, I realize that you can only keep a student's interest on any given subject for a limited period of time. However, there are a variety of assignments and subjects in this program. Each subject is a part of the learning process and complements what was learned in previous lessons. It is still best to structure an art curriculum where the student will be doing a little painting, drawing, penmanship, perspective, etc. during any given month to offer *variety* and *balance*.

Art appreciation is very important to the homeschooling family. Many parents feel awkward and vulnerable when it comes to selecting a proper art curriculum for their children, especially when selecting a program on art appreciation. There are so many to choose from, and art is a subject that can be a questionable investment both in time and finances. A very good source for enriching appreciation of art is your public library! It is a practical and prudent place for creating a program in art appreciation. With this in mind, we have created what we believe to be an efficient and educational program in art appreciation. It is an introduction into the world of art appreciation and should be a practical means of research and comparison. The library offers enriching material in art, and also supplementary materials may be ordered upon request. The encyclopedia also provides an excellent introduction to many of the artists and the different time periods of art.

*"Enthusiasm is one of the most powerful engines of success. When you do a thing, do it with all your might. Put your whole soul into it. Stamp it with your own personality. Be active, be energetic, be enthusiastic and faithful, and you will accomplish your objective. Nothing great was ever accomplished without enthusiasm."*

Emerson

We are also excited about teaching painting! *Feed My Sheep* offers a fresh approach to painting that should be an enlightening asset in the student's growth as an artist. It is a wonderful course for young and old, and can be a good balance for other subjects in the text. However, there are a three main concerns that go along with bringing painting into the home: the mess, the expense, and the lack of an extensive curriculum. Our objective in painting is to be prudent, efficient, and practical. Most of the lessons in *Feed My Sheep* will be done directly in the text, but the painting exercises will be done on the paint cards. The *"Paint Pac"* is a series of painting cards that accompanies the text. Each paint card is printed on a thicker paper than the paper in this text and is more suitable for painting. We will also use poster board for a painting surface because it is easily available, inexpensive, and durable.

Every effort was taken to make this a well-balanced text - both educational and enjoyable. We believe the lessons are easy to follow and will teach many of the fundamentals of art - helping to build a good foundation. The joy should come partially from the assignments, partially from the enthusiasm of the student, partially from the inspiration of the parent, and partially from the environment in the classroom. Remember, the teacher's main goal is to inspire the student *to begin* the work and to encourage the student to *complete* it. We have included two little friends (on the right and left) to assist and encourage you through the text.

Note: Colored pencils seem to be more colorful, enjoyable, and practical for our purposes than any other media. Therefore, our course in color and color theory will be constructed entirely around colored pencils and how to use them. There are many brands to select from, but we recommend choosing a quality set like Scholar Prismacolor. A set of 12 pencils will be good to start with.

# ART Materials

As mentioned, *Feed My Sheep* has been created to be comprehensive, practical, and efficient. A great deal of consideration has gone into structuring the lessons and materials to be cost-effective and instructional. The list may seem lengthy, but you may already have many of the supplies. Also, you do not have to purchase all the materials at one time. You may start by acquiring 1 through 6 on the list below, which will carry your students for some time. When you come to the assignments on painting, you can obtain the other materials.

1. 1 "2B" or "4B" Drawing Pencil
2. 1 Kneaded Eraser
3. 1 12" ruler
4. 1 Black Extra-Fine Marker Pen
5. 1 Box of 12 Colored Pencils
6. 9" x 12" Sketchbook
7. White Poster Board
8. Brushes*
9. Acrylic Paints*

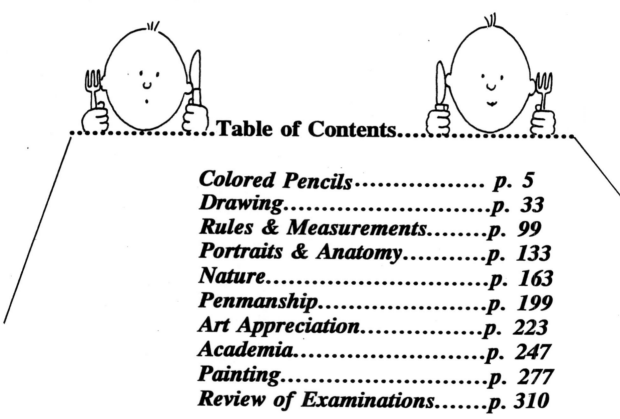

## Table of Contents

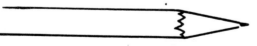

**Pointer:** *You should have three or four brushes: a fine point, or #2 for detail; a medium brush #4; and a larger brush, #6 or #8. A great starting set is the Grumbacher Artcraft packet of three brushes. A larger brush, like a #10, will be helpful for painting in large areas. For paints, we are going to use a pure pigment acrylic paint, like the Accent Blending Colors. We will use 2 oz. containers, and limit our colors to red, blue, yellow, and white.

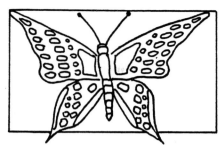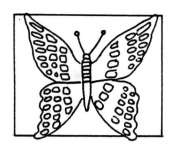

# Colored Pencils

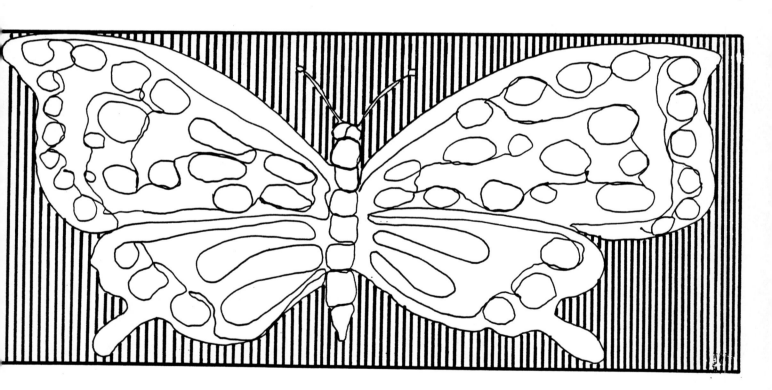

.............................
*"Beauty in art is the delicious notes of color one against the other."*

**Charles Hawthorne**

**Pointer:** Some students will not have the discipline to go through an entire chapter at one time. If your student finds any given chapter to be tedious, go on to another chapter and return to complete the chapter later. Again, it may be best to structure a program by offering the student a little painting, drawing, penmanship, etc. each month.

# Color

Color is a good chapter to start with because you will be able to use your colored pencils throughout the text. Even though many of these assignments are on drawing, you will be asked to draw them with a colored pencil and then color them in. Therefore, they are two-fold lessons: instruction in drawing and color.

We are going to use colored pencils because they are the most practical introduction to color. They are also inexpensive, and unlike oil paints, acrylics, tempera paints, and watercolors, they are not messy and are relatively easy to achieve good results.

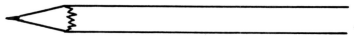

**Pointer:** We will do these lessons in the text; however, a sketchbook is also recommended. Whenever the student does a good job with any assignment, it should be done over again on a larger, better quality sheet of paper. This is a good practice for several reasons. First, it can be the start of a portfolio, displaying the student's best works. Second, it is always good to learn to work big, working small in the text to working larger in a sketchbook is a valuable exercise. Finally, the student may have a greater sense of accomplishment when working on quality paper in a sketchbook. Keeping a sketchbook can be an encouragement for the students to apply themselves and put forth their best effort.

We will use a standard set of 12 colored pencils. You may use any colored pencils that you like, but the pencils of choice for most homeschooling families are the Scholar Prismacolor pencils. They have a high quality of brilliance, soft lead, and are durable enough to last for a long time.

Finally, an inexpensive 9" x 12" sketchbook should do. I like the spiral bound because the paper seems to be more permanently attached than in a hardbound sketchbook.

**Pointer:** It is good to take care of your art materials so they will last. You can store your pencils in their carton when not in use, or put them in a jar. I like to keep mine in a jar because they are easier to reach and will not roll off the table. However, if you are going to store your pencils in a jar, make sure to *always have the points up!* This keeps a nice point on your pencils.

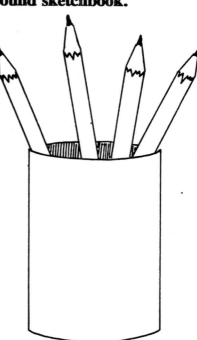

*"Do not have your concert first and tune your instruments afterward. Begin the day with God."*

J.H. Taylor

## Lesson #1: *Coloring with Line*

**A.**

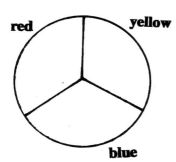

One of the first things we should learn when using colored pencils is how to color with *line*. Coloring with line allows us to see how one color relates to another, and also allows the colors to breathe. This means that there is not a heavy, flat application of color, but rather a light, see-through layer.

**E.**

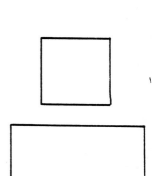

### Color Wheel

A *color wheel* is a chart used to better understand color theory. Do you know how to make a color wheel (A)? See if you can draw your own in E like the one in A. To draw a circle, you may want use the lid of a small jar. Divide your circle into three equal pie shapes using your ruler. Next, we are going to lay in the primary colors.

**B. Yellow Vertical Lines**

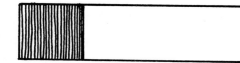

**C. Blue Horizontal Lines**

**D. Red Diagonal Lines**

**Primary Colors:** The primary colors are red, blue, and yellow. Let's practice coloring with straight, parallel lines. For the yellow pie shape, color with vertical lines (B), for the blue pie shape, color with horizontal lines (C), and for the red pie shape, color with diagonal lines (D). You may want to practice drawing each series of lines in the figure boxes first (B, C, & D). Then on the bottom of the page (F), draw some geometric shapes, such as squares, triangles, and rectangles. Draw these shapes with your ruler and a colored pencil. *Always draw with a colored pencil*; lead pencils do not blend well with colored pencils. Finally, color in your shapes with primary colors, coloring some with yellow using vertical lines, some with blue using horizontal lines, and some with red using diagonal lines.

**F.**

**Pointer:** It is very important that you always have a sharp pencil point when using colored pencils. You should notice how delightful it is to color with a sharp point. Please, do not let your points become round and dull. This takes away from the quality of your artwork. It is best to use an electric pencil sharpener, since it will give you the longest and sharpest point.

## Lesson #2: *Primary Colors & Creativity*

For this assignment, we are going to do three exercises: draw some geometric shapes using overlapping, do an abstract contour drawing, and finally, draw a kitchen chair. Also, with each of these assignments, we are going to use primary colors and color with line.

*Overlapping* is drawing one object slightly in front of another object. This gives you a better composition, and creates a sense of depth in your artwork (A). Draw several geometric shapes in figure box B making sure to overlap some of them. Color them in with primary colors, using horizontal, vertical, and diagonal lines.

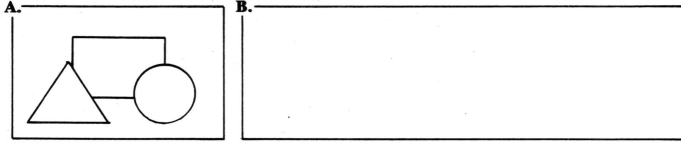

A contour drawing is when you draw one continuous line without lifting your pencil from the surface of the paper. This can create some interesting patterns and designs (C). Take one of your primary colors and do a contour drawing below (D). Again, color in each of the areas with yellow, blue, or red using vertical, horizontal, or diagonal lines.

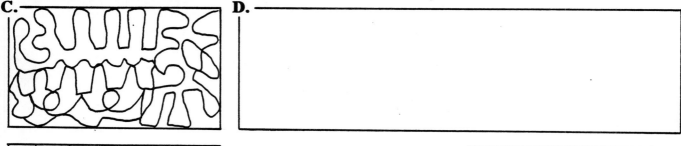

Finally, draw a chair and some other simple objects in your kitchen or dining room using your blue pencil. You may want to draw the design of the grain in your wooden flooring, the carpet, or the tile pattern (E). When finished, color in all of the areas using your primary colors (F).

E.

F.

8

# Lesson #3: *Secondary Colors*

Secondary colors are the colors which go in between the primary colors on the color wheel. They are colors that are made by mixing the primary colors on either side of them. For instance, green would go between yellow and blue, violet would go between blue and red, and orange would go between red and yellow. Again, color in the three primary colors in the color wheel (A), skipping a space between each. Then, place the three secondary colors (green, violet, and orange) in their proper positions. Use the light green, orange, and violet from your pencil set to color them in.

## Mixing Colors

Now, let's see if you can mix your own colors in the figure boxes below. First, place yellow in the leaf, and then add light blue over it to make a green. Take your yellow pencil to blend over the leaf again, and it should create a nice green. Color the balloon yellow. This time add light red and create orange. If it is too red, add some more yellow. In the third square, color the grapes a dark red, and then add blue. Make sure the violet you are making is not too blue or too red. When you are finished, print underneath each, the color combination you used. Some of these mixtures will not create a perfect secondary color – much depends on the colors, the pencils, and the application of color.

A.

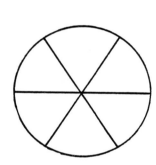   

Draw the scene below (B) in figure box C. Color everything with primary colors, using only your yellow, red, and blue. Mix in your secondary colors, creating green, orange, and violet. See how well you can blend the colors together and how colorful you can make the picture.

B.

C.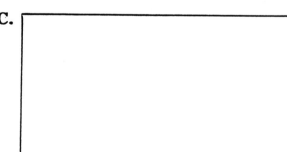

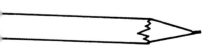

**Pointer:** Remember, some colors will not mix well together. For example, your red and blue pencils may not make a nice violet. However, learning the principles of mixing colors will always come in handy.

*"It's not how much color you use, it's how you use it."* **Philip Jamison**

## Lesson # 4: *Color Chart*

One of the keys to understanding color is being able to create pleasing, colorful pictures by mixing and blending many varieties of the same colors. For this assignment, take your colored pencils and blend them together below, seeing what other colors you can create. Do not use any browns or black in this exercise. Underneath each, print the colors you used. On the bottom of the page, color in your three favorite colors as a special reminder to use them. This color chart will be a good reference whenever you are coloring and need to find just the right color.

Here is a list of abbreviations that you may want to use to label each new color: B - blue, Y - yellow, R - red, O - orange, V - violet, G - green, B/G - blue/green, Y/O - yellow/orange, and so on.

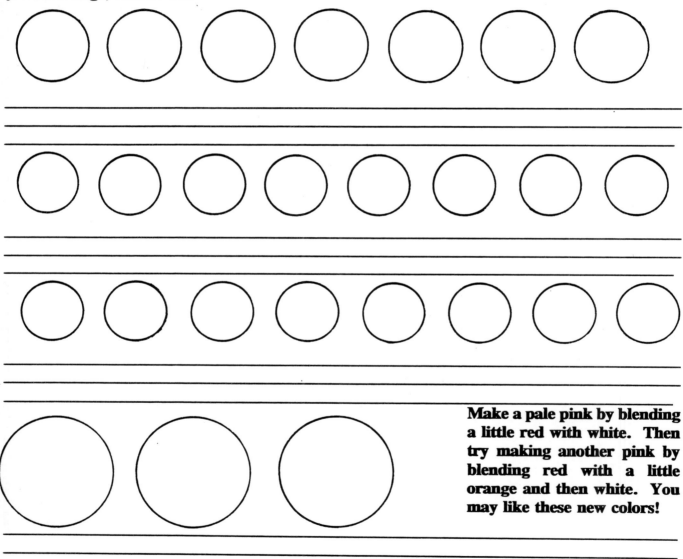

Make a pale pink by blending a little red with white. Then try making another pink by blending red with a little orange and then white. You may like these new colors!

**Pointer:** By mixing other colors, you can make lighter and more colorful browns and blacks. Try Y + O + V for brown, and R + Dk B + a touch of Y for black. Your brown and black colored pencils make excellent drawing pencils; however, use these colors sparingly.

# Lesson #5: *Making A Colorful Apple*

Most students simply color an apple red, a tree green, an orange orange, or a bunch of grapes violet. If you really look at these objects, you will see many other colors in them. When we color or paint, one of our main desires should be to make things colorful. Learn to see colors where others do not.

Let's color an apple below. First, draw the apple with your orange pencil, leaving a little window highlight in the upper right (A). We are going to imagine that sunlight is shining on the apple from the right side, thus having a light side and a shaded side. Now, color the apple with yellow vertical strokes. Do not color over your little window highlight which will remain white (B). Color over the yellow areas with orange vertical strokes. Next, color over your apple with red vertical strokes. For the shaded side, we are going to add dark blue vertical strokes; for the light side we are going to add more yellow. Now, color the entire apple red again, placing most of the red in the middle. When coloring, the purest colors always go in between the light side and the shaded side (C). If you are coloring an apple, the most red will be in the middle. Finally, let's color the shadow of the apple. This shadow is called a *cast shadow*. Lightly draw the entire outline of your cast shadow with a violet pencil. Then color the shadow with long horizontal lines of blue, violet, and a touch of red. Do not outline your shadow with a heavy line; rather let the color be its outline (D). Color the stem orange, yellow, and violet.

**A. Draw an Apple**　　**B. Color with Yellow**　　**C. Light and Shade**　　**D. Cast Shadow**

## My Apple

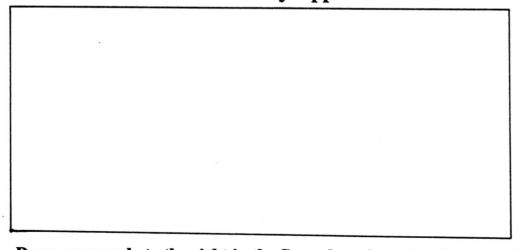

Notice how much color you have placed in your apple! Do you see how nice your colors look without using black for your shadows? It's only a beginning and you will learn more about color in the following lessons.

**Draw your apple to the right in the figure box above, leaving room for your cast shadow.**

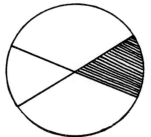

# Lesson #6: *Complementary Colors*

Complementary colors are colors that are across from each other on the color wheel. For instance, green is directly across from red and is its complement. Take a look at your color wheel in Lesson #3, and write down the complements of orange, green, blue, yellow, and violet.

The complement of red is GREEN.

The complement of blue is _____.

The complement of orange is _____.

The complement of yellow is _____.

The complement of green is _____.

The complement of violet is _____.

Learning how to use complementary colors in your artwork will greatly assist in understanding color theory. Complementary colors have two main purposes: for shading or dulling another color, and for use as a background color. For example, if you are going to shade a yellow ribbon, you could use its complement, violet, to blend into the yellow (A). If you wanted to add shading to an orange umbrella, you would blend in its complement, blue (B). Complements are a much better selection of color to shade with than black, and will make your pictures more colorful. Finally, complementary colors can be a good selection for backgrounds. You may want to color the background of the apple in Lesson #5 with its complement, which is green. However, *color your backgrounds lightly.*

Draw the ribbon with your yellow pencil, and then color the entire ribbon yellow. Color over the shaded areas lightly with its complement, violet. If it becomes too violet, you may want to add more yellow on top of it. Next, draw the umbrella with your orange pencil (B). Color the entire umbrella orange, and then color over the shaded area with its complement, blue. Finally, on the bottom of the page, color each entire circle (C) with one of the six colors on the color wheel: red, blue, yellow, orange, violet, and green. Then color over half of each shape with its complement. *Only use a touch of the complement, or it will overwhelm the other color.*

## A. A Yellow Ribbon

## B. An Orange Umbrella

C.

Color the entire shape with one color, and then go over half of it with its complement.

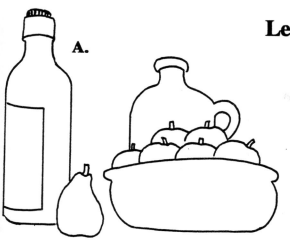

**A.**

# Lesson #7: *Monochromatic*

*Monochromatic* means one color. When you use one color with all its variations from light to dark, it teaches you to appreciate color more and to understand the many different ways you can use color. Some great artists of the past have gone through a "blue period". This was a time when all they did was paint with blue to learn more about color. You might as well go through your blue period too!

Copy the still life (A) below in B. Draw everything in with your light blue pencil. Then color everything with your light blue, dark blue, and white (adding just a little black). Color with line.

## Crosshatching

Another way to shade is by *crosshatching*, which is a series of parallel lines that dissect another series of lines. Crosshatching gives you a darker value. Try this in the square to the right.

**My Blue Period By:** _____

**B.**

**Pointer:** Do not forget to keep your pencils sharp and to shade with line, using either horizontal, vertical, or diagonal lines.

# Lesson #8:  *Green, Green, My Tree is Green*

Let's color a tree!  First, we should learn how to use the color green.  Most students simply use the light green pencil to color objects green.  However, when you are coloring large green areas like fields, hills, and woodlands, only one green will become tedious, and will not look picturesque.  Create a variety of greens in the figure boxes below and print the colors that you used underneath each.  Here are some greens for you to try: yellow + light blue, yellow + dark blue, yellow + light green, yellow + dark green, light green + blue, light green + red (the complement), dark green + blue, dark green + red, yellow + light blue + light green, yellow + dark blue + light green.  Can you mix any other greens?  Keep your chart as a reference for whenever you use green.

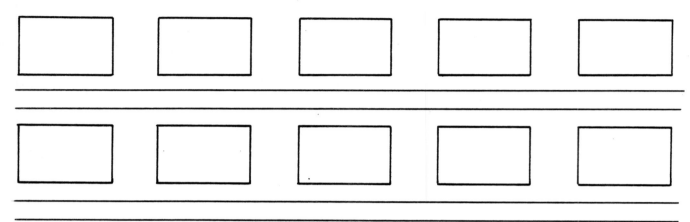

On the next page, draw and color six trees.  Sunlight is yellow, so yellow is the best color to lay in first for all the foliage.  Use diagonal lines (A).  Each tree will have sunlight coming from the right side.  Coloring a tree is similar to the apple you colored in Lesson #5: there is a light side and a shaded side with the most true color (green) being in between the two (B).  Leave the light areas of your tree more yellow than green to show the light.   Then take your light green and gently go over the yellow.  Finally, add dark blue diagonal lines on the shaded side.

Practice by adding colors to the three trees below.  Then draw and color six trees on the next page using six different methods of mixing greens as you did above (You may want to refer to pages 172 and 174).  Make sure to have a light side and a shaded side.  When studying a tree, you will notice that there are small pockets of shaded areas throughout the tree, as well as the entire area on the bottom which is also shaded (C).

**A.  Color Entire Tree Yellow**      **B.  Add True Green to Middle**      **C.  Shade with Blue**

**Tree #1**          **Tree #2**          **Tree #3**

**Tree #4**          **Tree #5**          **Tree #6**

*"A picture is an unusual combination of lines and colors that set one another off."*

Edgar Degas

## Lesson #9: *Warm & Cool Colors:*

Warm and cool colors create a certain mood. Warm colors are: red, yellow, and orange. Warm colors almost feel warm. They are light and lively and can create a bright feeling in your pictures. Cool colors are: blue, violet, and green. They almost feel cool. When using these colors, you can create a calm or peaceful mood.

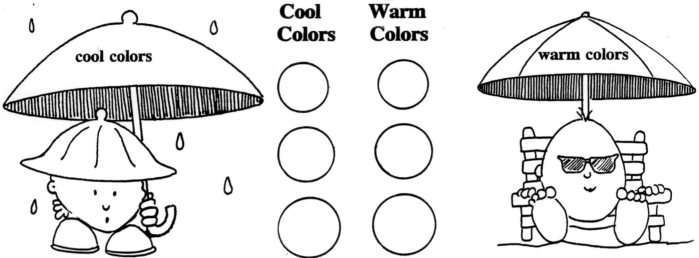

Copy our two friends above in the figure boxes below. See if you can add more to the pictures, maybe some flowers, distant trees, or a road sign. Show that one is somber by using all cool colors. Using vertical lines for coloring will add to the effect. Then in the other figure box, show that it is a warm, cheerful day by drawing and coloring everything with warm colors. Use diagonal lines for coloring. They will give your picture more life and vitality!

## Cool Colors: Somber

## Warm Colors: Bright & Cheerful

# Lesson #10: *Analogous Colors*

**A.**

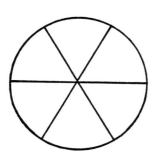

So far, you have learned about primary and secondary colors, complementary colors, and warm and cool colors. Now let's learn about analogous colors. First, color the color wheel with your colored pencils (A). Use horizontal lines to color in all six of the pie shaped sections. *Analogous colors* are any three colors that are next to each other on the color wheel. When coloring with analogous colors, your pictures have a wonderful sense of harmony, and the colors seem to sing together. For instance, you may want to use red, violet, and blue. Or you may select blue, green, and yellow. It does not matter which three you choose as long as they are next to each other. Also, mix and blend the colors!

Draw the two pictures below (B) in the picture boxes (C), coloring each with analogous colors. Make sure to use a colored pencil to draw with and draw lightly.

**B.**

### Analogous Picture #1

**B.**

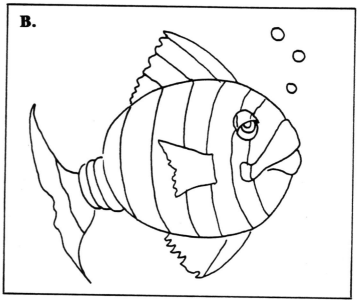

### Analogous Picture #2

**C.**

**C.**

# Lesson #11: *Blue Skies*

Skies are fun to color and not too difficult. However, there are some basic principles that you should know. The lightest part of a sky is near the horizon, where it meets the land or sea. If you look closely at the sky, you may see some very light violet near the horizon. Use your light blue and violet pencils for this area. As the sky ascends, it becomes slightly bluer and darker (A). You may want to add a little more violet and your darker blue for the top part of the sky. Remember, skies are light! The blue in your sky should always be the lightest color in your picture; do not make it too deep a blue. Hold up your picture of a sky and compare it with the actual blue in the sky outside to see if you made it too dark. A good way to start coloring skies is by using the broad side of your pencil.

Let's color a sky in B. This will be a blue sky and there will be no other colors except for some violets and variations of blue. Start with light blue at the horizon, using horizontal strokes. Add a little violet to this. As you color upward in your sky, add some more blue and violet, and then add some darker blue to the top. For the water use your dark blue pencil and horizontal strokes. Remember, the sky is always lighter than anything else, even the water.

**A.**
dark blue

light blue

violet, blue & white

**B.**

horizon line

When drawing or coloring water, use horizontal strokes. Skies should be well blended and smooth to give a flat appearance while the water usually needs a ripple effect to give the appearance of waves. Water is fairly smooth, or blended, near the horizon, but as it comes toward you, there should be the suggestion of waves and ripples made with horizontal lines. The closer the ripples are to you, the further apart the waves. Finally, add a little dark green and some violet to your water to give it depth and color variation.

## Lesson #12: Drawing & Coloring Clouds

Most students have a tendency to outline clouds. However, clouds should be drawn very lightly with either your violet or light blue pencil. Clouds are light and fluffy, like wisps or billows; they are not cotton balls (A). For now, keep the bottom of your clouds flat and make the tops puffy (B). Study the clouds in the sky and see how they are formed.

Also, clouds are not all white. Like apples, trees, and other objects they have form, with light and shaded sides. Notice where the sun is, and place your shading on the opposite side of your clouds. Try to remember how delicate clouds are, letting the blue color of the sky be their outline (C). The shaded side can be colored with violet or light blue (D). Practice by coloring the sky and the shaded side of the clouds below (E).

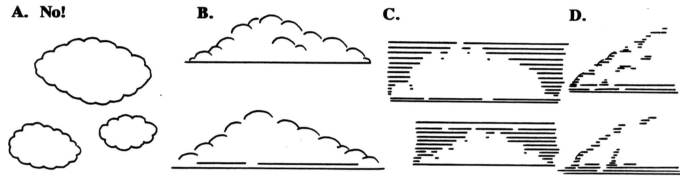

A. No!     B.     C.     D.

Let's draw and color a sky with clouds and a sunset in F. Draw your clouds with a sun just over the horizon on the water (see page 18). Color your sky the same way you colored your sky in the previous lesson. Color your sun with yellow and orange, and its reflection on the water with the same color. Finish by coloring the water the same way as you did on the opposite page.

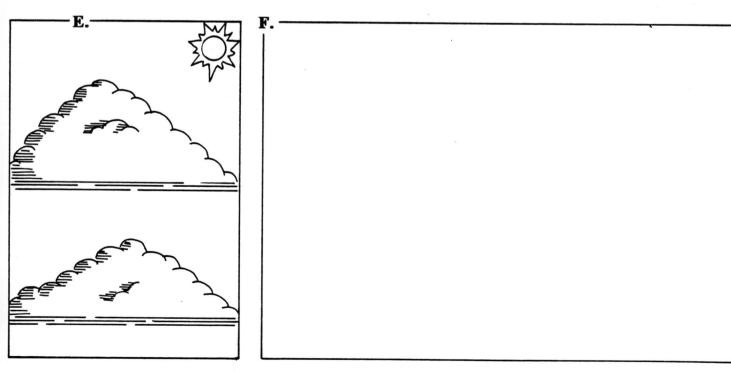

E.     F.

# Lesson #13: *Shading with Color*

Many students simply shade with black. Many times this can make your picture look too harsh and dull. There are so many other colors you can use to give your pictures life and color! In Lesson #6, we discussed complementary colors and how we can use them to color in the shaded sides of objects. For this assignment, you are going to color in the balloons below with a light side and a shaded side. There is a suggestion on the balloons of a light side and a shaded side. For example, a yellow balloon will first be colored entirely yellow, and then violet, its complement, will be added over the shaded area. After you have shaded each balloon with its complement, you may want to go over it again with the original color to lighten up the shaded area. For example, with the yellow balloon you may want to add some yellow over the violet. Color the balloons: red, yellow, blue, orange, violet, and green. Add the complement of each to the shaded side. Leave the little window of light in the upper right of each balloon to show where the highlight is. Finally, color the rest of the picture with an assortment of colors.

H E L P!

# Lesson #14: *Seeing Sunshine*

How do you color sunlight? There are many kinds of light and each one has a different color to it. The sun even casts a different color of light on objects at different times of the day. Claude Monet, a French impressionistic artist, had such a keen eye for light that he could tell the time of day by the color of the sunlight on his white wall. When the sun comes up in the morning the light is a cool yellow, like the yellow of a pale lemon. During the day, the sunlight becomes a brighter warmer yellow like a banana. Finally, near the end of the day, the sun has a yellow-orange light to it. For this assignment, we are going to color the pictures below with three different types of sunlight: morning light with light yellow, afternoon light with just yellow, and evening light with yellow and orange. Color the scenes below, coloring everywhere the sun is shining on the objects with the appropriate color of yellow.

**A. Morning - Light Yellow**    **B. Afternoon - Yellow**

**C. Evening - Yellow and Orange**

*"How good and pleasant it is when brothers live together in unity!"* **Psalm 133:1**

## Lesson #15: *Harmony*

Harmony in color is like harmony in music. Harmony in art means a pleasing arrangement of colors. When we color, we should try to use a little of the same color here and a little of it there, like a bee going from flower to flower. For instance, you may want to use the same blue for the sky, the shaded areas of a road, and the shaded areas of a tree. Harmony means that you may want to use the same yellow for the sun as for the light areas in the grass and trees in the previous lesson. Harmony makes melody both in music and in art.

Do you remember coloring with harmony in any of the previous assignments? How about Lesson #10, when we colored with analogous colors? Color the picture below using harmony with your colors; a little color here and a little color there.

# Lesson #16: *Colorful Combinations*

Can you see colors where others can not? Many great artists have seen color where other eyes have not: a red sky, orange grass, violet trees! For this assignment, let's color things the way they are not! Yellow skies, orange trees, blue grass - creating a world of unusual colors.

Imagine a picture: a dream of wonderful colors; children playing; large bright flowers; shimmering snowflakes; leaves with new patterns blowing across a colorful rainbow. Draw and color the picture below which you have imagined, creating a world of colors!

*"There is a time for everything, and a season for every activity under heaven."*

**Ecclesiastes 3:1**

# Lesson #17: *Coloring a Season*

Let's design a month for a calendar. You can copy from a picture of the season if you like. Use *contour line* to draw all of your detail. To do a contour drawing, do not lift your pencil from the paper from beginning to end. Let your line wander in and out, over and under. Create nice designs and patterns throughout your picture that remind you of that month and season of the year. Make sure to use a colored pencil to do your drawing. When finished, color it with colors that will help express the time of the year, like warm or cool colors. You may even want to use analogous, complementary, or primary colors. Write the calendar month above your picture, and the color theory you used, i.e. analogous colors, on the bottom of the page. Practice your drawing with contour line on scrap paper before beginning.

**My Calendar Month is:** _____

**The Color Theory I Used is:** _____

# Lesson #18: *Coloring an Ol' Western Still Life*

**A.**

Let's do another type of interesting drawing. For the first part of this assignment, use three colored pencils: light brown or orange, dark brown, and black. First, take your light brown or orange pencil, and color the entire figure box (B) to *"tone"* the white paper. When you have completed this, draw in the still life (A) with your dark brown pencil. Next, shade part of the objects with the dark brown. Take your black pencil and add a few darker areas. What do you think of the final picture? Did you create a nice effect, like something out of the old west? In figure box C, color the square orange and use light brown, dark brown, and black to draw and color the picture (A). Finally, color figure box D yellow, and then draw and color any picture you like with light brown, dark brown, and black. How do you like working on a *toned* surface?

**B.**

**C.**

**D.**

# Lesson #19: *Coloring the Tropics!*

For this assignment, we are going to color a flamingo, a porpoise, a hibiscus flower, and a tropical fish. We are going to create some bright colors, and only use brown and black sparingly.

**Flamingo:** In Lesson #4, we practiced mixing new colors. One such color was pink. Lightly color the flamingo below with red. Add a little orange, and then blend with white. What color should the water be? Try a light blue/green. Green is the complement of red and should be a pleasant choice. Select a soft green for the circle in the background that will not overwhelm your beautiful flamingo. Remember, most of the time background colors should be lighter and softer. The tip of his beak is black and his eye is yellow.

Flamingo

Porpoise

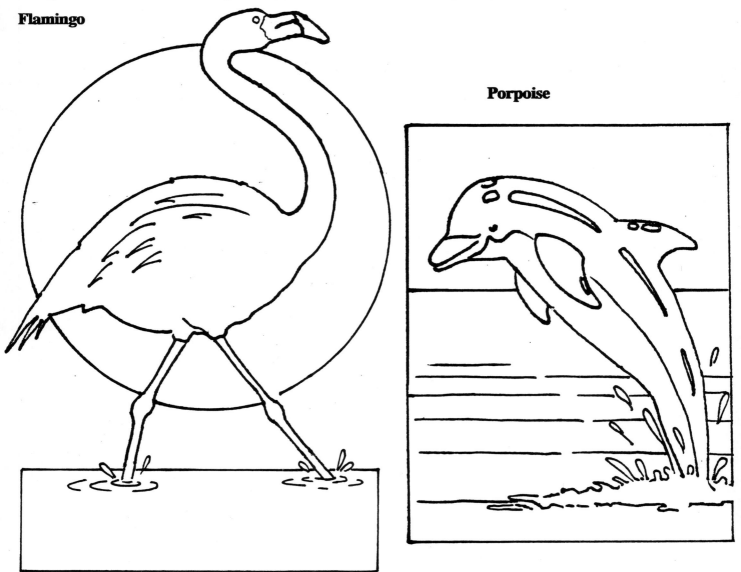

**Porpoise:** To color the porpoise, use light blue, dark blue, and violet. These colors are next to each other on the color wheel. Such colors are called *analogous*. Color the porpoise first with your light blue pencil. Make sure to color with line, either horizontal, vertical, or diagonal. Do not color the highlights around the curve of his back; these will always remain white. Add violet in the middle area, and a dark blue to the underbelly.

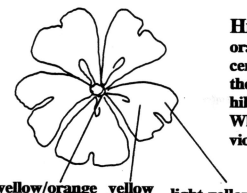

**yellow/orange  yellow   light yellow**

## Hibiscus: Our flower is going to be yellow with a little orange blended into it. The deepest yellow will be near the center of the flower and will become paler near the ends of the petals. Color the hibiscus below, and then draw a hibiscus with a yellow pencil on a plain sheet of white paper. When finished, color in the background with a very light violet.

**Hibuscus**                                    **Angelfish**

**yellow/orange     black**

## Tropical Fish: Our Juvenile Angelfish is going to have yellow/orange stripes. The rest of the body will be black. It is better to lay down light colors first, as darker colors may smear when coloring next to them. Therefore, start with yellow in the stripes, adding a little orange. Finally, color in the black areas. To create a black, you can blend dark blue, red, and dark green.

# Lesson #20:  *A Panorama of Color*

**For this assignment, color the picture below using some of the color theories you have just learned.  Do you remember how to color a sky, a sunset, the clouds, the water, the greens, the flamingo, the porpoise, and the hibiscus?**

**Pointer:**  We do not encourage tracing, but sometimes it may be necessary.  One way of tracing is to tape your picture to a window and then tape another plain sheet of white paper over it.  This will allow you to see the image more clearly.

*"No eye has seen, no ear has heard, no mind has conceived what God has prepared for those who love Him."*

I Corinthians 2:9

**Pointer:** Another way to trace is to take a picture, turn the sheet of paper over, and cover the area you want to trace with pencil lead. This will create a carbon. Then, turning your picture over, place a plain piece of paper under it. Outline your picture with a sharp pencil point, and it will trace onto the bottom sheet of paper.

# Lesson #21: *A Bouquet of Colorful Flowers*

**A.**

Copy the flowers (A) and color them below (B). How are you going to shade your flowers? What colors are you going to use: primary colors, warm and cool colors, analogous colors, etc? What color are you going to use for light on your flowers and leaves? Are you going to create harmony with your colors? Before starting, write the color theory you are going to use below, and explain why you want to use these colors.

**B.**

*"If you get simple beauty and naught else, you get about the best thing God invents."*

Robert Browning

## Lesson #22: *Coloring the Cover*

Have you noticed the colors on the cover of this book? Let's see if you can color a nice picture below. First, color the sky blue just as you did in Lesson #11. Keep it light, using your light blue pencil. For the rainbow, color each band a different color. Then, use a light blue/green for the trees far back on the horizon, a yellow green for the grass, and another green for the trees next to the school house.

Color the school house red, but add some orange to it to give it more color. Use several different greens for the leaves and petals that frame the picture. Color the flowers with soft warm colors. For instance, instead of a red flower, color it orange and red. Color some flowers violet. Color the sunflowers around the arch with yellow and a little orange.

How do you color a white sheep? The same way you colored a white cloud in Lesson #12. On the shaded sides of the sheep, use a little violet and blend with white.

When you are finished, draw the entire picture on a plain white sheet of paper and color it in. Start your drawing lightly. Be creative with your colors!

**Pointer:** It is always good to do a practice study of the colors you are going to use before beginning your finished picture. One way of doing this is to make several copies of the original, and experiment with your colors on these copies before doing your finished work.

# Lesson #23: *Color Examination*

**Use your colored pencils and color in all of the answers below (4 points each):**

1. The complement of red is ◯

2. The complement of violet is ◯

3. The complement of green is ◯

4. The complement of blue is ◯

5. The complement of yellow is ◯

6. The complement of orange is ◯

**Color in the blanks (5 points each):**

7. The primary colors are red, yellow and [          ] .

8. Three colors that are next to each other on the color wheel are [     ][     ][     ] colors.

9. The only color that cannot be made by mixing the primary colors is [               ] .

10. Yellow and blue make [              ] .

11. Blue and red make [          ] .

12. Red and yellow make [         ] .

13. The warm colors are [         ] , [         ] and [         ] .

14. The cool colors are [         ] , [         ] and [         ] .

15. Two colors that should not be used in the beginning are [         ] and [         ] .

**Color the pictures below using the proper color theory (5 points each):**

**16. Analogous Colors**

**17. Monochromatic Picture**

**18. Cool Colors**

19. On a plain piece of paper, draw and color a picture of the sun setting over a farmland with trees, barn, fence, etc. What color theory are you using, and why? (16 points)

(Answers on page 310)

# Drawing

*"I can't tell you how happy I am to have taken up drawing."* **Vincent Van Gogh**

# Drawing

Before beginning our course in drawing, let's discuss several pointers that will assist you in learning to draw.

**Pointer I:** Use a drawing pencil. A regular pencil has a hard lead and a light line, whereas a drawing pencil has a soft lead and a darker line. Use either a "2B" or "4B" pencil. They are both fairly dark in line and good to draw with. You will find the marking "2B" or "4B" on the side of the pencil.

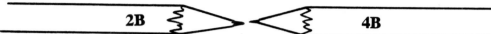

**Pointer II:** Have a sharp pencil point. Your drawings will look much nicer when the lines are crisp, made from a sharp point. An electric pencil sharpener will give you the best point on your pencils for drawing.

**Pointer III:** Hold your drawing pencil correctly. It is best to hold your pencil as far back from the point as is comfortable. You may think you have more control holding the pencil close to the point, but actually, you will have more control holding your pencil farther back. Holding a pencil in this manner also gives you more freedom in drawing, and can make drawing a more enjoyable experience.

**Pointer IV:** Try not to erase. When you get in the habit of using erasers, you lose your confidence as an artist. It is better to draw lightly, and then after sketching everything the way you want, go over it again with darker lines.

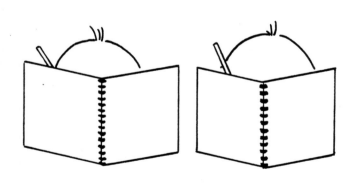

**Pointer V:** Have a sketchbook. Every time you do a good drawing, it should be drawn again in your sketchbook. Your sketchbook should be a display of your best work. Have respect for your sketchbook; it is something to show to others. Many of the assignments in *Feed My Sheep* are to be done directly in the text. However, some of the figure boxes are small. It would be good to redo some of your best drawings on larger paper in your sketchbook.

**Pointer VI:** Practice drawing each day. Also, it is good to study from life and not to copy. Try to draw objects that are in a good light, so you can study form.

*"In the beginning God created the heavens and the earth. Now the earth was formless and empty...."*

## Lesson #24: *Beginning Drawing*

In the beginning, *"the earth was formless and empty"*. For the art student, beginning means starting with an *"empty"* piece of paper..."*without form."* Many people believe a person is born with a *God-given talent*. This may be true to a certain degree, but drawing can be learned just like science, math, and English. It is more a matter of hand-eye coordination, seeing what is before you and being able to control your pencil to make it do what you want it to do.

For today's assignment, we are going to learn how to make *ellipses* and *lines*, two very important fundamentals in learning how to draw. This lesson may not be too much fun, but neither is taking your vitamins; however both are good for you! First, draw straight lines in the boxes below. All these lines are to be drawn *freehand*, which means without the use of a ruler. Do not go too fast, but see if you can draw controlled, straight lines. In the first square, draw horizontal lines; in the second square, draw vertical lines; and in the last one, draw diagonal lines. Remember, keep your lines parallel and close together.

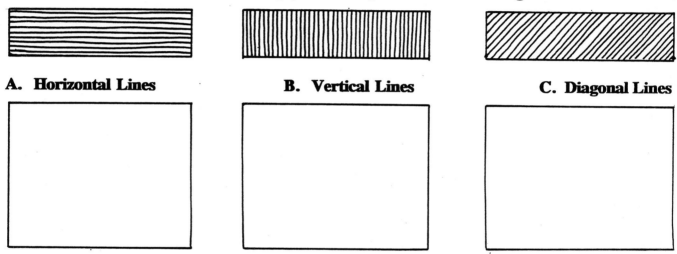

**A. Horizontal Lines**          **B. Vertical Lines**          **C. Diagonal Lines**

An *ellipse* is a circle seen on an angle. Look at a roll of tape or a jar, and you will see they are made up of ellipses. To draw an ellipse, lock your hand, wrist, and arm together, and make an elliptical motion with your pencil above the paper. Bring your pencil down and lightly draw the ellipse, going around four or five times. When finished, you should have the shape of an ellipse. Fill the figure box below with ellipses.

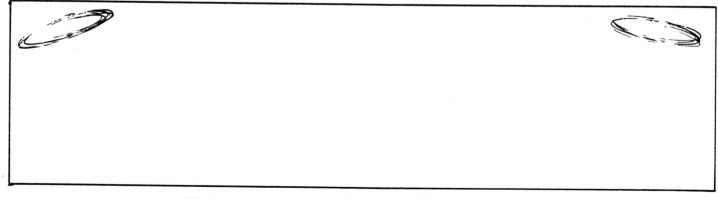

**Pointer:** Drawing lines and ellipses are two of the best exercises that you can do to improve your drawing skills. Practice them regularly.

# Lesson #25: *Long Lines & Circles*

### A. No!

### B. No!

Now let's see if you can make some long, horizontal lines. Draw the lines with control, and keep them as straight as possible. Do not stop every inch or so (A), and do not draw the lines so fast that you have no control (B). Draw your freehand lines in the long figure box below (C).

**Figure Box C**

Next, we are going to make long, thick and thin lines. To make a thick and thin line, put more pressure on the pencil, and then less pressure, more pressure, less pressure, and so forth. Thick and thin lines can create delicate lines for drawing things like a glass vase, tree limbs, or flowers. Draw a series of long, thick and thin lines in figure box D.

**Figure Box D   Thick & Thin Lines**

## Circles:
## Freehand Circle

## Traced Circle

**F.**

**E.**

There are basically three ways to draw a circle: freehand, tracing, or using a compass. For this assignment, we are going to practice drawing circles by using the first two approaches: freehand and tracing. To draw freehand circles, use the same principle as you did for drawing ellipses - lock your hand, wrist, and arm, and lightly go around four or five times to create the shape of a circle (E).

To trace a circle, find a coin, bottle lid, or other round object approximately the size of the circle you desire. Hold it securely on the paper with your finger, and bring your pencil point all the way around it without stopping (F). Practice drawing circles freehand (G), and by tracing them with an object (H).

**G.**                                          **H.**

# Lesson #26: *Ellipses Go Around and Around*

**Look at the lid or other object that you used to trace in Lesson #25. It is round. However, if you hold it at an angle, it becomes more oval or like an *ellipse*. Drawing ellipses will help show that objects are *round*. For this assignment, find five objects which are round in shape: jars, cups, glasses, etc. Place them on the table in front of you, and draw each, making sure to sketch every ellipse that you see in the objects. Start by drawing lightly.**

**Jars**  **Cups**  **Glasses**

# Lesson #27: *Ellipses & Umbrellas*

Can you draw an umbrella? Start by drawing an ellipse (A). Then, place a round top on it (B). Next, draw a light, straight line from the top down through the center of the ellipse (C). Finish your umbrella by putting a little tip on the top, making the pole with two controlled lines and giving it a handle. Finally, draw designs on the top (D). For this lesson, fill the figure box below with floating umbrellas. Make some bigger than others. Draw them with one of your colored pencils, and then color them in. Use lines and darker values to show the inside of each umbrella.

A.          B.          C.          D.

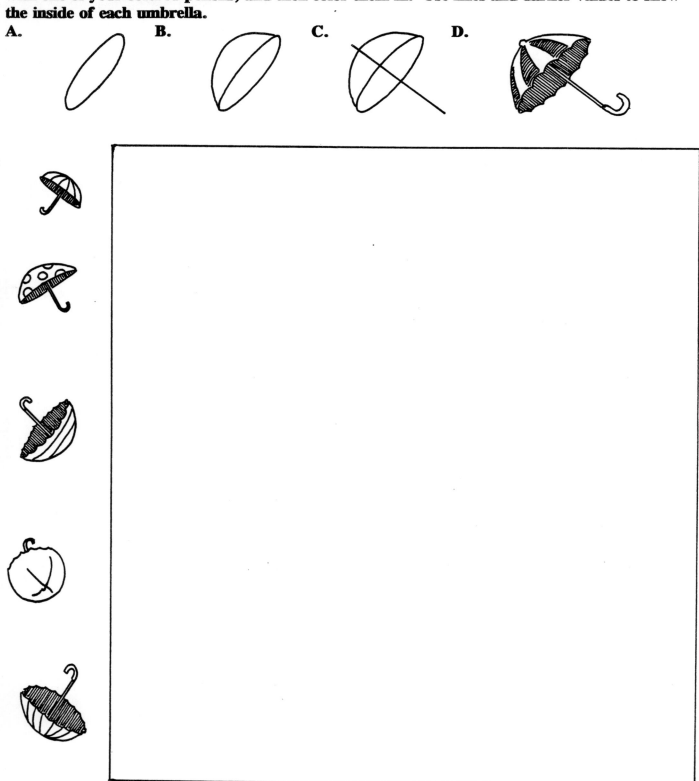

## Lesson #28: *Around the Head it Goes*

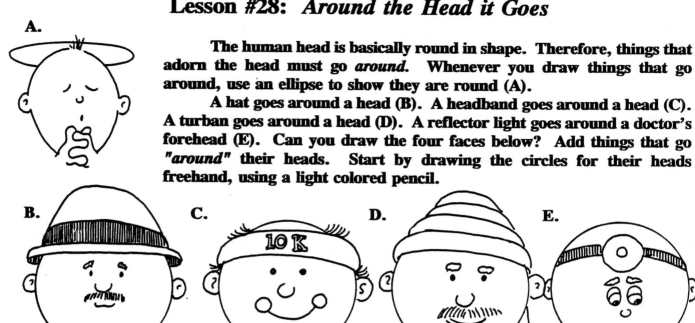

**A.**

The human head is basically round in shape. Therefore, things that adorn the head must go *around*. Whenever you draw things that go around, use an ellipse to show they are round (A).

A hat goes around a head (B). A headband goes around a head (C). A turban goes around a head (D). A reflector light goes around a doctor's forehead (E). Can you draw the four faces below? Add things that go *"around"* their heads. Start by drawing the circles for their heads freehand, using a light colored pencil.

**B.**     **C.**     **D.**     **E.**

# Lesson #29: *Circles & Funny Faces*

**Fill the next page with funny faces using as many circles as possible. Trace some of the circles, and make some of them freehand. See if you can create some interesting faces by using circles, polka dots, and dots for the eyes, ears, noses, glasses, clothing, and so forth.**

*"You who are simple, gain prudence; you who are foolish, gain understanding."*

✸ Funny Round Faces ✸ Funny Round Faces ✸ Funny Round Faces ✸

# Lesson #30: *What's in the Pantry?*

Let's fill grandma's pantry with jars of preserves. Draw a label on each jar to show what's in it: pickles, jam, beets, relish, etc. Remember, a label goes around a jar the same way a hat goes around a head (A). Place some jars in front of you to study.

Fill the shelves below with jars - big jars, small jars, fat jars, and thin jars. Place some partially in front of others. This is called *overlapping*. When you overlap, lightly draw the entire objects, even the parts you can not see, and then darken just the parts you see. This will help you draw the correct form of each jar. Also, stack some on top of others (B).

Make sure to draw labels on all the jars by drawing ellipses (C). If you want to letter the labels, draw ellipses within the labels as guidelines (D).

A.

B.

C.

D.

# Grandma's Pantry

# Lesson #31: *Cups & Bottles*

In the very first lesson on drawing, we learned how to draw lines and ellipses. Let's see what we have remembered from that lesson, trying to use those techniques in this assignment.

First, let's use an *axis line*. An axis line is a straight, vertical or horizontal line used as a guideline when drawing an object. The axis line assists in keeping your objects straight up and down, and not looking like the leaning Tower of Pisa (A). An axis line is also a light guideline used to make sure the same proportions are drawn on both sides of the object (B). Remember to draw every ellipse, and use controlled lines to draw the sides of your objects (C).

**A.**

**B.**

**C.**

**D.**

Draw a cup in D and a bottle in E. Use a vertical axis line for each. You may use a ruler for drawing your axis lines, but do not use a it for anything else in your drawing. Keep your axis lines light. They are supposed to be a part of your drawing, but not a big part. You may want to use your yellow colored pencil for this.

A *still life* is an arrangement of inanimate objects or things that do not move. In F, place two cups in front of a jar and glass, and draw this still life.

**E.**

**F. Still Life with Cups & Bottle**

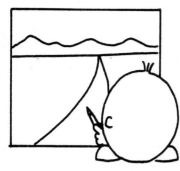

# Lesson #32: *Freehand Cubes*

A cube is a 3-dimensional drawing of a square. It shows depth by giving the impression of the sides fading into the distance on a piece of paper. Paper is 2-dimensional: wide and long. A standard sheet of paper, like the paper in this text, is 8 1/2" wide and 11" long. Unfortunately, you cannot step into a piece of paper to show depth or a third dimension. Therefore, we have to create the illusion of *depth*, by making things look like they recede or go back into the distance. One way to do this is by using *perspective*. This is a term which we will study later, but for now let's see if we can draw cubes and give them the illusion of depth.

Draw some 3-dimensional cubes below. First, draw a square (A) in the figure box on the bottom of the page (E). Then draw the three sides going back into the distance (B). Make sure these lines are all angled to show that somewhere back in the distance they will connect. If one line is angled in the wrong direction, it will throw off your entire box (C). Make controlled lines for the sides of your cubes (D).

A.    B.                        C.    *No!*              D.

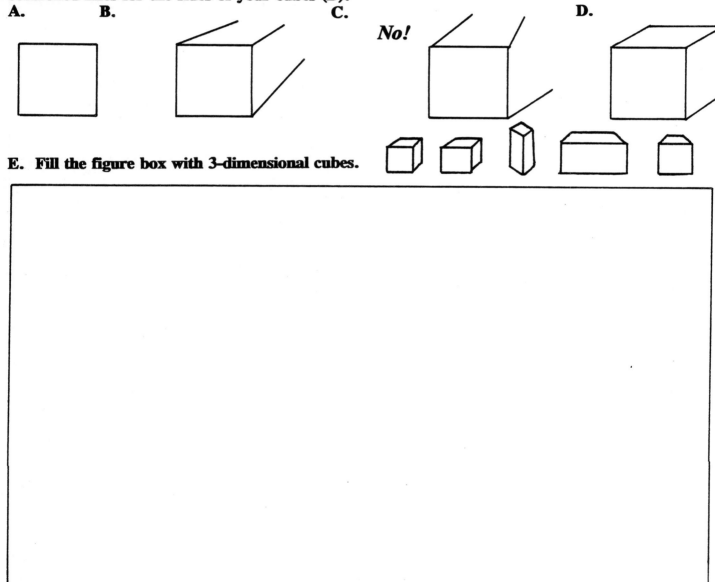

E. Fill the figure box with 3-dimensional cubes.

# Lesson #33: *Transparent & Opaque*

*Transparent* means being able to see through something. For instance, glass is transparent. *Opaque* means that light cannot pass through and is the opposite of transparent. Black paint on a window would make it opaque. Today we are going to create more cubes, making some of them transparent and some of them opaque. A transparent cube will show all the sides and everything within the structure, as if it were made of glass (A). An opaque cube is like a cardboard box, and you cannot see within its confines (B). When drawing cubes and boxes, all the lines must be parallel, except those which recede into the distance. For instance, the top and bottom horizontal lines are parallel (C), and the side. vertical lines will be parallel (D). Using these principles of freehand perspective to show depth, draw an aquarium, a toaster, and dresser drawers on the bottom of the page. One last thing: when drawing the sides of your objects that are going back into the distance, end them wherever you like to make your object appear larger or smaller (E).

A.      B.      C. **Parallel Lines**      D.      E.

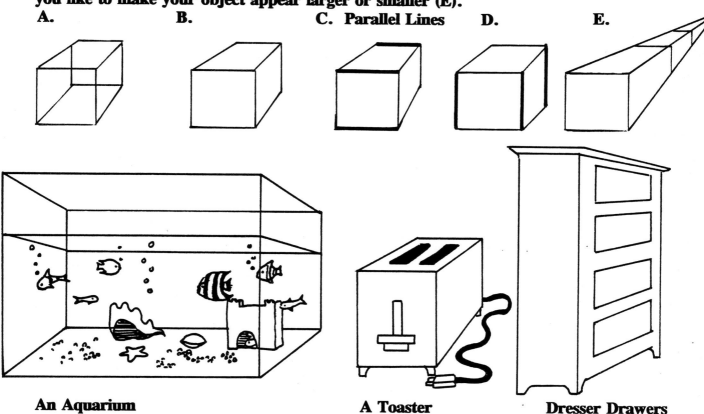

**An Aquarium**          **A Toaster**          **Dresser Drawers**

# Lesson #34: *Light & Values*

Let's add light and shade to 3-dimensional boxes. By placing a small sun to the right (A), we'll know the direction of our light source. If your light is coming from the right, you will shade the left side of your objects (B). For these assignments, use *line* for shading. In drawing, you do not want to make the shaded areas too heavy or too dark. Line is good to use because it makes shaded areas transparent.

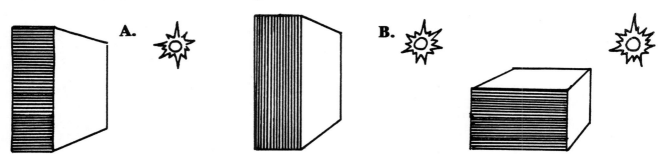

Create some 3-dimensional boxes on the next page, using a light source and shading part of each with *line*. Have at least one box with an open top, and make the value inside the box darker by shading with crosshatching (C). *Crosshatching* is a technique in drawing where one set of parallel lines crisscrosses another to create a darker value. Draw four boxes *freehand* (without the use of a ruler) on the top of the next page, shading one side of each. Then, on the bottom of the page, draw four more boxes, but use a ruler to create each box and for the lines you use for shading (D). Drawings that are done with rulers or any other mechanical devices are called *technical drawings*.

**C.**

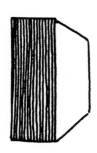 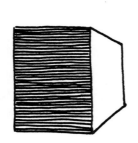 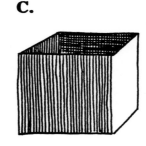 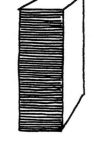

---

**D. Add Technical Lines**

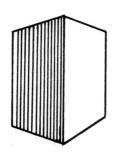 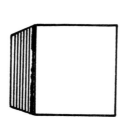 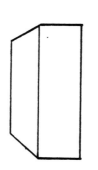 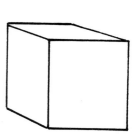

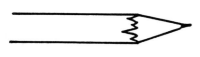

**Pointer:** Remember, the lines on the sides of your cubes or boxes are drawn at an angle to show that somewhere in the distance they will connect.

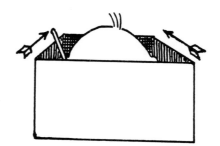

**Draw four 3-dimensional boxes above the line. Do these *freehand*. Next, draw four 3-dimensional boxes below the line using a ruler. Place some boxes in front of you to copy.**

# Lesson #35: *Texture*

*Texture* is the visual, surface appearance of something. For instance: a soft, spongy surface like a sponge; a coarse, granular surface like a tree trunk; or a shiny, metallic surface like a tea kettle. There are several ways to create texture when drawing. One is with thick and thin lines, which we learned in Lesson #25. Let's practice thick and thin lines again below (A), just to make sure you know how to draw them. Remember, the more pressure you place on your pencil point, the darker and thicker the line; the less pressure, the lighter and thinner the line. Draw long, horizontal lines going straight across, thick to thin, thick to thin.

**A. Thick & Thin Lines**

To draw a knot in a piece of wood, start with a small ellipse that is pointed on each side (B), and then continue out making larger and larger pointed ellipses. Move your pencil from thick to thin, thick to thin. Practice drawing a knot on textured wood in (C).

**B.** 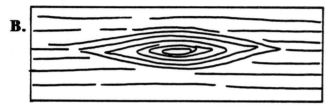    **C.**

**D.**

Let's add some texture to a tree trunk. The light will be coming from the right, so the shaded side will be on the left (D). *Always place more texture in the shaded areas, and less texture in the light areas.* Use long, thick and thin, vertical lines to shade the tree and to show that the *texture* of the tree is bark. You may even want to draw a knot (E).

**E. Draw Tree Trunk Here**

Short, quick strokes are another way of adding texture, like when you are drawing grass. It is important to remember that these strokes always go away from the object (F). With a sharpened green pencil, draw some grass below (G), and then complete the textured effect on the porcupine with an extra fine black marker (H).

**F.**     **G.**     **H.**

48

# Lesson #36: *Fuzzy, Fluffy Creatures*

**A.**

**B.**

The same principle applies for furry animals, like a cat, dog, or mouse; the strokes move away and are thinner near the end (A). Whiskers are the longest strokes on the animal and should be done with one quick movement away from the face. Practice this long, quick stroke on a scrap piece of paper. When drawing detail in fur, it is the same principle as drawing bark on a tree; always add more texture in the shaded areas. Notice the face of the porcupine (A) and the body of the cat (B). In the areas where light is on their bodies, there is very little detail or texture.

Do not outline your animals with a heavy dark outline (C). When drawing animals with fur, use thick and thin lines going around their bodies and let the texture of the fur be the outline (D). Draw the three animals below. Sketch your animals lightly, and then add the fur as a darker detail over your guidelines.

**C.** *No!*   **D.**

# Lesson #37: *What Goes Around*

**Many students do not know how to draw things that go *around*. For instance, a rope that wraps around a pole is thicker than the sides of the pole. It is not flat. Remember this when drawing: a hand going around a glass; a rope going around a pole; a monkey's tail going around a limb. All have to be thicker than the object they go around. Let's draw the three animals below on the next page, showing their hands and tails wrapping around objects. To give your drawing more impact, you may want to add *contrast*. Contrast is the difference between light areas and dark areas. Notice how the monkey stands out more because a darker value was placed behind him, defining his image. Start by drawing the animals very lightly. Shade with line, show more texture in the shaded areas. Use thick and thin lines.**

**Pointer:** If your drawing starts to smear, you may want to place a small piece of paper under your hand.  This will keep both your drawing and your hand clean.

# Lesson #38: *Drawing a Birdhouse*

**A.** *No!*

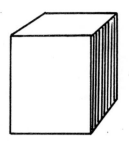

**B.**

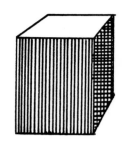

Let's see if we can put together several of the principles just learned and build a birdhouse. First, draw a freehand cube, and then add another value to it by shading. *Values* are the different gradations from light to dark that you use in your drawings. Do not simply have a light side and a dark side (A), but allow for many different gradations of light and dark (B). Do a value study (C) from light to dark, just like the one below (D). The lightest area is the white of the paper, and the darkest value can be done with crosshatching, like the boxes on page 46.

**C. Value Study**

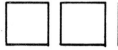  **D.**

On to the birdhouse. Although your finished drawing will be on page 55, practice these exercises on page 54. First, we are going to learn about your *vantage point*, which means the position from which you view something. If the birdhouse is up high, we will be looking up at it and will see the bottom. Therefore, when we draw the cube for the birdhouse, we will draw it so the bottom will be showing (E). Review Lesson #32 on drawing cubes. Using a ruler, draw a vertical line down from the center of the bottom of the cube, and another vertical line dividing the side (F). One line is for the pole to the birdhouse, and the other is a guideline for the center of your A-frame roof and doorway.

**E.**

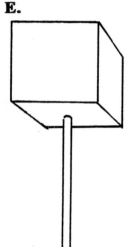

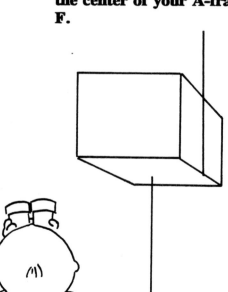

**F.**

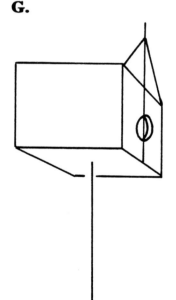

**G.**

**H.**

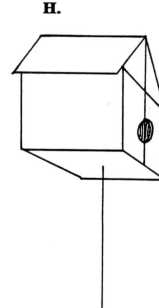

Now, complete your roof by making a triangle, connecting to the top of the vertical line you have just drawn (G). Add the top horizontal line to the roof, making sure it is parallel with the bottom lines. Finally, draw the slant for the rear of the roof at the same angle as the front (H).

*Jesus replied, "Foxes have holes and birds of the air have nests, but the Son of Man has no place to lay his head."*

Matthew 8:20

I.

Place an entrance in the front of the birdhouse. This is made by drawing a long ellipse using a vertical guideline as its center (I). You will be able to see inside part of the hole because of your *vantage point*. Place another ellipse next to the first one to show the thickness of the wood. Make the pole thicker by adding another long, straight line down the side of the vertical guideline you drew in the beginning. Draw the sun in the upper left corner. Add texture by placing thick and thin vertical lines on the shaded side of your birdhouse. Remember, more texture on the shaded side, less on the light side. There will also be some shading on part of the pole (J) and the bottom of the birdhouse. Finally, your darkest values will be the bottom of the birdhouse and inside the doorway. Use crosshatching for these areas. Draw and color your birdhouse on the next page with colored pencils.

J.

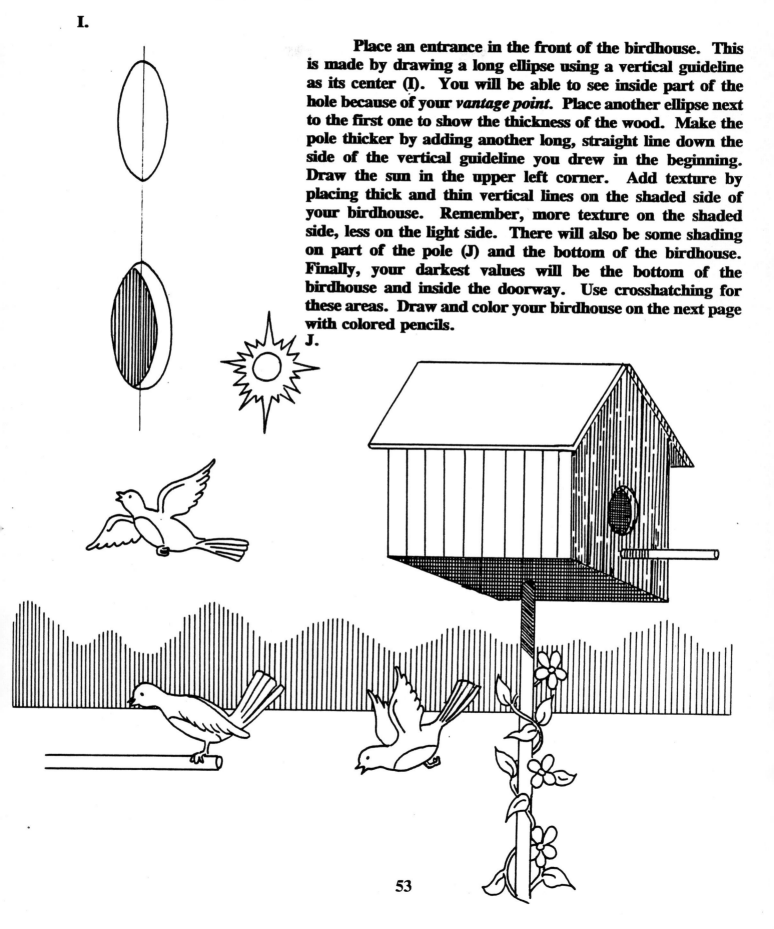

53

*"There is nothing in which the birds
differ more from man than the way in which they
can build and yet leave a landscape as it was before."*

Robert Lynd

**My Birdhouse by:** _____ **Date:** _____

**Practice drawing your birdhouse above.**

# Lesson #39: *What About Birds?*

Now we are ready to draw and color an entire scene with a birdhouse, sky, trees, and even a bird! Let's give our composition a foreground, middle ground, and background. As mentioned in the first chapter, things in the foreground are larger and have more color, whereas things in the background are smaller with less color. We will place a bird on a branch in the foreground, the birdhouse in the middle ground, and the distant trees and hills in the background. Notice the illustration on page 53.

*Composition* is defined as the way you compose or place things in your picture. It is always good to have something looking into the picture instead of away from it. For instance, a bird on the left side of your picture should lead the eye into the artwork (A). A bird on the right should be looking in, bringing the eye back into the picture (B).

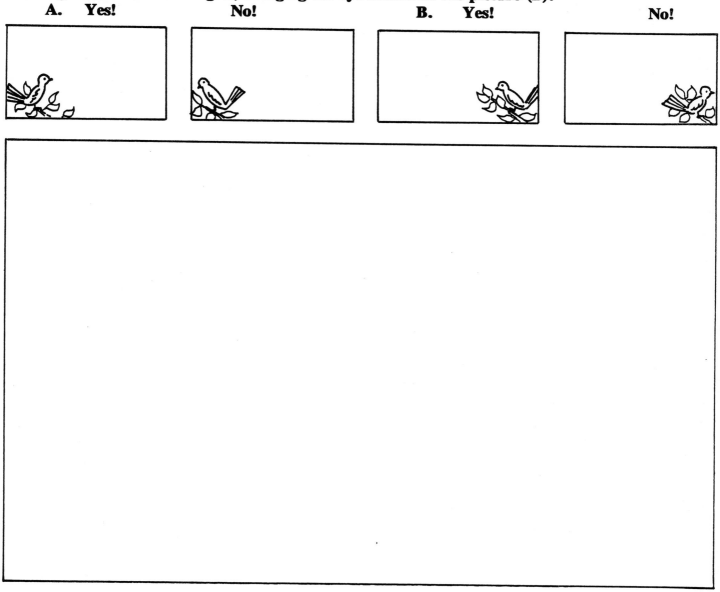

A.   Yes!                    No!                    B.   Yes!                    No!

Draw your picture above with a violet pencil. You may want to practice your colors on scrap paper before completing your final picture. Make the roof red and the pole light blue. For the darkest areas of the birdhouse, use dark blue, dark green, and red. Can you draw and color some flowers winding their way up the pole? Again, refer to page 53.

# Lesson #40: *Drawing Eggheads*

**A.**

Can you draw an egg? It seems simple, but it's not as easy as it looks. However, it is similar to drawing an ellipse. Place several eggs in front of you, and see if you can draw them on the top of page 57. Take your time. Start off lightly and go around four or five times to create the proper shape. Then go around your best lines to form the egg (A).

Now let's draw some egg people. Sketch them standing in line receiving tickets for the ice skating rink. Overlap your egg people, placing one slightly in front of another. Overlapping will help create depth. Remember, when overlapping, draw the entire object lightly and darken just the area that the eye can see. This will give your objects better form (B). Give them funny faces, feet, and hands. Add bowties, hats, glasses, and other accessories! Draw your funny egg people on the bottom of the next page.

**B.**

56

**Egg People Going To The Ice Skating Rink**

*"Life is music if one be rightly in tune and in time."* **Anonymous**

## Lesson #41: *Drawing Eggheads with Texture*

Let's draw some egghead portraits with texture. There are three ways to draw a portrait: the front view (A); the three-quarters view (B); and the side view or profile (C). For this assignment, we are going to draw our egghead characters in the front view. Can you add texture to your eggheads? You may want to try adding beards, mustaches, whiskers, eyebrows, hair, etc. Draw at least five eggheads below.

**A. Front View**     **B. Three-Quarters View**     **C. Profile**

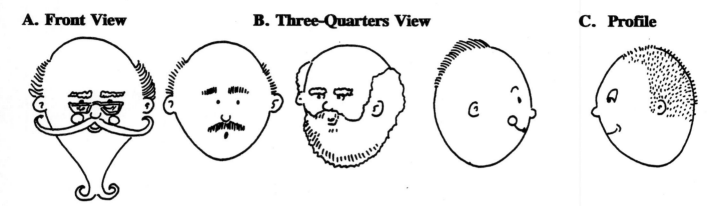

# Lesson #42: *Drawing a Picket Fence*

Today you are going to do a drawing of a picket fence. Use a light blue pencil and your ruler for this assignment. When doing a freehand drawing, try to draw everything without the use of a ruler. This will teach *control*. However, we will use a ruler for this exercise to keep the lines straight. First, set up guidelines for the top and bottom of your picket fence, drawing horizontal lines across the paper (A). Space your pickets, measuring at a distance of 1" apart, and marking each on the top and bottom guidelines (B). Next, draw a vertical axis line down from each of the 1" markings (C). Your picket posts are going to be 1/2" wide, so mark 1/4" to one side of your axis line, and 1/4" to the other side (D). Come down 1/4" from your top guideline, and draw another horizontal line parallel with your top and bottom guidelines. This is for the points of your picket fence (E). Finally, connect the corners to the top point of the fence to make each point. Practice drawing some more pickets on the fence below.

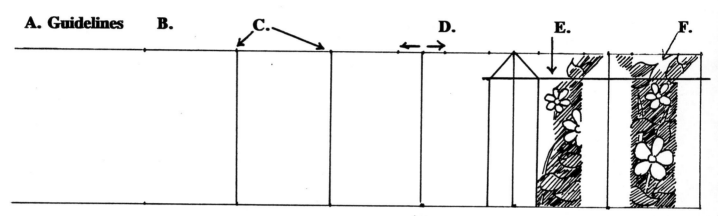

Finally, draw your own picket fence. Start by drawing it lightly with your light blue pencil in the figure box below. Be sure you have a sharp point. *Do not outline* your fence with dark lines when you are finished, but color some greens behind your fence like bushes or trees. This will give a nice contrast between the light of your fence and the dark of the vegetation, and will also give you an outline for your fence without having to draw it (F).

*"Vision is the art of seeing things invisible."* **Jonathan Swift**

## Lesson #43: *Negative Space*

*Negative space* is the area around your subject matter. For instance, when drawing the handle on a tea cup, the student should see the negative space inside the handle, as well as the handle itself in order to draw it correctly (A). The same goes for the picket fence in Lesson #42. If we can see the shapes that go inside and around the fence, it will help us to draw the fence more accurately.

Today we are going to draw a still life of cups and mugs. Find three cups or mugs of different sizes and shapes, and arrange them so they overlap each other. Place the handles to the sides to see the shapes within each handle. Draw your cup still life below (B) with your violet pencil. Draw a light straight axis line for each cup to keep your objects balanced when drawing them. Sketch as many ellipses as necessary to show the cups are round. Draw a horizontal table line behind the cups. Color them with cool colors: violet, light blue, and dark blue. Use vertical lines for shading, and use crosshatching inside the cups for a darker value. Finally, color the background lightly with orange, light blue, and dark blue.

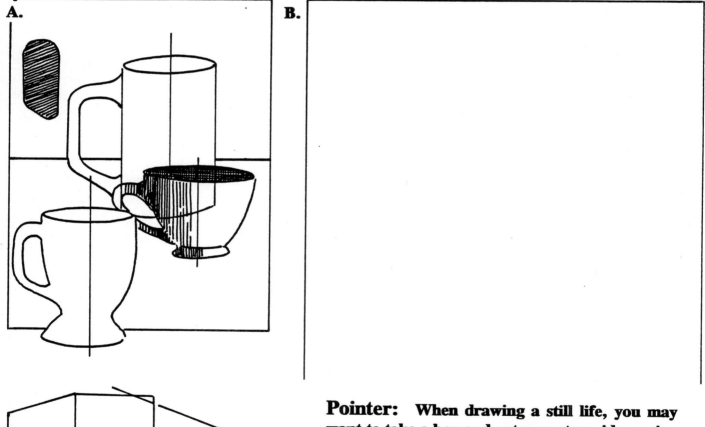

**Pointer:** When drawing a still life, you may want to take a box and cut away two sides, using the remaining two sides and bottom to make a *shadow box*. Take black paper and tape it to the sides and bottom of the box. Then, situate objects in the box the way you would like to draw them. Finally, direct a good light on your subject matter, and you will have something exciting to draw.

# Lesson #44: *Cast Shadows*

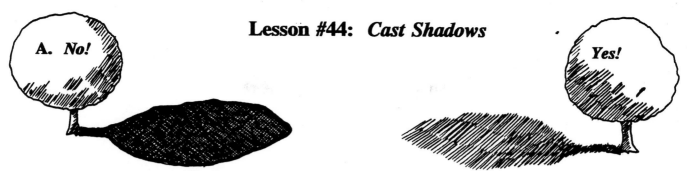

A *cast shadow* is the shadow cast by an object upon the ground or other surface. Notice the long cast shadow of a tree during early evening. Shadows should be drawn softly and transparently. In other words, do not draw a heavy outline around your shadows or darken them too much (A). Shadows are light and delicate, and you should be able to see into the shaded areas.

A cast shadow is darkest near the object, and lighter as it goes away from it. Set up a candlestick, an apple, and a bottle in front of you (B). Use a strong light source, like a spotlight. Bring the light down low on your objects to produce longer shadows. Draw your three objects in C using your light blue pencil, and then shade with your light blue, violet, and dark blue pencils. Use some crosshatching. Remember, do not outline your shadows!

B.

C.

# Lesson #45A: *Still Life*

    As mentioned in other assignments, a still life is a composition of objects that will not move. A still life is great to draw because it is stationary and allows you to work on it whenever you like. It is easy to set up and you can be creative in the way it is composed or situated. A still life is also excellent subject matter for a *shadow box* (see pointer on p. 60). When setting up a still life, do not simply place the objects in front of you and start drawing. Learn to take your time, positioning every object to make a pleasing composition. Overlap some of the objects and turn them to their best sides. A good rule to remember is to set the smaller objects in the foreground and the larger objects in the background (A). Also, the closer an object is to you, the further down the paper it will be in your picture. Use light axis lines for all your objects and ellipses when possible (B). Also, be aware of the negative space between the objects to help you in drawing them with proper proportions (C).

**A.**                                   **B.**                                   **C.**

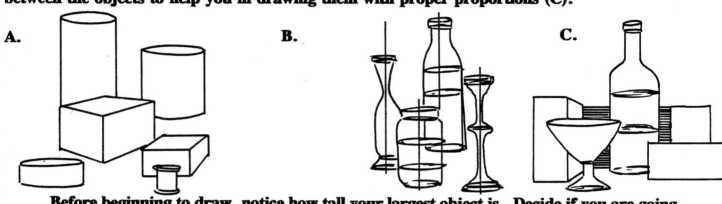

    Before beginning to draw, notice how tall your largest object is. Decide if you are going to have a *horizontal* or *vertical* composition. Some students take their paper and start drawing without considering if they want to use their paper vertically or horizontally. Wait a moment to decide, and then turn your paper accordingly.

### Is Your Composition Long or Wide?

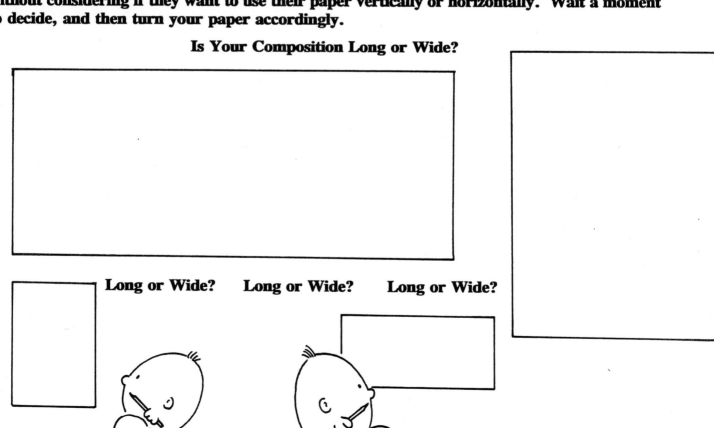

Long or Wide?     Long or Wide?     Long or Wide?

*"Fine art is that in which the hand, the head, and the heart of man go together."*

Ruskin

**A.**

**B.**

Now it's time for you to look around the house and find some objects you would like to draw. Compose them into a pleasing still life, recognizing that larger objects should be situated in the background. Use your entire paper when drawing, trying not to make your objects too large or too small (A & B). When overlapping, lightly draw the entire object, even the parts you cannot see. Use your drawing pencil for this assignment, and draw your still life on the bottom of the page. Have a good light source and shade with line.

**My Still Life by:** _____  **Date:** _____

# Lesson #45B: *Still Life with Boxes*

We are going to place several boxes or rectangular shapes in our still life, along with objects that are round, such as jars, vases, and bottles. Find a very small box, a book, and another box about the size of a baking soda container or cereal box. Surround these objects with objects that are cylindrical in shape and have ellipses. Situate everything in a pleasing way, with larger objects in the background. Do you know how to draw a freehand box? The same principles are for books and any other square or rectangular shape. All lines that recede in the distance will have to eventually connect, and all vertical lines remain vertical.

First, draw everything with one of your colored pencils below. Then, select one of the color theories from the first chapter to color it in: primary colors, warm or cool colors, complementary colors, analogous colors, etc. Have a light source and color with line.

**Still Life by:** _____ **Date:** _____

# Lesson #46: *Contour Drawings*

In Lesson #2, we experimented with contour drawings by creating abstract patterns and designs for coloring. Let's develop this a little further today. Remember, for contour drawings, never lift your pencil from the paper, but make one continuous line, in and out, over and around. Find a toy animal or ceramic object and place it in front of you. You are going to do three contour drawings of it below. In the first figure box, draw the object in front of you without looking down at your paper the entire time. Continue to keep your eyes fixed on the object in front of you. You may be pleasantly surprised with the results! In the second figure box, you can look down at your paper and see where your line is going. Finally, in the third figure box, take the best of both contour drawings, and put them together for a third, very creative drawing. Use a different colored pencil for each drawing, and color them in using either warm, cool, or analogous colors.

**A. Contour Drawing Without Looking Down**　**B. Contour Drawing Looking Down**

**C.  Creative Contour Drawing**

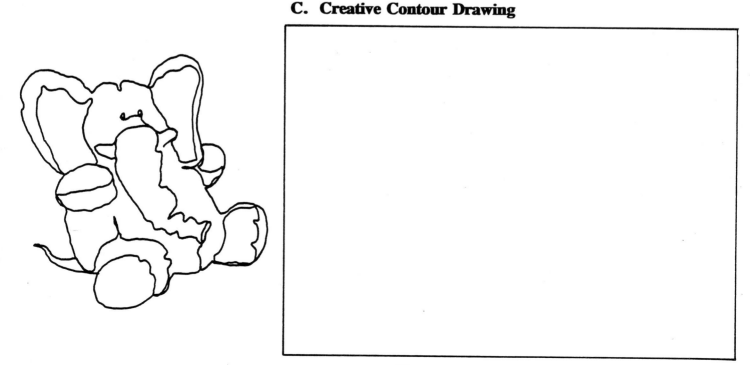

*"I have come to give you life and to give it to you more abundantly."* **John 10:10**

# Lesson #47: *Bringing Inanimate Objects to Life*

For this assignment, either use the same figure from the previous lesson or find another toy to draw. Place the object in front of you in different positions, turning it a little to one side and then the other. You will be surprised at how different it looks when you see it from different angles! Does it have moveable parts? Can you move its arms, legs, or wings?

Notice my little friend below. In one drawing his wings are raised, in another he is seen from a side view, and in another a profile view. Draw your inanimate object from six different angles on the next page. Use your drawing pencil and start with the basic shapes first (A), then put in your details. Finally, see if you can draw your subject matter in different styles. Notice that I drew *Mr. Owl* first with a simple outline, then with a contrasting dark background, then with bold black and white, and finally with diagonal lines.

**A.**

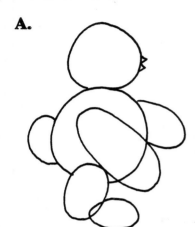  

**Pointer:** You may want to place your subject matter up on a box so you will have a better vantage point. This will give you a more dynamic view than looking down at it.

# Lesson #48:  *A House With A Picket Fence*

You have learned how to draw a birdhouse and how to draw a picket fence.  Let's see if you can now draw a house with a picket fence in front of it.  Using your drawing pencil, draw a 3" by 3" square (A) on the next page, placing it near the center of the page.  Do not use a ruler for this lesson; we will do all of the drawing, except the guidelines, freehand.  Make it 3-dimensional by adding a side (B).  Next, using a ruler, draw a vertical guideline directly through the center of the square (C).  This will be used to center the door, the window, and the top of your roof.  Draw your A-frame roof by connecting the top two corners to the vertical guideline (D).  Draw a front door and an attic window using the same vertical guideline to center both of them.

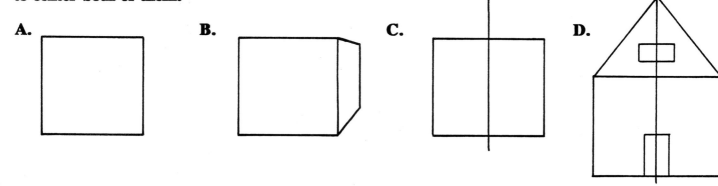

A.        B.        C.        D.

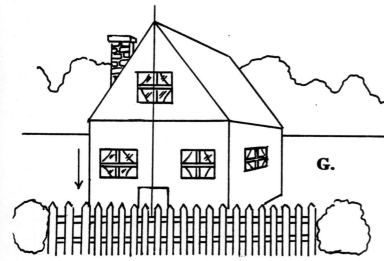

G.

Next, draw the back of your A-frame roof at the same angle as the front (E).  These lines have to be parallel, or at the same angle.  The top line of your roof has to be angled to connect with the other lines on the side of the house somewhere in the distance (F).  Even the windows on the side of the house have to follow the same lines as the other lines on the side of the house.  Remember, all vertical lines must remain straight up and down (G).  Can you place a chimney on your roof?  Finally, add a picket fence to the front.  How about a bird on a branch (H) in the foreground, some flowers, and distant trees?

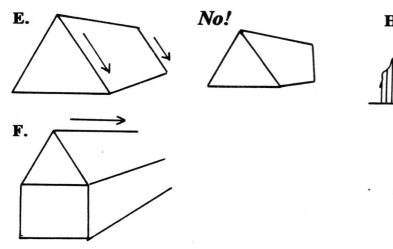

E.        *No!*

F.

H.

**Pointer:** Drawing is like putting pieces of a puzzle together; it takes some thinking. It is just a matter of putting one piece properly next to another to build a good drawing.

# Lesson #49: *Looking Up & Looking Down*

When drawing, we always have to consider where our *eye level* is. If we are looking down at an object, we will see it differently than if we are looking up at it. For this assignment, draw a cup, a jar, and a small box, each from a different vantage point.

First, draw these objects at eye level, meaning you are not able to see the tops or bottoms of the objects. Then draw them as you sit on the floor, looking *up* at them. (It is better if you place them on a glass shelf or table so you can see their bottoms). Finally, place the objects on the floor, looking *down* at them. Use your drawing pencil and draw them in the figure boxes below.

**A. Cup/Eye Level**

**B. Jar/Eye Level**

**C. Box/Eye Level**

**Cup/Looking Down**

**Jar/Looking Down**

**Box/Looking Down**

**Cup/Looking Up**

**Jar/Looking Up**

**Box/Looking Up**

# Lesson #50:  *Puddles, Ponds, & Reflections*

Drawing a reflection in the water is similar to drawing a reflection from the mirror, with the exception of ripples.  As mentioned in Lesson #11, a basic way to express water is with horizontal lines.  The closer the waves or ripples are to you, the wider apart they will be.  A reflection goes in and out with the ripples.  Even if it is only a small puddle, it is good to put one or two tiny ripples in to suggest water.  Using a combination of colored pencils, draw and color the objects below in the figure boxes.

71

## Lesson #51: *Drawing Bridges*

**A.**

Do you remember the entrance we drew for the birdhouse in Lesson #38? We were able to look in and see the side of the doorway (A). Look at a piece of cantaloupe; we are able to see inside past the curve. In both illustrations the same shape is repeated on the inside as it is on the outside. Now, look at the bridge, and notice how the bottom of the bridge has the same principle as the entrance to the birdhouse and the cantaloupe. It is the same semi-circular shape as the front, only farther back (B).

**B.**

**C.**

**D.**

Let's draw the scene above on the next page, showing the underside of the bridge, along with the inside of the rowboat. Draw everything lightly with your blue pencil, and color with an assortment of colored pencils. However, do not use browns or black.

To draw the stones on the side of the bridge, draw one row and then the next row above that, beginning each row in the middle of the one beneath it (C). Old stones like the ones on the bridge have irregular shapes but are still drawn with the same principles as rows of bricks.

To draw sea oats, or weeds, in the foreground, use long quick strokes going up from the ground the same way you put the whiskers on the animals in Lesson #36. Finally, the ripples in the water are long, thick and thin lines (D). The closer the ripples, the darker they are; the farther away, the lighter the lines. Show the reflection of the bridge and the boat in the water?

*"We cannot become what we need to be by remaining what we are."* Max De Pree

Draw and color your bridge scene above. See if you can create some rust colors for the stones in the bridge and some greens for the distant trees and the grass embankments. Use both green and violet and some blues in your water. Check your color chart on p. 10 for a wider variety of colors to choose from.

# Lesson #52: *Over the Hills and Through the Dales*

**A.**

There are many ways to show *depth* in your pictures. One way is to use perspective, another is to use lighter colors and less detail in the background, and a third way is to use a wandering road that meanders into the distance.

**B.**

**C.**

Observe the three roads. In A, notice how the road swings in and out and up and down the hills. In B, the road does the same as A, but not with as much swing. Can you see how the road is not connected as it starts up again at the bottom of the two distant hills? Finally in C, the long "S" curve winds its way into the distance. In all three, the roads become thinner as they head toward the horizon. Draw the three roads below with your light green colored pencil. Draw some trees, a farm house, and someone walking on the road. Try coloring your roads pink or violet, instead of black or brown.

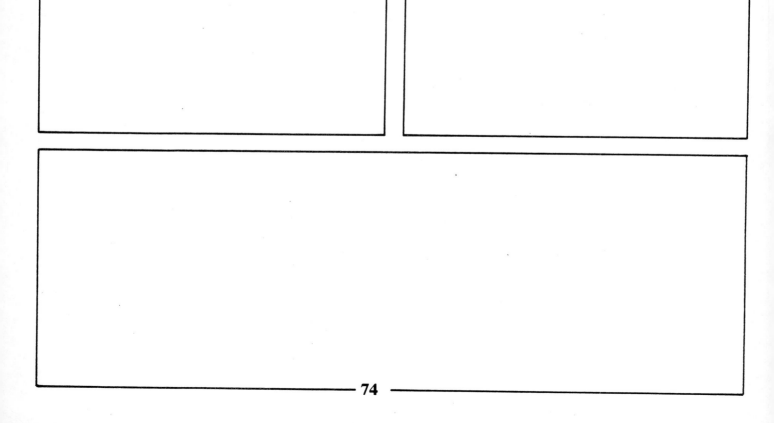

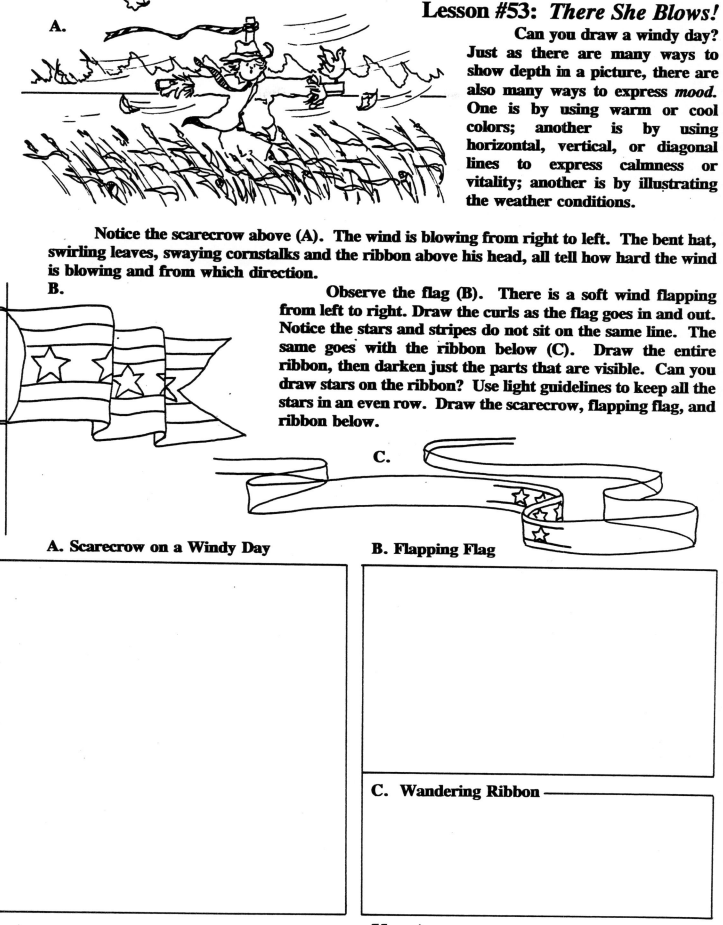

**A.**

# Lesson #53: *There She Blows!*

Can you draw a windy day? Just as there are many ways to show depth in a picture, there are also many ways to express *mood*. One is by using warm or cool colors; another is by using horizontal, vertical, or diagonal lines to express calmness or vitality; another is by illustrating the weather conditions.

Notice the scarecrow above (A). The wind is blowing from right to left. The bent hat, swirling leaves, swaying cornstalks and the ribbon above his head, all tell how hard the wind is blowing and from which direction.

**B.**

Observe the flag (B). There is a soft wind flapping from left to right. Draw the curls as the flag goes in and out. Notice the stars and stripes do not sit on the same line. The same goes with the ribbon below (C). Draw the entire ribbon, then darken just the parts that are visible. Can you draw stars on the ribbon? Use light guidelines to keep all the stars in an even row. Draw the scarecrow, flapping flag, and ribbon below.

**C.**

**A. Scarecrow on a Windy Day**

**B. Flapping Flag**

**C. Wandering Ribbon**

*"I don't know a better definition of an artist than one who is eternally curious."*

**Charles Hawthorne**

## Lesson #54: *Detail, Detail, Detail, Detail, Detail, Detail.....*

Do a drawing with as much detail as you can possibly put into it! You may want to draw a lace pattern, an old piece of machinery, the inside of a radio, or some jewelry. Do your drawing below. You have a choice of doing it in pencil or with colored pencils. Take your time, place as much detail in your drawing as possible, and make sure your pencils are sharp!

# Lesson #55: *Suggestion*

Sometimes it is good to put in a lot of detail, and other times it is good to *suggest*. Suggestion means to draw enough to let the eye and mind know what it is, but not to draw everything. When drawing the bricks on the side of a house (A), you do not have to draw every brick. The same with the leaves on a tree (B). Many students like to draw every single leaf when all that is really needed is the suggestion of just a few. Even the bark on a tree does not have to be completely illustrated (C), as we learned in Lesson #35. Only a very little grass on a hill has to be drawn (D). Learn to *suggest*. This is a beautiful part of drawing and leaves much to the viewer's imagination. Draw a brick house, a tree, and a grassy hill in the figure box below (E) suggesting only a little of the detail.

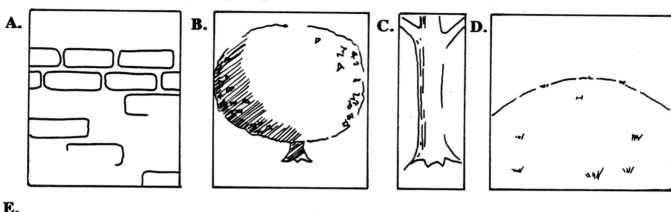

A.   B.   C.   D.

E.

# Lesson #56: *Contrast*

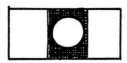

*Contrast* is the value difference between light and dark in a specific area of your picture. Placing a light object against a dark background creates an image with impact. Contrast can give you a very bold illustration!

There are many ways of creating contrast. You can place a lighter object against a darker background by using horizontal, diagonal, or vertical lines (A, B, C). For an even darker contrast, you can use crosshatching (D). You can even reverse the process and place a dark object next to a light background (E). Draw my little friend in the figure boxes below using a different method of contrast in each illustration. You can even try contrast with color by using light colors against dark colors or warm colors against cool colors.

A.                  B.                  C.                  D.                  E.

Create some of your own doodle characters below. Use bold color contrast, warm against cool, or light against dark, to create different effects as illustrated above.

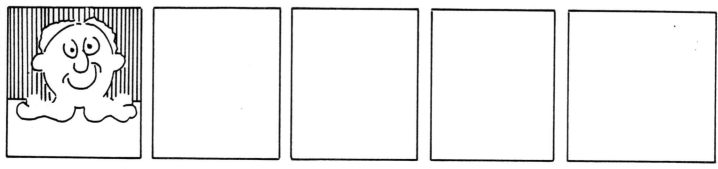

# Lesson #57:  *Focal Point*

The eye likes to do several things when looking at a picture. It likes to read from left to right, the same as it reads the page of a book. It likes to relax in areas where things are suggested, as in Lesson #55, and it likes to relish on detail! A good technique in drawing is to suggest around the area that is of most interest; this will allow the viewer's eye to enjoy that area of detail, which is called the *focal point.* You may also want to have darker values and more contrast in the area of most interest to you.

Do you have a game with a lot of little pieces to it? Place a handful of them on a piece of paper, and draw them using a focal point. Put the most detail and values in the area of your focal point, and let the rest softly fade out to the sides by simply suggesting with light lines and not much detail. Finally, you do not always have to place your focal point in the center of your paper, it can be on the left, right, top, or bottom of your picture also. Do your drawing of game pieces below. Use your black colored pencil for this assignment.

**Focal Point to the Left**

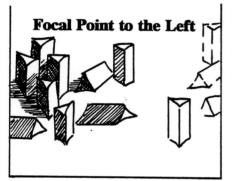

**Focal Point in the Center**

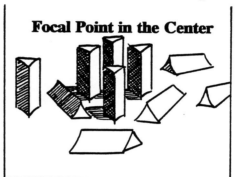

**Focal Point to the Right**

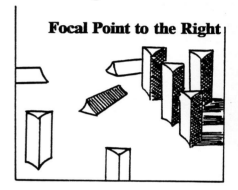

# Lesson #58: Dot....Dot....Dot....Dot....Dot....Dot....

Dots can be a delightful approach to drawing. However, they can also be tedious and time consuming if the student has to draw in large areas. Another name for this is *stippling*. Stippling means to apply, by small touches, dots or flicks. It is done mainly by the use of a pen or pencil. Still another term for using dots is *pointillism*. Pointillism is the application of small strokes or dots of color that blend together from a distance. Let's practice with dots below and see what happens!

**A.**                                                                      **B.** *No!*

Always make sure to have a light source. You can show the form of objects by placing more dots in certain areas to create darker values and shading (A). When drawing, remember to let the light come into your objects; do not have cookie cutter shapes by giving all your objects a heavy outline (B). Use only a few dots around the lighted side. There is also more than just a light side and a shaded side to objects. If you look closely, you will see that there are many different values that go from light to dark. Do a value study with dots in C, going from light to dark, using an extra fine black marker.

**C. Value Study**

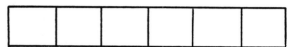

Draw the objects below in the spaces provided. Lightly draw a circle with your "2B" drawing pencil, and then start placing dots within the object with your extra fine black marker (D). Next, draw a box and place the dots within it with your black pen (E). Finally, use your pencil to draw the cylinder, and then place in the dots with your pen (F). Remember, *do not outline everything*. Let the light enter in on the light side of your objects. Take your time.

**D.**                          **E.**                          **F.**

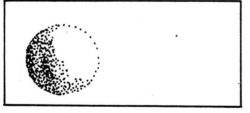

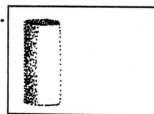

Let's do a small picture below using colorful dots (G). Draw the scene in H with your light green pencil. Color it in with dots. Use yellow, green, and blue dots for the field and tree. Place a little red in some of the green areas. Dot your sky with light blue and violet, leaving room for clouds. Dot the barn with orange, yellow, and red. Make sure you have a light side and a shaded side. Be colorful and creative!

**G.**                                              **H.**

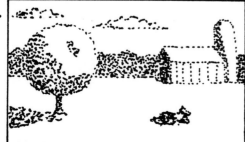

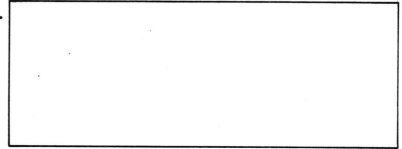

# Lesson #59: *Beach Ball Shop*

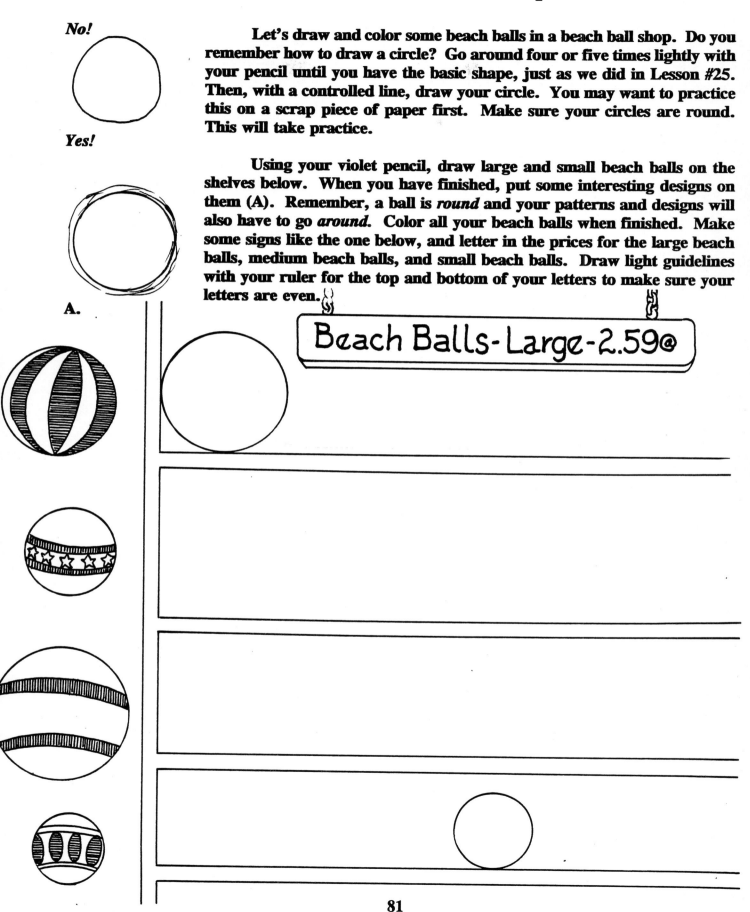

**No!**

**Yes!**

**A.**

Let's draw and color some beach balls in a beach ball shop. Do you remember how to draw a circle? Go around four or five times lightly with your pencil until you have the basic shape, just as we did in Lesson #25. Then, with a controlled line, draw your circle. You may want to practice this on a scrap piece of paper first. Make sure your circles are round. This will take practice.

Using your violet pencil, draw large and small beach balls on the shelves below. When you have finished, put some interesting designs on them (A). Remember, a ball is *round* and your patterns and designs will also have to go *around*. Color all your beach balls when finished. Make some signs like the one below, and letter in the prices for the large beach balls, medium beach balls, and small beach balls. Draw light guidelines with your ruler for the top and bottom of your letters to make sure your letters are even.

Beach Balls-Large-2.59@

# Lesson #60: *Up, Up in the Air in My Colorful Balloon!*

**A.**

**B.**

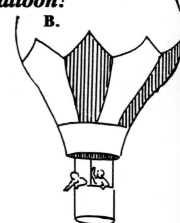

Making hot air balloons is like making beach balls. Let's make some balloons floating in the sky. See if you can find pictures of hot air balloons to copy. *Overlap* them by placing one in front of another to create depth. Place the larger hot air balloons in the foreground and the smaller ones in the background (A). Draw them with your light blue pencil. Give them patterns and designs and color them in. Finally, draw some people riding in the balloons. Do not draw little stick figures. Instead, *suggest* the people by drawing them with simple shapes (B).

## Up, Up in the Air!

# Lesson #61: *Trucks & Cars*

One of the best ways to learn how to draw trucks and cars is by using toy replicas. Find some toy trucks or cars and draw three of them below. Or you can draw the same vehicle from three different positions.

When drawing tires, remember that they are round, and if you see them from an angle draw them with *ellipses* (A). Also, drawing cars and trucks is similar to drawing freehand cubes and boxes like we did in Lesson #32. Draw the basic rectangular shape of the vehicle, and then round it off and put in the details (B).

**A.**　　　　　　　　　　　　　　　　　　**B.**

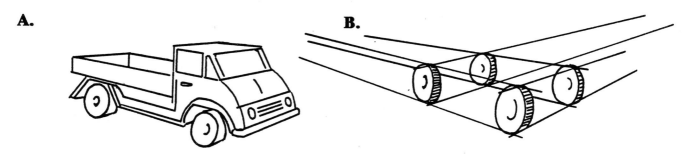

**Pointer:** Set your subject matter on a box to bring it close to your eye level. Many times this will make for an interesting drawing and be easier to draw than looking down at it.

# Lesson #62: *Pineapples and Patterns*

The more we observe the things around us, the more aware we become of how they are structured. We start to notice certain patterns and designs that God has used in creating everything. An example of this is a flower (A). Everything comes out of the center to form a delightfully simple pattern. A snowflake also has a pleasing pattern (B). A pine branch has a nice pattern (C); even a ripple, when we throw a pebble in water, has an interesting pattern (D).

**A.**   **B.**   **C.**   **D.**

Now let's look at a pineapple and observe its pattern. It would be best if you had a real pineapple in front of you; but if not, a picture will do. Studying a pineapple will reveal some of God's little secrets in creation. If you look closely, you will see a pattern of diamond shapes going around the pineapple (E). You will also notice that the leaves on the top come out from a central point (F). Understanding these two things will assist in drawing a pineapple. First, draw its basic shape with your yellow pencil going around four or five times. A pineapple is a long, vertical ellipse (G). After you have drawn this shape, draw a series of diagonal lines that go *around* it (H). Then, draw another series of diagonal lines the other way (I). Notice that you have created the little diamond patterns that make up a pineapple. Look closely and you will notice that each diamond shape is divided in halves (J). Finally, as mentioned, each leaf comes out of the center of the fruit. Draw the leaves in lightly, showing the entire leaf. Make some leaves twist around like a ribbon, and darken the underside (K).

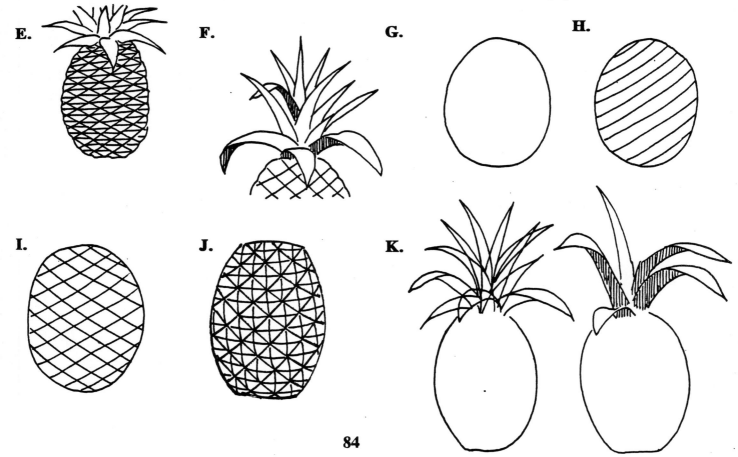

84

*"A work of art is reality filtered through the personality of the artist. That's what makes one artist different from another."*

**Phillip Reisman**

Using your yellow pencil, draw a large pineapple above. Lightly draw the basic shape of the pineapple and then its top. Place in the diamond patterns with diagonal lines and divide them as shown on the previous page. Finally, color in your pineapple. What colors do you see? Be colorful and creative!

# Lesson #63: *Drawing Animals*

There are basically four ways to draw animals: copying from pictures, copying from photographs, working from life, and drawing from memory. The easiest way is to copy, and the most difficult is working from life. Drawing from life is difficult because animals move around quite a bit. ALso, most students do not have a lot of animals readily available to observe. So, we will start by drawing from pictures.

Each animal is made up of basic geometric shapes. For instance, when drawing a cow, start with the geometric shapes below, rectangles and squares (A). Notice the basic shapes that make up the cat's posture (B). Do you see any geometric shapes that make up the horse (C) and the dog (D)? Draw the four animals below on the following page, or find other animal pictures to draw from. Make sure to start by drawing the basic geometric shapes.

A.

B.

C.

D.

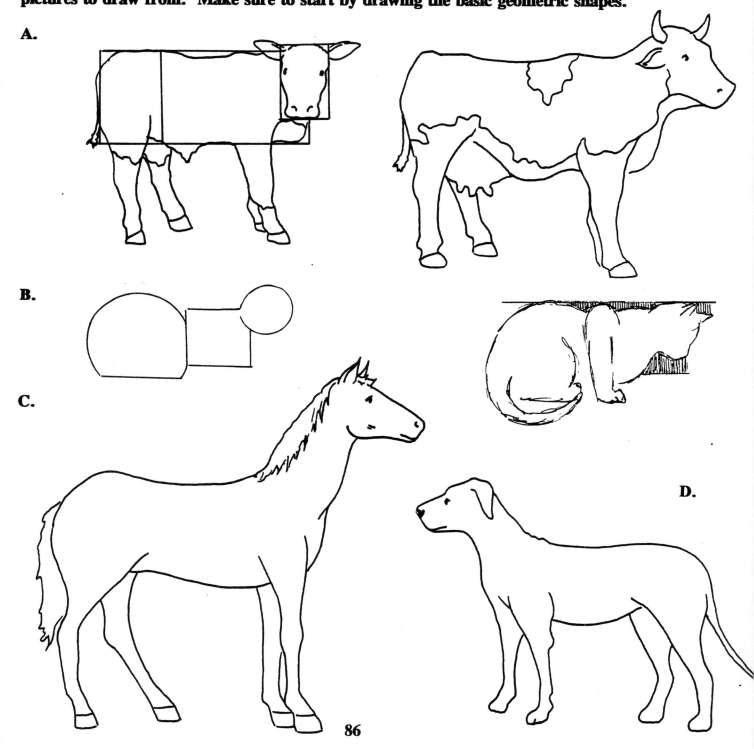

*"God made the wild animals according to their kinds, the livestock according to their kinds, and all the creatures that move along the ground according to their kinds. And God said that it was good."*

**Genesis 1:25**

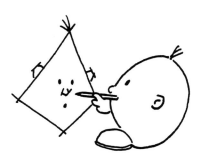

**Pointer:** Draw with *angles*. Start light and draw every curve with straight lines. As your subject matter comes into focus, you can round off many of the areas. Drawing with angles will show the form of your subject matter better when finished.

# Lesson #64: *Creating Creative Creatures*

Let's create some new animals. You may want to look at pictures for this assingment. Take parts from different animals and put them together to make four new animals on the next page. You can add other interesting features to your new creatures (A). Use your orange colored pencil to lightly draw them, then color your creative creatures with a bright assortment of colors. Write a brief description below each animal. What is the name of your new animal? What does it like to eat? How big is it? Is it friendly? Where does it live?

A.

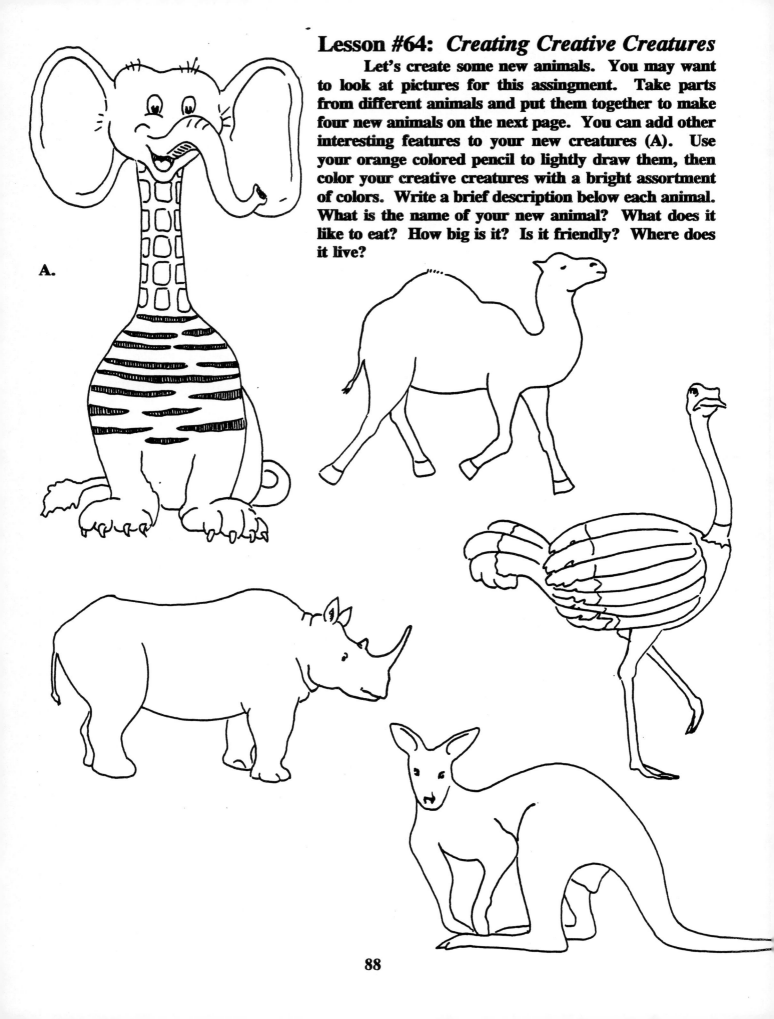

88

# A New Species of Animals!

**Animal #1:**_____

**Animal #2:**_____

_____
_____
_____
_____

**Animal #3:** _____

**Animal #4:** _____

_____
_____
_____
_____

# Lesson #65: *Copying the Masters*

*Masters* are great artists from the past and present whose art has withstood time and serves as a standard of excellence. Studying and copying the works of the masters is a great way to learn about art, giving you a better understanding of their individual styles and a better appreciation of quality art. Studying the masters can also be a great source of inspiration. As mentioned, the best form of study in drawing is to study from *real life*, objects that are in front of you. This teaches you to see *light* and *form*. You will not learn as much copying from pictures and photographs. Only occasionally do we recommend such copying

You will learn a great deal from studying their work, understanding how great artists create with form, color, line, and composition. You will also learn some of their techniques. Students *glean* from generations before them; taking some of the best qualities of the masters and incorporating them into their own work. However, we do not grow to be copyists, becoming just like other artists, but rather we become more enriched in our own unique way by the many things they have taught us.

We are going to learn more about artists in the chapter titled *"Art Appreciation"*. For now, go to the library and look up the works of four of the artists below, copying their pictures on the next page and below, creating a gallery of your own. Your assignment will be to find two master drawings to copy in pencil, and then two copies of paintings that you can do with colored pencils. Place the name of the artist and the title of the picture below each piece of artwork. Can you draw a frame around the pictures as shown below?

**Masters to Study:**
>    Leonardo Da Vinci
>    Michelangelo
>    Raphael
>    Rembrandt van Rijn
>    Vermeer
>    Albrecht Durer
>    Claude Monet
>    Carl Bloch
>    Thomas Eakins
>    John Singer Sargeant
>    Winslow Homer
>    Charles Russell
>    Norman Rockwell

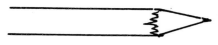

**Pointer: Continually copy artwork by the masters. Take your sketchbook to the library and draw their works. This is one assignment that you can do on your own. It will provide you with plenty to do and will also teach you about composition, color, and design.**

# ART GALLERY

Name: _____ Title: _____   Name: _____ Title: _____

Name: _____ Title: _____   Name: _____ Title: _____

# Lesson #66: *Treasure Hunt*

There is a wealth of interesting material to draw around the house. Some things are more beneficial to draw than others. The more you study from life, and the more you study works from the masters, the better your taste will become for subject matter that is worthy of drawing and painting. Today we are going to search for things to draw: a light bulb, two bottles, three clothespins, a lamp, and a doorknob. Find each of these objects. Set them on a piece of dark colored paper, and give them a good light source like the light from a window or lamp. Use your drawing pencils, and draw and shade with line.

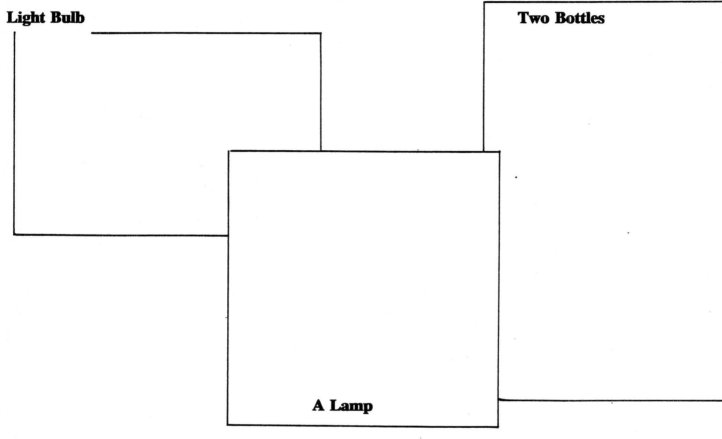

**Light Bulb**

**Two Bottles**

**A Lamp**

**Three Clothespins**

**A Doorknob**

# Lesson #67: *Rustic Still Lifes*

Today we are going to draw three still lifes, making them look like they were done a long time ago. This is similar to Lesson #18. Find several simple objects: a teapot, some apples, a vase, grapes, a cup, etc., and place them in an interesting position near the light of a window. For this assignment, use only your light brown, dark brown, and black pencils. First, lightly place a smooth layer of color in the three figure boxes below with your light brown pencil. Then, draw in the first still life with your dark brown pencil, and shade it with dark brown and black. Set up two more still lifes and do the same. You will find that coloring the surface of your paper, or *toning* it, creates an interesting effect. Finally, try taking an eraser and erasing some areas of your objects that are in light.

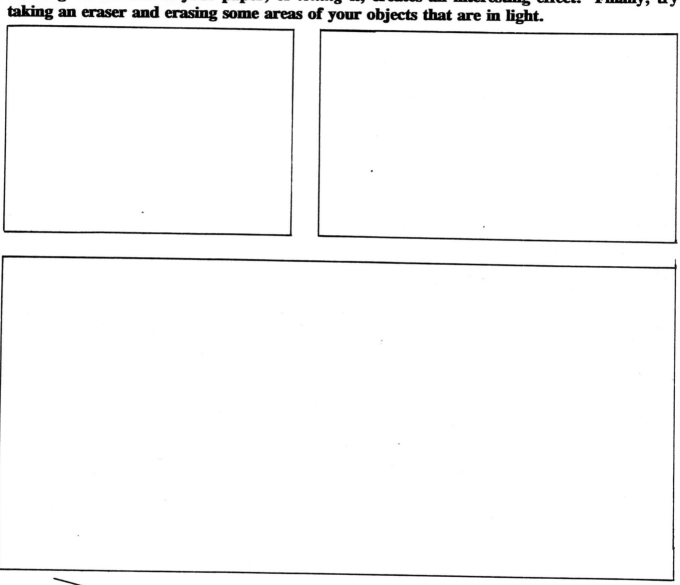

**Pointer:** When drawing objects from life, try drawing them larger in one drawing, and smaller in another. How about standing up to look down at what you are drawing, or sitting down to look up at your subject matter. You may want to draw the same thing first with a drawing pencil, then with colored pencils, and then with your black pen. Finally, turn your objects around to get a good vantage point.

# Lesson #68:  *A Golden Treasure Chest*

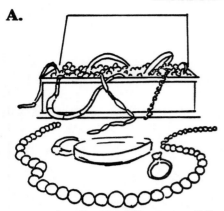

Let's draw a treasure chest of jewelry (A).  Set up a jewelry box and some jewelry in a pleasing composition, and draw it below with your violet pencil.  Have a focal point where you show the most detail and contrast between light and dark (refer to Lesson #57.)

As the necklaces and bracelets wind forward, they will become larger.   Therefore, you may want to draw things larger than they really are as they come forward.  If someone was standing in front of you with his hand outstretched, you would make the hand larger than it really is to suggest depth (B).  This is called *foreshortening*.  Foreshortening can create a more dynamic illustration.  Complete your picture with an assortment of colored pencils when you have finished the drawing.

# Lesson #69: *Independent Studies*

Students need to learn how to work *independently* in order to be their own source of inspiration and encouragement. A good way to do this is to simply go out and draw things around you for 30 minutes each day. Below is a list of things that you may want to draw independently. Can you think of anything else to draw?

Go to the library and study the works of the great masters. See what they selected to draw and paint. This will assist you in finding good subject matter to study.

## Independent Studies

A Pair of Scissors
A Stapler
A Striped Shirt
A Window Latch
A Wrench
A Candlestick
Toothbrush & Toothpaste
Containers Under the Sink

A Jar of Pencils
A Houseplant
A Tractor
A Chair
A Set of Keys
A Baby Doll
An Old Tire
Parts of Machinery

**My List:**

_____
_____
_____
_____
_____
_____
_____
_____
_____
_____
_____
_____
_____
_____
_____

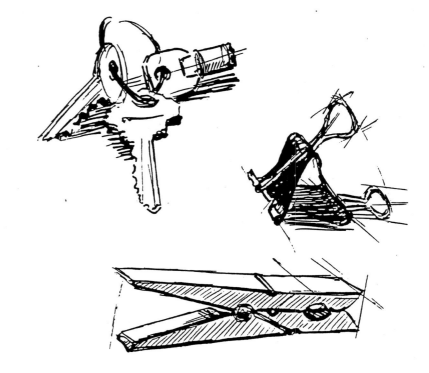

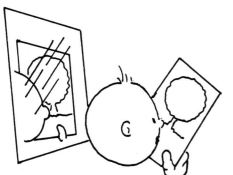

**Pointer:** A good way to evaluate your work is to hold it up to a mirror. A mirror will show you the opposite image of your drawing and will make your mistakes more obvious. Try this with some of your drawings and see what happens! Mirrors do not lie.

*"There has never been a man in our history who led a life of ease whose name is worth mentioning."*
**Theodore Roosevelt**

# Lesson #70: *Keeping a Daily Journal*

Keeping an art journal is very important! Artists in the past used to keep beautiful journals - drawing the things around them and writing their thoughts about each day. An art journal is something like a diary with a lot of artwork in it. However, diaries are generally private, whereas an artist's journal is *open* and pertains to observations of higher learning. A good comparison of a diary and an art journal would be *The Diary of Anne Frank* and the journals of Leonardo Da Vinci.

Simply stated, an art journal is a sketchbook of your drawings and thoughts. As your journal begins to develop, it will begin to have its own personality. No two journals are alike! It will be something to have and cherish forever, sharing those bygone days with friends and family.

Journals are a wonderful way of investing your time. Most students have wandered away from quality time by watching too much television, playing too many computer games, or just spending time doing nothing. Learn to spend your time wisely.

One of the most important purposes of a journal is drawing, but you can also add other things like postcards of places visited, tickets from shows, letters from friends, cut flowers, magazine articles, and pictures. However, the essential ingredient of a quality art journal is the drawings that fill the pages.

See if you can fill a page of your journal with drawings of things around you, and your thoughts about the day. Journaling should inspire you to work independently, encourage you to draw from life, and help you practice penmanship. Try to include other things in your journal, such as: the date, what the weather is like, your thoughts, things you have learned, and so forth. Be creative! Fill the next page with your thoughts and drawings!

_____

_____

_____

_____

_____

_____

_____

_____

# Lesson #71:  DRAWING EXAMINATION

**I.  Matching:  Match the word with the correct definition by placing the correct letter next to the word (3 points each).**

| | | | |
|---|---|---|---|
| 1. | Overlapping | A. | Dark values against light values. |
| 2. | Ellipse | B. | Suggesting various surfaces in drawing. |
| 3. | Negative Space | C. | Vertical or horizontal guidelines. |
| 4. | Foreshortening | D. | The direction and type of light in your drawing. |
| 5. | Freehand Perspective | E. | Placing objects in front of other objects. |
| 6. | Values | F. | The use of mechanical instruments for drawing. |
| 7. | Light Source | G. | Crisscrossing lines used to create darker values. |
| 8. | Contrast | H. | The area or space around objects. |
| 9. | Focal Point | I. | Exaggerating proportions to show depth. |
| 10. | Suggestion | J. | Different shades of lights and darks in drawing. |
| 11. | Axis Line | K. | Two-dimensional. |
| 12. | Shadow Box | L. | Used as a backdrop for still life studies. |
| 13. | Contour | M. | An arrangement of inanimate objects. |
| 14. | Composition | N. | The way subject matter is situated in a picture. |
| 15. | Texture | O. | The place where the eye is directed to in a drawing. |
| 16. | Crosshatching | P. | 3-dimensional objects drawn without mechanical tools. |
| 17. | Drawing Paper | Q. | A circle seen on an angle. |
| 18. | Cast Shadows | R. | Shadows of objects on the ground or table. |
| 19. | Still Life | S. | Leaving out much of the detail. |
| 20. | Technical | T. | A continuous line drawing. |

**II.  Fill in the blank:  Place the correct answers in the blank spaces (4 points each).**
1. Three famous artists are_____, _____, and_____.
2. _____ are the gradations from light to dark in a drawing.
3. In drawing, you should always shade with_____.
4. The first thing you should decide before drawing is, is your composition going to be vertical or_____.
5. One of the most important things we can learn in drawing is what the famous French master once stated, *"Draw _____ young man, plenty of _____."*

**III.  True or False.  Place a T or F next to each statement (4 points each).**
1. An "HB" pencil has soft lead, and will give you a dark line.
2. When setting up a still life, it is good to place the smaller objects in the foreground.
3. You should look up at your subject matter every three seconds.
4. Like reading, the eye desires to move from left to right in a picture.
5. An ellipse is the top of a box.

(Answers on page 310)

# Rules & Measurements

*"Line upon line - precept upon precept."* **Isaiah 28:10**

# Lesson #72: *Inches & Guidelines*

In the previous chapter, we learned how to draw *freehand*, that is, without the use of a ruler or any other mechanical device. In *Rules & Measurements*, we will learn ways of creating technical drawings.

If you desire a good understanding of mechanical drawing, it would be beneficial to have a drawing board (A), a triangle (B), and a t-square (C), along with masking tape, a ruler, and a pencil. For this course, however, the main tool will be a ruler.

**A. Drawing Board**

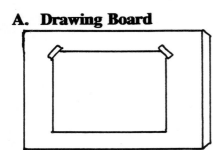

**B. Triangle**

**C. T-Square**

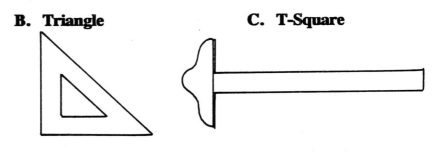

First, take your ruler and hold it against the line below. See if you can mark off these dimensions: 1 1/8", 1 1/2", 1 6/8", 2 3/4", 2 15/16", 3 3/16", 4 1/4", 4 1/2", 5 3/8", 5 7/8", 6 1/16", 6 6/16", 7 1/4", 7 3/4", and 7 14/16". Place the beginning of your ruler exactly on the mark to the bottom left and start marking off each measurement (A). Place the correct measurement above the markings on the line.

**A.**

## Guidelines:

Whenever doing technical drawings, you should draw guidelines on the bottom of the page and letter your name, grade, and date. You will be required to do this for many of the assignments in this chapter. Let's practice below. First, place two marks 1/2" up from the bottom of the page, one mark to the left side, and one to the right. Using your ruler, draw a horizontal line and connect the two marks. Connecting two measured marks on the side of a straight piece of paper will give you a parallel line with the paper. Come up 1/4" from this line and place two more dots, one to each side and connect another line. These lines should go all the way from one side of the paper to the other. Finally, come up another 1/8" and mark off two more dots, connecting them with your ruler. Starting near the center of the page and moving to the right, letter your last name first, first name and then middle initial. Then letter your grade and date. Letter very lightly at first to make sure you will have enough space.

Name

come up 1/8"
come up another 1/4"
come up 1/2" from the bottom
of the page

9th Date

# Lesson #73: *One-Point Perspective*

*Perspective* is a technique used to show *depth* in your pictures (A). Today we are going to use perspective to draw two boxes that go back in the distance and connect at the *horizon line*. The horizon line is where land meets sky. All the lines that go back to the horizon line will connect at a point called the *vanishing point* (B). In one-point perspective, the vanishing point is where all of the lines converge that go back into space. Connect the corners of the box below (C), to the vanishing point (B) as shown in A.

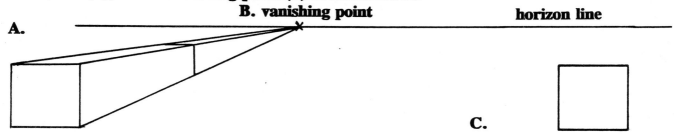

**A.**

**B. vanishing point**      **horizon line**

**C.**

Next, draw two 1" squares below, one to the left, and one to the right of the vanishing point. Place them below the horizon line. Make sure the top and sides of your boxes are *parallel* (D). Use your ruler for all lines. Connect all the corners of the squares to the vanishing point, just as you did above (A). Finally, draw guidelines on the bottom of the paper, and print your last name, first initial, grade, and date as illustrated in Lesson #72.

**D.**      *No!*

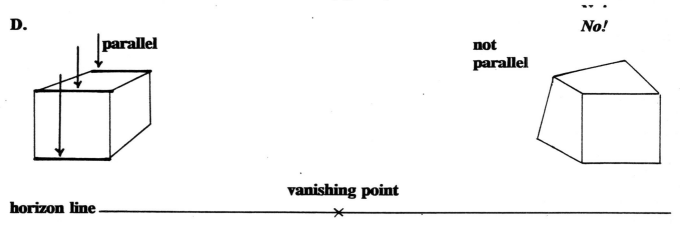

parallel

not
parallel

**vanishing point**

**horizon line**

**Draw 1" square above** .                    **Draw 1" square above**

**Place Guidelines here:**

# Lesson #74: *Cones, Cubes, Spheres, and Prisms*

## Two-Dimensional Shapes:

As mentioned earlier, everything that we draw on paper is two-dimensional. It has only two dimensions: height and width. There is no depth to paper. Let's start today by drawing some *flat* objects. Using your ruler and other mechanical devices, draw the two-dimensional shapes on the next page. First, draw each shape lightly in pencil to have an idea of how it is going to look, and then use your ruler to create straight lines (A). For making the circle, you can use a compass, the top of a small container, or a coin. After you have drawn the objects, draw guidelines 1/8" and 1/16", and letter underneath each what geometric shape it is (B).

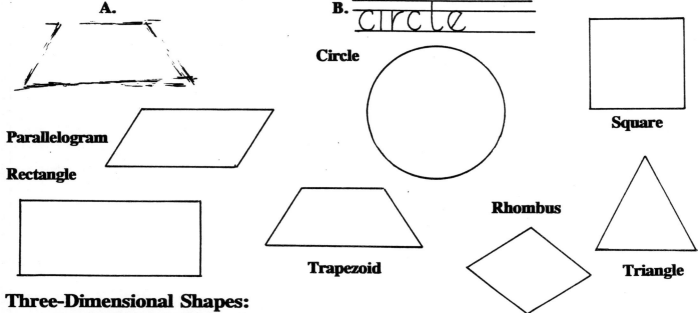

## Three-Dimensional Shapes:

Three-dimensional shapes show *depth*. Therefore, the artist will be using one dimension for height, one dimension for width, and a final dimension to show that it has depth. Below are some solid forms which show depth. Have you noticed that some of the names have changed from those above? See if you can draw these on the next page. Remember, all sides that go back into space will eventually come together. You will have to draw ellipses for the cylinder freehand. Make sure to letter each object using your guidelines.

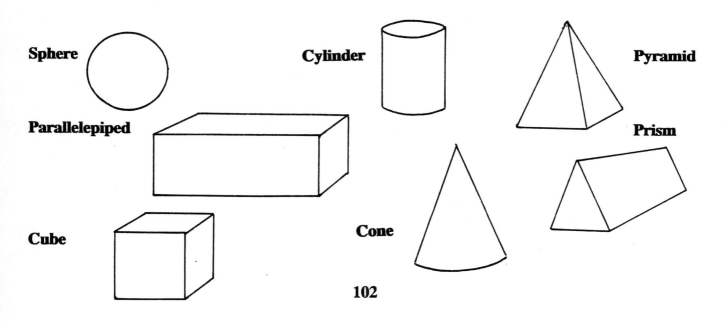

# Two-Dimensional Objects

# Three-Dimensional Objects

**Pointer:** When creating technical drawings, it is good to place a border around your paper. For our assignments, there will already be a border (as above). However, to make another border, draw a 1/8" top and side borders inside the one already provided. For the bottom border, come up 1/4" from the bottom line and draw a line. Finally, come up another 1/8" and 1/16", and draw guidelines for your name.

# Lesson #75: *Drawing a Cathedral*

*Cathedral:* The Greek word cathedral means *"seat"* or *"throne".* The word cathedral is sometimes used to mean a large church.

In the early years of Christianity, nearly 2,000 years ago, church was held in believers' homes. The disciples of Jesus traveled from place to place spreading the gospel, ministering, and appointing some believers to be apostles, prophets, evangelists, pastors, and teachers. As Christianity grew, the affairs of the Church became increasingly more complicated, and the buildings, churches, and cathedrals became larger and larger. Can you design a cathedral or church? Draw it first on a scrap piece of paper, and then do your final drawing below using your ruler and a sharp pencil.

# Lesson #76: *Old McDonald Had a Farm*

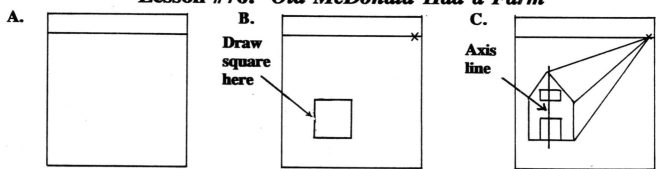

A.

B. Draw square here

C. Axis line

In Lesson #73, we learned how to make three-dimensional boxes using one-point perspective. Now, let's draw a building using one-point perspective. First, place a horizon line high up on the picture plane (A). Do this below in the large figure box (F). Then, draw a 1 1/4" square below your horizon line and to the left side (B). Place an axis line down the center of the square, and use this as a guide for the center point of your "A" frame roof, the center of your hayloft, and the center of your door (C). Finally, place an "X" on the far right of the horizon line, and connect the top and sides of the barn to the "X" or *vanishing point*.

Complete the barn by drawing the rear of the roofline at the same angle as the front (D). Do the same for the rear side. All vertical lines should remain straight up and down. You can make your barn as long or short, as you like (E). Finally, draw a silo, distant trees, and some farm animals to complete your picture.

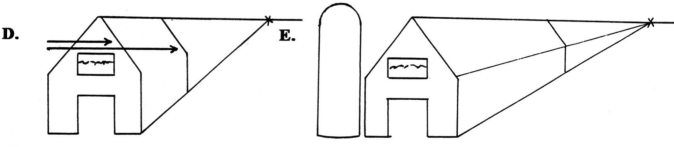

D.

E.

F.

# Lesson #77: *An Old Western Town*

   Let's see if you can draw an old western town on the next page. Turn the text around and use the paper horizontally (next page) for more space. First, draw a 1/4" border around the top and sides of the page, and a 1/2" border on the bottom. Then, draw the guidelines for your name on the bottom. Place the horizon line near the top of the picture plane, placing an "X" in the center of it for your vanishing point (A). Lightly sketch how large you want your buildings to be. Then take your ruler and draw guidelines from the tops and bottoms of the buildings to your vanishing point (B). Notice how the lines grow farther apart the closer they come toward you. Draw the fronts of your buildings between these guidelines. Use the vanishing points and guidelines for the wooden sidewalk, the signs on the buildings, and the windows and doors (C). You can even add some light guidelines for the lettering on your signs (D). Study the drawing below and try to copy it on the next page, using guidelines for your sidewalks, roofs, doors, signs, and windows. Can you add some people, horses, wagons, and distant mountains? Remember, keep all your vertical lines straight up and down. This is a difficult assignment. If you become frustrated, have someone assist you.

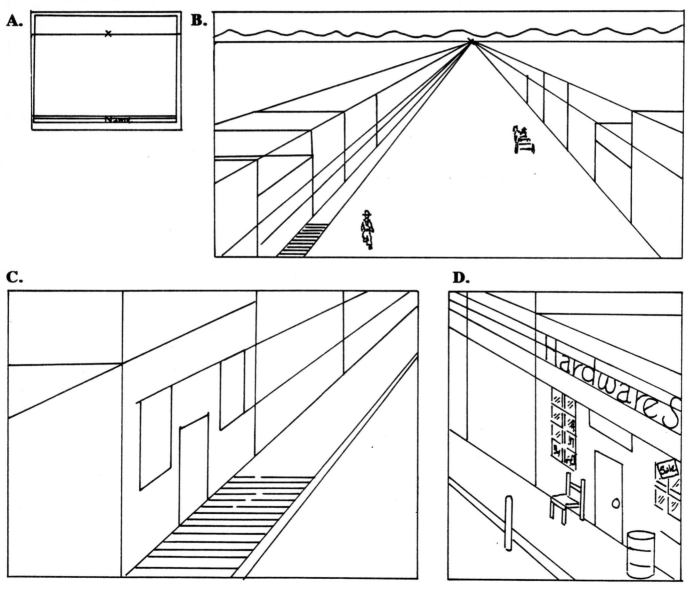

A.

B.

C.

D.

**Pointer:** The first thing you should do before starting a drawing is to figure out whether your composition is long or wide and adjust your paper accordingly. For instance, this scene is *wide*; therefore we will use our paper horizontally for more space and a better composition.

# Lesson #78: *Floating Books*

**A.**

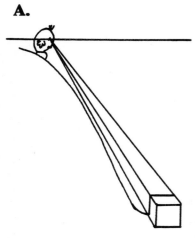

**B.**

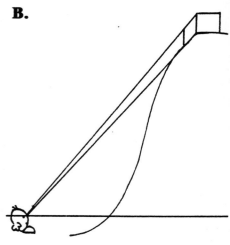

As mentioned in Lesson #73, the horizon line is where the sky meets the earth or sea. In perspective, another name for the horizon line is eye level. If you are looking down, you will have a high horizon line and vanishing points (A). If you are in a valley looking up, you will have a low horizon line (B).

We are going to draw some books floating in space (C), with the horizon line in the middle. Try to keep in mind that all lines will connect to the horizon line.

You will be looking up at some books and down at others. You will be able to see the tops of some books, and the bottoms of others. See if you can draw three-dimensional books floating in space (D). Before beginning, lightly draw a few books, and learn how to connect them to the vanishing points (as you did with boxes, barns, and houses). If this assignment is too difficult for you, turn to Lessons #82 and #86, and return to it at a later time.

**C.**

**D.**

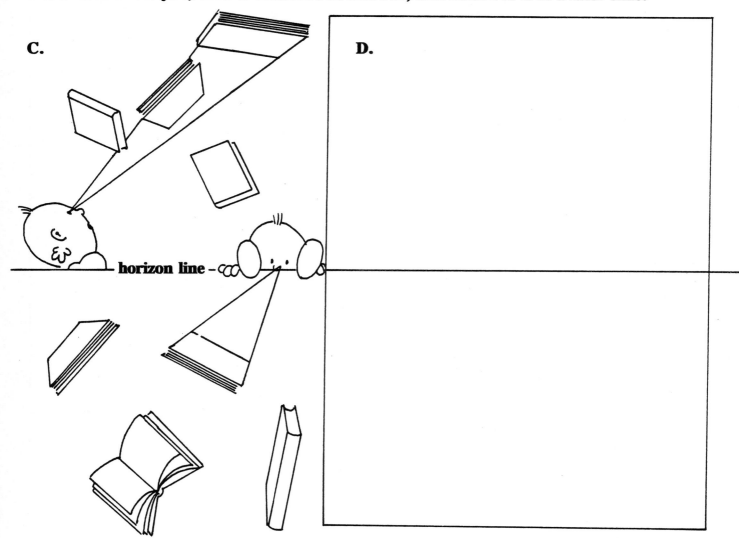

horizon line

108

# Lesson #79: *Dimensions & Dimensions*

**A. Overlap**

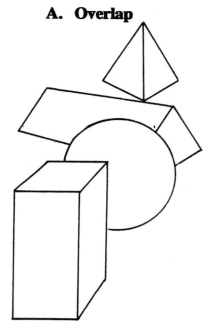

For this assignment, create a picture using the three-dimensional objects that we studied in Lesson #74: prisms, cubes, spheres, etc. We are going to use our light blue colored pencil to draw them, making sure to *overlap* some to show *depth* (A). Place the horizon line near the top of the picture plane. Extend the horizon line out to the right and left of the paper (B). Draw light guidelines coming from the tops and bottoms of the objects to points on the horizon line. Draw your objects in C.

**C.**

**B.**

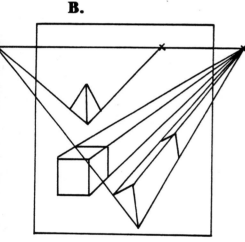

**Pointer:** When you have objects sitting at different angles (above) place several vanishing points on the horizon line. Each object will have to be drawn to its own vanishing point. Depending on the angle of the object, some of the VP's will have to go off the paper (B).

# Lesson #80: *Floor Plans*

Floor plans are blueprints for building a house. The floor plan below is seen from a *bird's-eye view*. Let's say our floor plan is going to be 1/8" per foot. That means every 1/8" you draw on your paper will actually represent 1'. We will make a one story ranch house for simplicity. Notice below how the doorways and the windows are illustrated, as well as the shrubbery around the house (A). Design a two-bedroom house with a kitchen, living room, dining room, garage, and one bathroom in figure box B. This will take some thinking, and you might want to do a rough draft on another sheet of paper. Use guidelines and letter each room when finished. Make sure you have a sharp pencil.

**A.**

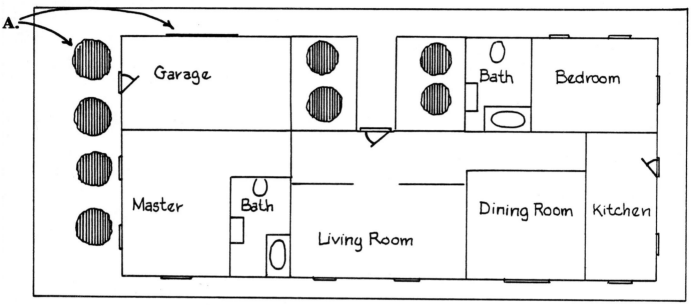

**B.**

# Lesson #81: *Adding the Detail*

**A.**

**B.**

In an earlier lesson, you learned that you did not have to add all the details when drawing bricks on the side of a house; merely *suggesting* them would be good enough. However, with some technical drawings, it is good to show all the detail. For this assignment, draw two houses below, placing all the details on the front of each: one with brick, and the other with siding. Give each house a front door, two windows, and an A-frame roof.

To make straight lines across your house for the siding and bricks, measure equidistant 1/8" points up each side (A). Connect the horizontal lines with your ruler to make guidelines for your siding or bricks. With bricks, draw one layer and then start the second layer in the center of the first row. The third row will be the same as the first row. Use a ruler to draw the bricks and keep them even (C).

**C.**

**Brick House**                    **House with Siding**

**Pointer:** One of the reasons for using mechanical drawing tools is that it saves time. When using a t-square, place 1/8" marks on one side of the house, and slide your t-square down to draw and connect each line. Since your t-square will be *parallel* with the side of your drawing board, it will always give you parallel lines.

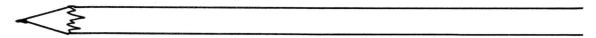

**Pointer:** If you have the desire to go a little further with mechanical drawing, you should obtain a drawing board, t-square, and triangle. A drawing board has a flat, smooth surface on which to tape your drawing paper. It also has a straight, smooth edge for your t-square to slide up and down (A). Your t-square is for making horizontal lines (B), and is a brace for making vertical lines with your triangle (C).

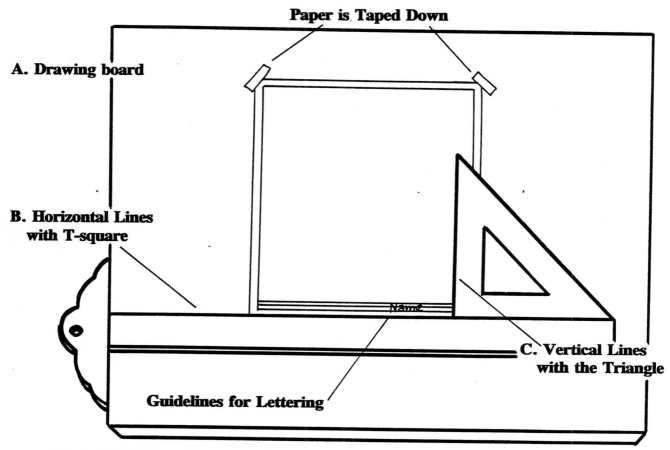

Begin by holding the t-square flush against the side of the drawing board, situating it low enough to place the bottom of the paper on. When the paper is perfectly even with the t-square, tape down the top left and right corners with masking tape. (Some students use tacks to hold down their paper, but this will eventually put holes in your drawing board, creating a rough surface.)

When you have your paper perfectly in place, it is a simple matter to draw vertical and horizontal lines. If you want to place a 1/4" border around the top and sides, measure 1/4" from the edge of the paper. Use the t-square for making horizontal lines, and the t-square and triangle for vertical lines. For the bottom border and guidelines for lettering, measure a mark 1/2" from the bottom, and then another mark 1/4", and another 1/8". The bottom border is always slightly larger than the top and side borders. Use your t-square to draw horizontal lines across your paper, dissecting the mark. The triangle can also give you a perfect 45 and 90 degree angle by placing it flush on the t-square.

This is only a basic introduction to get you started. There are plenty of good books in the library on technical or mechanical drawing, often referred to as *drafting*.

# Lesson #82: *Two-Point Perspective*

*Two-point perspective* is when you have *two* vanishing points instead of one (A). It also means you will have two sides going back in space instead of one (B). Connect the top and the bottom of the line in figure box (C) to the two vanishing points on the horizon. Draw the sides to your box with vertical lines.

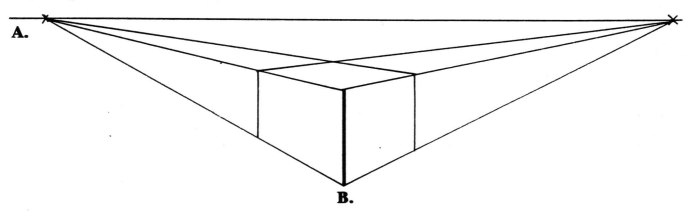

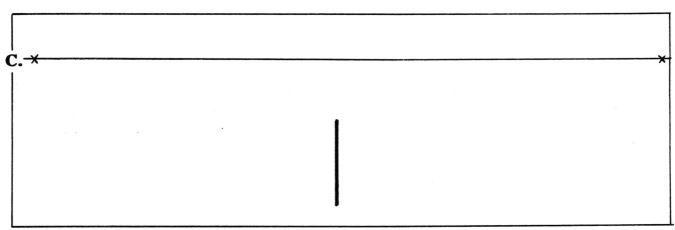

Now, do the entire two-point drawing on your own. First, draw the horizon line and place the vanishing points to the far sides. Draw a vertical line in the center, as shown in B, and connect the top and bottom to both vanishing points. Finally, draw the sides with vertical lines. Letter your name on the bottom using guidelines.

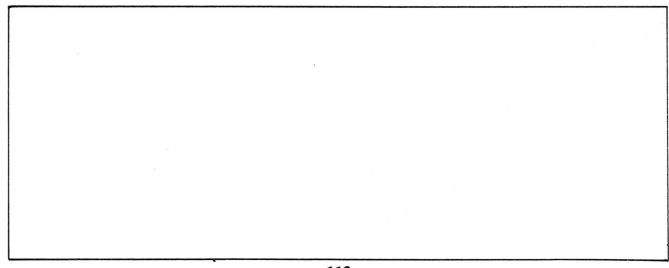

# Lesson #83: *Creating a House*

Let's take the same principles from Lesson #81, and create a house using two-point perspective. Follow the same procedures as in the previous lesson by drawing your horizon line and adding two vanishing points, one to either side of this line. Place a vertical line in the center of the page and below the horizon line. This is going to be the corner of your house. Connect the top and bottom to the vanishing points, then draw the sides with vertical lines. Lightly draw two windows and a door on one side of the house, and three windows on the other side (B). Then, taking your ruler, connect the top of the windows on one side to one VP and the top of the windows on the other side to the other VP. Connect the bottom of the windows in the same manner. Finally, do the same with the door. Do your drawing below (C).

**A.**

**B.**

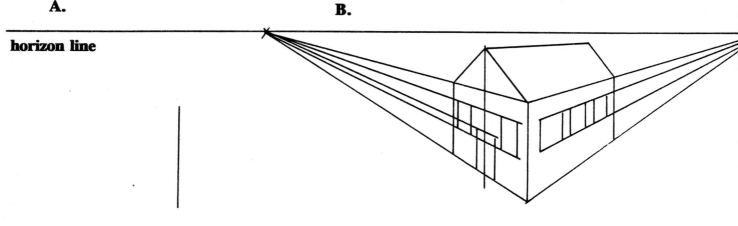

horizon line

**C.**

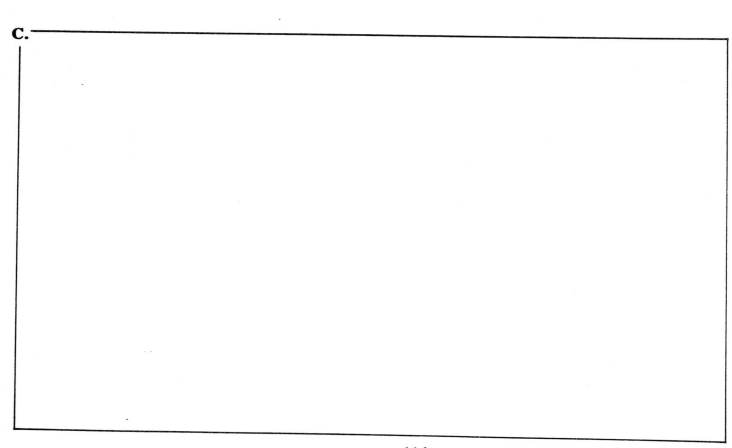

# Lesson #84: *Boxes & Cubes*

Do you remember how to draw cubes using freehand perspective (Lesson #32)? For this assignment, draw a box using one-point perspective (A), and another box using two-point perspective (B). These will be technical drawings, done with the use of a ruler. Let you guidelines go through the other boxes if need be. Then, draw two more boxes using freehand perspective: one point for one and two points for the other (C). Remember, freehand perspective is without the use of a ruler. Draw the four cubes in figure box D.

**A. One-Point Perspective**   **B. Two-Point Perspective**   **C. Freehand Perspective.**

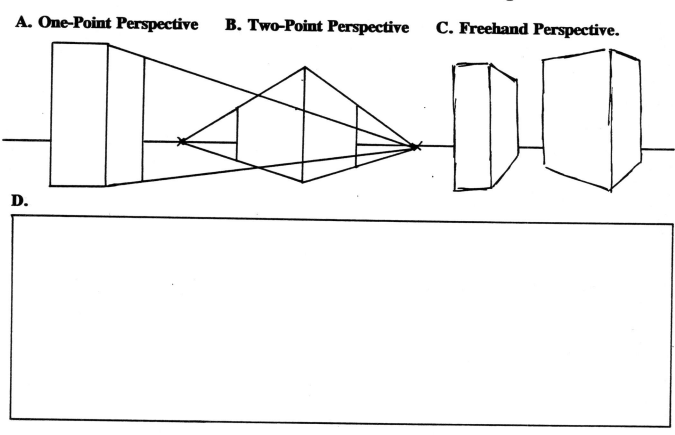

**D.**

Draw several three-dimensional boxes using one-point and two-point perspective in E. Situate them so some will be using one-point perspective and some two-point perspective (observe the boxes above). Draw all of them freehand, making some tall, some short, some thin, and some wide.

# Lesson #85: *Labeling Boxes*

**A.**

**B.**

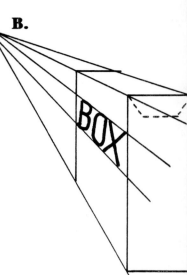

In Lesson #30, we learned how to place a label on a round object. The label and even the guidelines had to go *around* the jar or bottle (A). Now, let's learn how to place a label on a box. For all lettering you will need to use guidelines, just as you use guidelines for lettering your name. Guidelines in perspective will connect to a vanishing point (B). When letters recede in the distance, they become smaller and closer together. For this assignment, take a cereal box, and using one-point perspective, see if you can place the lettering on the box with guidelines in C. Use your violet pencil for this exercise, and color when finished. Letter your name on the bottom.

**C.**

# Lesson #86: *Looking Up/Looking Down*

Let's learn how to draw three-dimensional boxes from different *vantage points,* or eye level, looking up and looking down. This is somewhat similar to Lesson #78. If you are looking down on an object, you will have a high horizon line. In this position, you will see the top of the box (A). If you are looking up at an object, you will have a low horizon line. In this position, you will see the bottom of the box (B). If you are looking straight at a box, you will see neither the top or the bottom (C). Draw a box next to the ones illustrated below (A, B, & C) using the same horizon line and vanishing point.

A.     A.  Looking Down

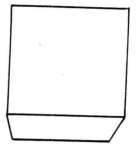

B.

horizon line

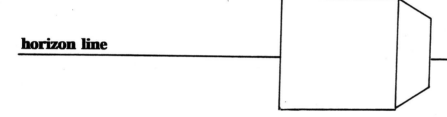

C.  Looking Straight

A.

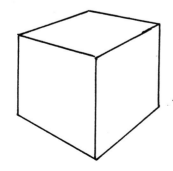

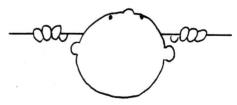

B.  Looking Up

# Lesson #87: *Overlapping Floating, Colorful Boxes*

**A.**

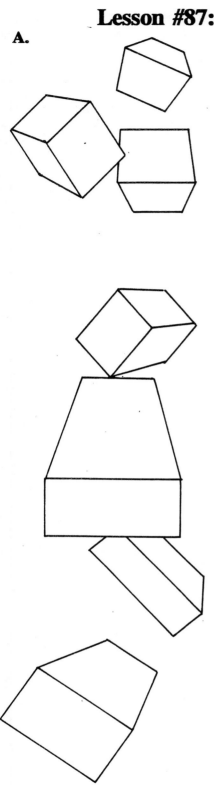

Let's see if you can make some floating boxes. Your eye level will be near the bottom of the paper. Imagine where your vanishing points would be. Lightly draw your boxes freehand, making them different sizes. Can you overlap some by placing one in front of another (A)? Overlapping creates depth. Do your drawing of floating boxes below.

# Lesson #88: *Stop! Yield! Slow!*

Today we are going to make road signs. All the signs are going to be made with geometric shapes (A) and a ruler or other mechanical device, such as a compass or triangle. Start with your yellow pencil, and lightly draw some of the geometric shapes from Lesson #74 and any other geometric shapes to create your own traffic signs. Make guidelines for all your lettering, and keep your letters the same thickness (B). Practice by lettering STOP (C). Draw five different designs for your traffic signs below (D). You may want to make a sign for "Yield," "Slow," "R/R" (railroad crossing), children at play, etc.

# Lesson #89: *What Else is in the Pantry?*

In Lesson #30, we filled Grandma's pantry with jars. Now, let's fill Grandma's pantry with cans, jars, and boxes: one shelf above eye level, one at eye level, and one below eye level. Draw some jars and cans on the next page, making sure to use ellipses to show they are round. Then, draw some boxes using one-point and two-point perspective, putting the boxes at different angles on the shelves (A & B). First, make a long horizon line across the middle of the next page that goes off your paper, and place your vanishing points far out to the sides (C). Then, draw three shelves and boxes, cans, and jars. Let's place one shelf above eye level, one below eye level and one at eye level. Label and letter all your containers using guidelines. You may want to place some cereal boxes, cans, and jars in front of you to have something to look at. Draw lightly and then add more color to Grandma's pantry when finished. Using guidelines, letter your name above the bottom border.

**A. One-Point Perspective**　　**C. Let Your Horizon Line Go Off the Paper**

**B. Two-Point Perspective**

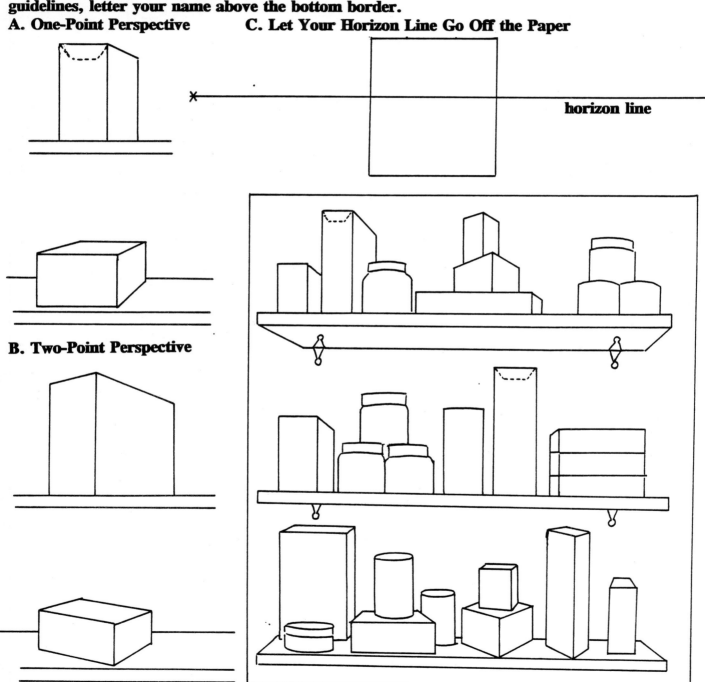

# Grandma's Pantry

# Lesson #90: *Shading With Line*

For this assignment, draw some boxes that are different heights and widths. With your drawing pencil, draw five different size boxes below (B). Use one-point perspective and a light source coming from the right (A). Place your vanishing point in the center of the horizon line. Shade the left side of the boxes with vertical lines using your ruler.

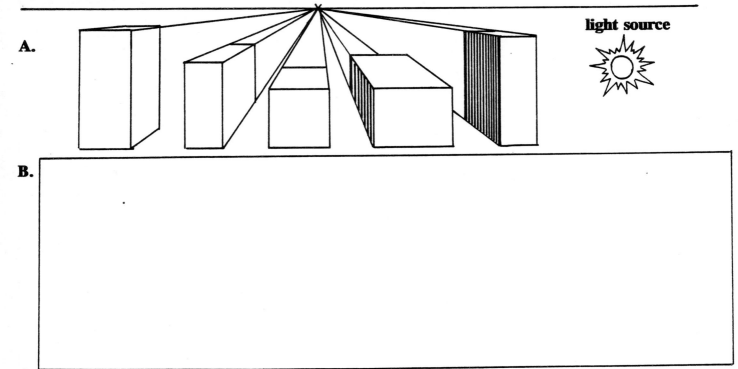

**A.**

light source

**B.**

For this part of the lesson, use two-point perspective. Draw a horizon line near the top of the figure box (below), and place your VP's to the far sides. However, this time the boxes are going to be open at the top, and the light will be coming from the left. Shade the right side of the boxes with vertical lines and use crosshatching to create a darker value inside the open tops (C). Notice that we are adding more *values* to these boxes.

light source

# Lesson #91: *Depth, Overlapping, & Color*

Draw some of the three-dimensional shapes found on the bottom of Lesson #74, along with some boxes like the ones below. Show depth using one-point perspective. Draw lightly with your violet pencil, placing your horizon line high on your picture plane (B). Mark the vanishing point in the center. Draw a series of lines from this VP to the foreground, and then place your objects inside these lines. Notice how your objects become smaller as they recede in the distance (A). Finally, overlap some of the objects to create more depth. Using your ruler, color the objects in the foreground with warm colors and vertical lines, and the objects in the background with cool colors and vertical lines.

**A.**

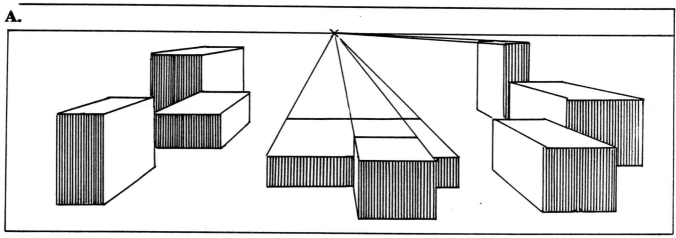

**B.**

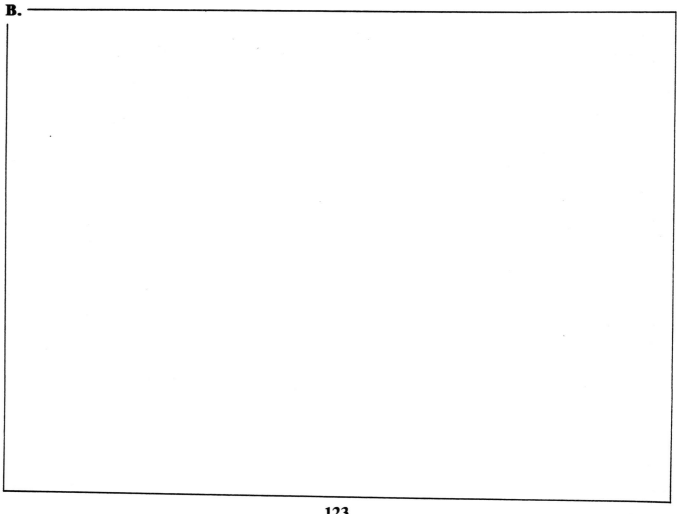

# Lesson #92: *Papetti's Grocery Store*

Today you are going to draw Papetti's Grocery Store. Start by drawing the grocery store using one-point perspective (see Lesson #76). You are also going to create signs for his store by using guidelines. Can you add boxes on the front porch for the fruits and vegetables, and letter the signs for each (A)? Place signs in the windows and on the porch (B). Draw siding or wood planks on the building using vertical lines. Finally, draw Papetti standing on the front porch (C). Use your ruler and drawing pencil to draw the scene below on the next page. You may want to turn your paper horizontally for a better composition.

**A. Fruits & Vegetables**

**B. Signs in the Windows**

**C. Papetti**

**Pointer:** Sometimes it is difficult to extend your vanishing points off the paper. The text may move and the edges, or binding, of the book may interfere with a straight line. However, try to keep your paper in a firm position and draw your lines as precise as possible. If you find it too difficult to work in the text, tape a single sheet of paper on the table to draw on.

# Lesson #93: *Fire Engines*

In Lesson #61, we designed a truck using freehand perspective. On the next page, we will design a fire engine using two-point perspective. Again, you may want to turn your page horizontally instead of vertically to allow for a better composition and more room to draw. First, draw a vertical line for the front corner of your fire engine below the horizon line (A). Have your VP's extend far to the sides (B). Using your orange colored pencil, connect one side to one VP, and the other to the other VP. Then make a long rectangular box (C). Add the details to your truck, using a ruler when possible. Remember, everything on one side of the truck goes to one vanishing point, and everything on the other side to the other vanishing point (D). Can you also draw some of the truck's accessories (E)?

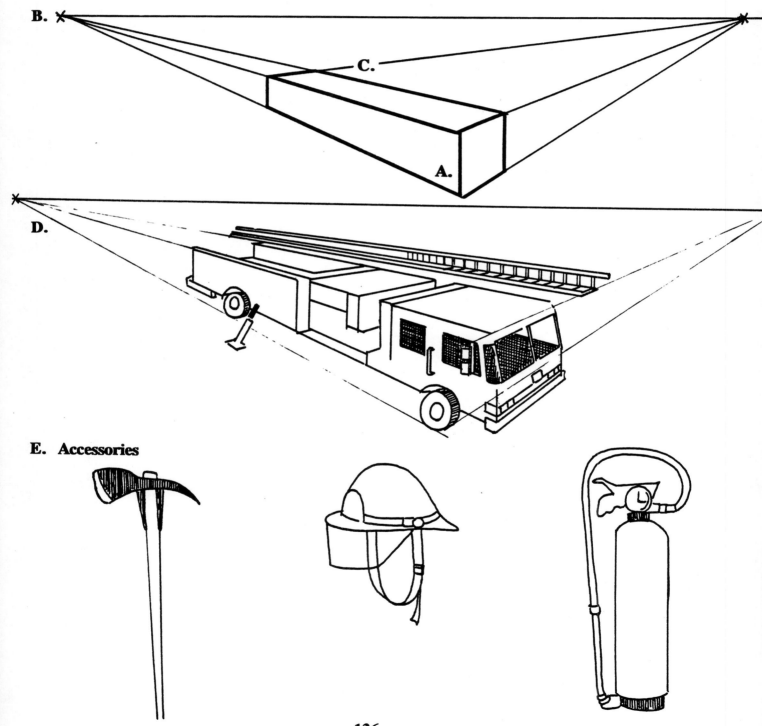

E. Accessories

126

**Pointer:** Drawing the fire engine this way and having to turn the text around will be more difficult because you will not be able to copy as well at this angle. However, you will have a more pleasing composition and will have more space to draw your truck.

# Lesson #94: *Grid Drawings*

Grid drawing is a good way of copying something exactly as it is. We are going to copy the picture of hands below (A) using a grid. To do this, draw a light grid over the picture (as in A), on a plain sheet of white paper. Place your lines 1/4" or 1/2" apart. When you are done, you will have perfect squares covering the picture. The next step is to draw another grid exactly like the first, and copy the picture frame by frame (B). Lightly number the squares on the picture-grid, and on the grid you have just drawn. For today's assignment, draw a grid on the top of the following page with the same amount of squares as the hands below (A). Then, copy the hands square by square. Doing a grid drawing is like drawing many little pictures to make one large picture.

A.

B.

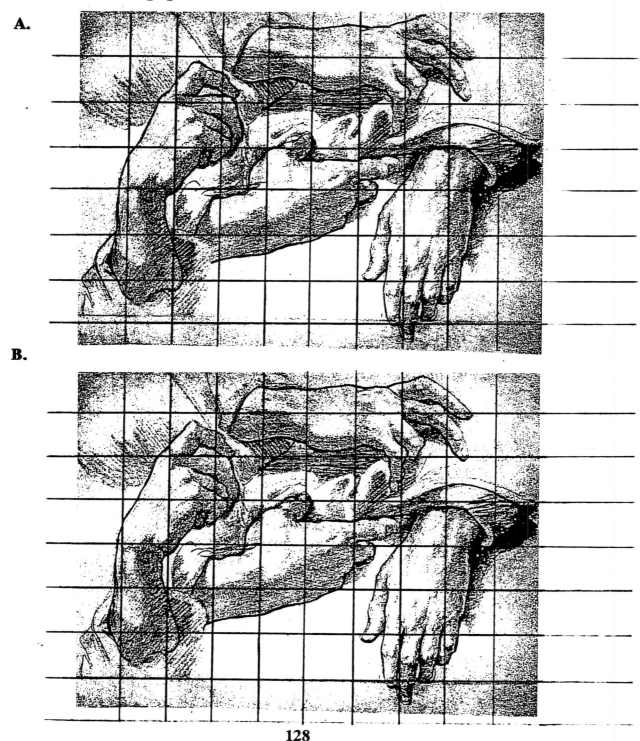

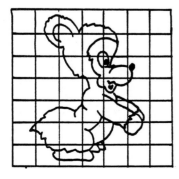

Lightly draw your grid above, and number the squares. Keep all the lines parallel with the sides of the paper by measuring two equidistant points from the side of the paper, and connecting the marks. Draw light grid lines. Your picture should be the focus of attention, and not the lines. Practice by drawing the little bear in the grid on the right.

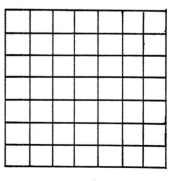

# Lesson #95: *Creative Grids*

**A.**

**B.**

There are many creative and fun ways to make a grid. For this assignment, grid the picture of the clowns below. First, using a ruler and your red pencil, connect the dots on either side of the picture. This will make seven equal squares. Then, draw a grid on page 131 using the same number of squares as in the picture below, but making the squares, or frames, different sizes and shapes. Make some longer, wider, thinner, etc. (A). There are many possibilities with grids that you may want to try. Copy (B) on the top of the next page using your own creative grid.

Draw your grid above. First, draw a large 7" square approximately the same size as the clown picture on page 130. Use your ruler for all straight lines. Then, draw each grid, or frame, with different proportions. Notice the grid example of the clowns to the left. Each square has the same picture in it as in figure box B, only they are larger, smaller, thinner, or wider. Copy the picture frame by frame. What do you think of doing a drawing like this?

**Name:**_____     **Date:** _____

# Lesson #96: RULES & MEASUREMENTS EXAMINATION

**I.   Fill in the blanks (5 points each):**
1.  The _____ _____ is where land meets sky.
2.  The _____ _____ is where all the lines connect that recede in the distance.
3.  _____ _____ means the same as horizon line.
4.  _____-point perspective is where all the lines converge to 2 points on the horizon line.
5.  A piece of paper is _____-dimensional.
6.  Perspective shows _____ in drawing.
7.  A _____ drawing is done with a ruler, t-square, compass, and/or other mechanical devices.
8.  _____ are used for lettering to assure that the letters are all the same height.

**II.   Draw 2 boxes below on the same horizon line. However, draw one with one-point perspective, and the other with two-point perspective (15 points). Refer to pafe 115.**

_____

**III.   Using your ruler, draw parallel guidelines and letter your name, last name first. Make the lower case (smaller) letters 1/4", and the capitals 3/8". Refer to the bottom of page 100. (15 points).**

**IV.   Draw an "A" frame house below, using one-point perspective. Draw two windows on the side, and place a door and two windows on the front. Give the house siding, and place shingles on the roof. Refer to Lessons #76 and #81. (30 points).**

**(Answers on Page 310)**

 # Portraits & Anatomy

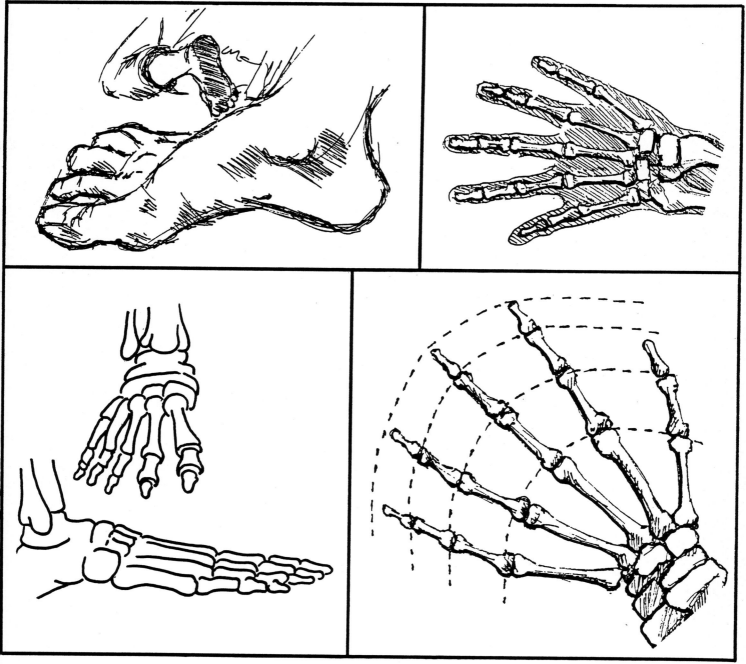

*"So God created man in His own image, in the image of God He created him."*

**Genesis 1:27**

# Lesson #97: *Drawing the Human Figure*

Do you know how many head lengths the mature human figure is?  How far the hands extend down to the side of the figure?  Where the mid-section or mid-point is?

The mature figure stands eight head lengths tall, and the hands extend down five head lengths from the top of the head (A).  The mid-section is under the pelvis, not the belly button.  These are called *proportions*, and the more we know about correct proportions, the easier it will be to draw the human figure.

Draw the skeleton (A) in the space below (B).  Use guidelines, and letter all the parts.  Look in the mirror and see if you can notice where your clavicle bone is.  Can you feel it?  What about your patella?  Rib cage?  Pelvis?  When you have completed the illustration, color in the different areas of the skeleton:  femur, patella, clavicle, etc., using warm and cool colors, and coloring different parts of the skeleton with different colors.  Use the color chart below for a coloring code (C).

**A.**

1

2

3

4

5

6

7

8

skull

clavicle

scapula

rib cage

humerus

radius

ulna

pelvis

femur

patella

tibia

fibula

**B.**

Color Code:  Skull     Clavicle     Scapula     Rib Cage     Humerus     Radius

Ulna     Pelvis     Femur     Patella     Tibia     Fibula

# Lesson #98: *Putting Meat on the Bones*

One of the most difficult things for young students to learn is how to put meat on the bones of their human figures. Once we begin to draw figures correctly, it becomes easier. Below are some stick figures in different positions. Draw the same figure next to each, and put meat on the bones. Also, draw clothing on them. On the bottom of the page, draw some stick figures skating and fishing (A and C). Then, draw them again with meat on their bones (B and D). Use your drawing pencil for this assignment.

**A. Skating**          **B.**                    **C. Fishing**          **D.**

# Lesson #99: *The Knee Bone's Connected to the Leg Bone!*

One of the easiest ways to draw the human figure is by connecting hot dog shapes and egg shapes. Let's draw the head with an egg shape (A). Add a larger egg shape for the rib cage (B). Below the rib cage, draw a shape that is like a round square, which will be the pelvis area (E). The egg shape and circle/square represents the rib cage, stomach and pelvis area, or torso. *Torso* means that part of the human body without the appendages: hands, feet, legs, arms, and head. Draw two long hot dog shapes connecting to the pelvis, which will be the upper legs (F). The biggest bone in the body, the femur bone, is located in the upper leg. Now, draw two slimmer hot dog shapes below the top sections of the leg (G). There are two thinner bones in the bottom part of the leg, the tibia and the fibula. The bottom and the top part of the leg are the same length; however, the top is wider than the bottom. For the feet, draw two short, fat hot dogs (H). The top of the arms are wider hot dog shapes than the bottom of the arms (C) because there is another large bone, the humerus, in the top part. The lower arm is like the lower leg, having two bones, the radius and ulna (D). The hands are short hot dog shapes, like the feet. Copy the figure below, and label all the parts, using guidelines for the lettering. Observe the skeleton on page 134. When you are finished, clothe your figure.

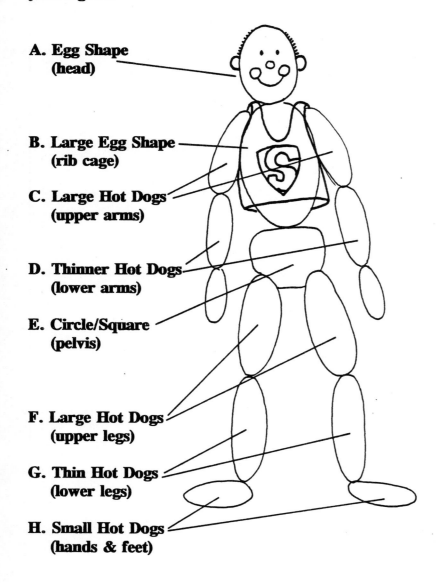

**A. Egg Shape**
(head)

**B. Large Egg Shape**
(rib cage)

**C. Large Hot Dogs**
(upper arms)

**D. Thinner Hot Dogs**
(lower arms)

**E. Circle/Square**
(pelvis)

**F. Large Hot Dogs**
(upper legs)

**G. Thin Hot Dogs**
(lower legs)

**H. Small Hot Dogs**
(hands & feet)

No!

## Lesson #100: *Little People*

For this assignment, fill the page with little people, but do not draw stick figures. See if you can draw each in the position described: a man sitting, a woman walking with a shopping cart, a boy bouncing a ball, someone sleeping, a man running, a boy flying a kite, a man with his hands above his head. Can you draw other "little people"? Try to remember the proportions that you have just learned. Are you drawing in the pelvis area? Are the upper arms and upper legs a little larger than the bottom extremities? Is the figure eight head lengths tall? Clothe your figures when finished.

# Lesson #101: *Smoothing out the Rough Spots*

Below are a series of *"hot dog"* figures. Smooth out the hot dog shapes, and try to make the outline of the figures more like the one in A. Always start by drawing lightly, and use hot dog shapes, ellipses, and egg shapes. Remember your proportions! How many head lengths is the figure? How far down do the hands extend? Where is the mid-section of the figure? Are you including the pelvis area? Draw some of your figures below, and then fill the next page with animated figures.

A.

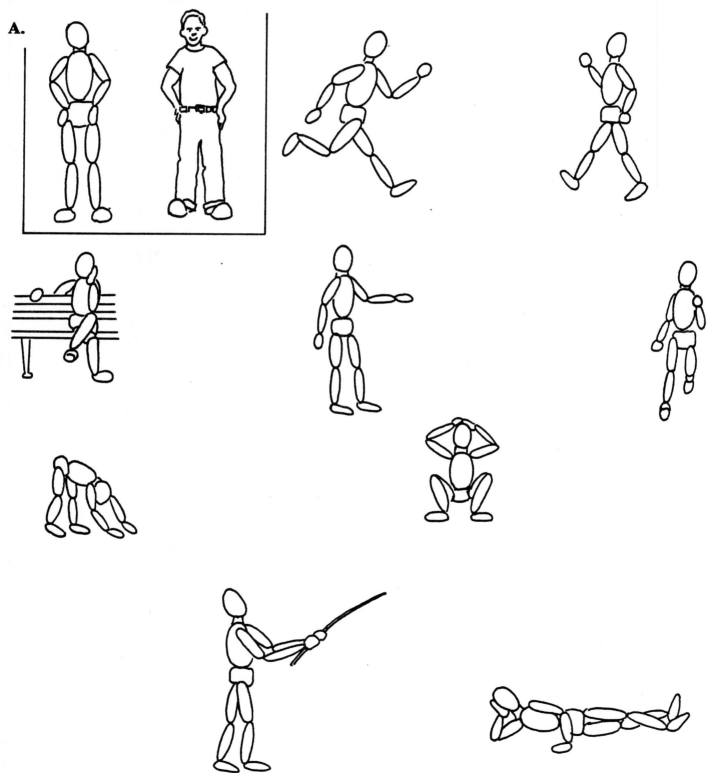

**Fill this page with people!  Lightly draw the figures with hot dog shapes.  Smooth out the features of the shapes, and put clothing on each when finished.**

# Lesson #102: *Drawing a Three-Fingered Hand*

Hands are one of the most difficult things for the young student to draw. Many times the student tries to hide the hands (A), erases them (B), or simply draws little circle-like hands (C). To build your confidence, we will start by drawing a simple, cartoon hand with three fingers and a thumb. First, draw a circle (D). Next, add three hot dogs for the fingers, and one smaller hot dog for the thumb (E). Draw a three-fingered hand below (F), and then draw a three fingered hand going around objects: a hand that goes around a hammer (G), hands that go around a basketball (H), and hands that go around a bat (I).

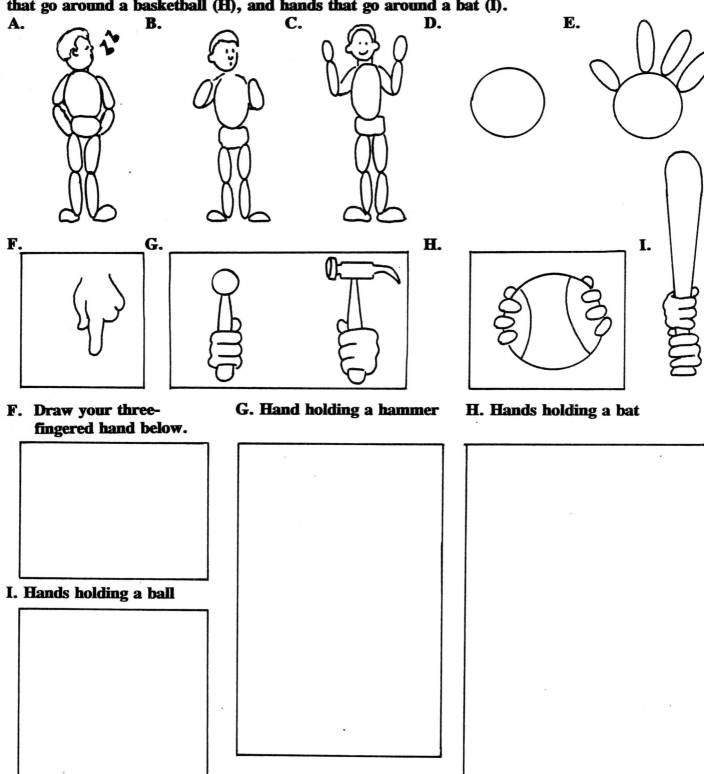

A.  B.  C.  D.  E.

F.  G.  H.  I.

**F. Draw your three-fingered hand below.**

**G. Hand holding a hammer**

**H. Hands holding a bat**

**I. Hands holding a ball**

140

# Lesson #103: *Going Around & Over*

For this assignment, you are going to draw a four-fingered hand going around a banana, with the banana peel overlapping the hand. Remember, whenever you draw something with thickness, like a rope (A) or finger (B) going around an object, it must be wider than the object at the point where it goes around.

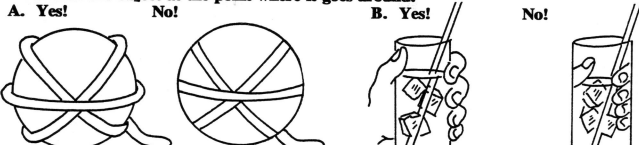

**A. Yes!**      **No!**            **B. Yes!**      **No!**

**C.**

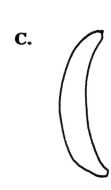

Start by drawing *lightly* to show how everything is constructed, even how parts look which are not seen (E). When drawing the hand with the banana, draw the entire banana first (C). Next, draw the hand going around the banana (D). Finally, draw the banana peel going over the hand (E). Darken just those areas that are seen (F). Draw your hand holding a banana in the figure box below (G).

**D.**

**E.**

**F.**

**G.**

# Lesson #104: *Rectangular Man*

Let's try another approach to drawing the human figure by creating the figures with long rectangular shapes for the arms and legs. This is going to be similar to Lesson #99, except we will use rectangular shapes instead of hot dog shapes for some of the parts of the body. Remember, the head (A) and torso, which is the chest and stomach (B), will remain chubby hot dog shapes, or ovals. The pelvis (underneath the chest and stomach) is another chubby hot dog (C). Next, attach the arms and legs. Each arm and leg is made up of two rectangular shapes (D). Finally, complete your *rectangular man* with two hot dog shapes for feet, and two small circles for hands (E).

**A. Head**  **B. Torso**  **C. Pelvis**  **D.**  **E.**

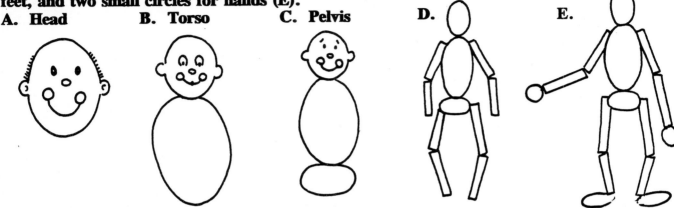

Practice drawing *rectangular man* on the next page. Make one figure running, one lifting weights, one sitting on a chair, and one walking. See if you can add more figures in other creative positions.

142

**Pointer:** Draw your *rectangular men* lightly, and then go over them to soften the curves of the arms, legs, and body. This will make them look more realistic.

# Lesson #105: *Clothing the Figure*

**A.**

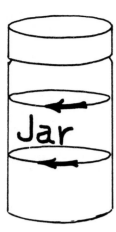

Whenever you draw clothes on a figure, you must remember that clothes go around the body, because the body is *round*. It is the same principle as placing a label on a jar; it goes around (A).

Draw the figure below and place clothing on him. Remember, a headband goes around his head (B), the T-shirt collar goes around his neck (C), the shorts go around his waist and legs (D), the wristbands go around his wrists (E), and even the shoes go around his ankles (F). Draw the figure below (G), and show how the clothing goes *around* his body.

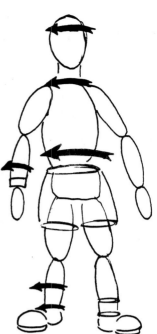

**B. Headband**

**C. Collar**

**D. Shorts**

**E. Wristbands**

**F. Shoes**

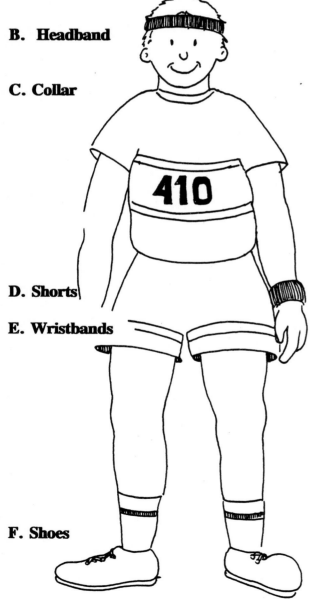

**G.**

# Lesson #106: *Creating Flesh Tones*

Most students have a limited number of colored pencils, making it a bit difficult to create unique colors, like flesh tones. However, we should be able to combine colors to make skin tones. Everyone's skin color: yellow, red, brown, or white, has a slightly orange undertone. The *undertone* is the underlying color. Therefore, start with your orange pencil. For a Caucasian, simply blend white over a light, soft layer of orange. For an African American, use a little brown over a light layer of orange. For an Indian, use orange, very little red, a touch of light brown, and blend with white. Finally, for an Oriental, use a light layer of orange, a little yellow, and then blend with white. Practice the four different flesh tones in the circles below, and then color in the four figures.

**Caucasian**    **African American**    **Indian**    **Oriental**

**Angled Point**

**Pointer:** There are several ways to color with colored pencils. One is with a sharp point, and the other is with a point that is dull or angled. For flesh tones, it is better to work with a dull or angled point, which will give a soft blended area. Practice coloring like this, softly blending the colors together.

# Lesson #107: *Completing the Figures*

Below are several figures that need to be completed. Can you add the extremities?
*Extremities* are limbs of the body such as arms, legs, hands, and feet. Color when finished.

# Lesson #108: *Placing People in a Picture*

Let's place people by the seashore. Draw some of them in the water, some on the boat, and some of them on the beach. How about children playing with shovels and buckets near the sand castle? Draw people in beach chairs, sitting under beach umbrellas, and walking on the beach. Finally, place seashore designs in the frame around your picture, and color everything when finished.

# Lesson #109: *People in Perspective*

We can use perspective for people the same way we use perspective for objects. For today's assignment, draw a horizon line in the figure box below, and place a vanishing point in the center. Draw two lines going out from this point on both sides (A). Using these as guidelines, draw your people, making them smaller as they go back in the distance (B). Draw everything with your yellow pencil. Then, draw in the details, and color when complete.

**A.**            **B.**

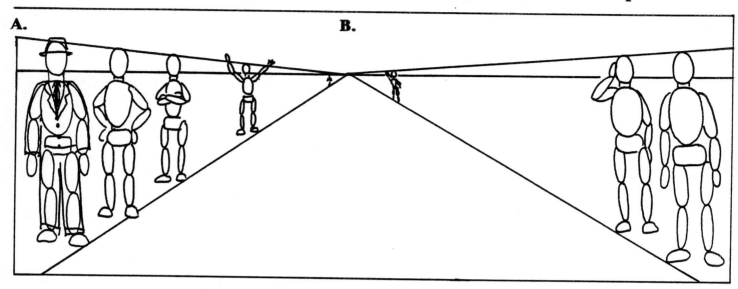

**People in Perspective**

# Lesson #110:  *Four-Fingered Hands*

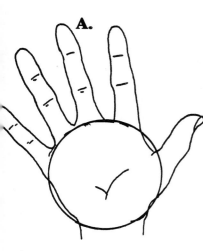

**A.**

**B.**

In Lesson #102, we learned how to make three-fingered hands.  Today we are going to add another finger!  Start with a circle (A), and add the four fingers and thumb.  Place them a littler closer together, and draw them a little thinner to give them room to go around the palm.  Look closely at one of your fingers.  Notice there are two knuckles and a fingernail (B).  Knuckles are where bones connect.  In the long rectangle below (C), draw one of your fingers.  Suggest where the knuckles are, and draw the fingernail.  For fun, you may want to draw one of your parent's fingers. In the larger figure box (D), draw your hand in any position.

**C. Draw your Finger**

**D. Draw your Hand**

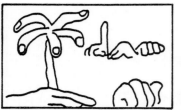

# Lesson #111: *A Landscape of Hands*

For this assignment, create a landscape of hands. Place your hand in different positions to create trees, clouds, fences, rocks, and so forth. See how creative you can be with this exercise. Use your yellow pencil to sketch lightly, and then color with warm colors.

# Lesson #112: *Putting Hands on People*
### Below are some people doing different activities.  Draw hands on each of them.

# Lesson #113: *Tug of War*

For this exercise, draw two rows of people going from this page over to the next. First, complete the row of clowns, keeping them all the same size. Use the guidelines provided for the top of the head, the chin, the bottom of the pelvis area, and the bottom of the feet. Connect their hands, and give them creative, colorful outfits.

8 head lengths

Mid Section

**On the bottom of these two pages, complete the two lines of men in the tug of war, making them the same size. These are strong men so make them muscular. Can you put different expressions on their faces? Make sure to draw their hands going around the rope.**

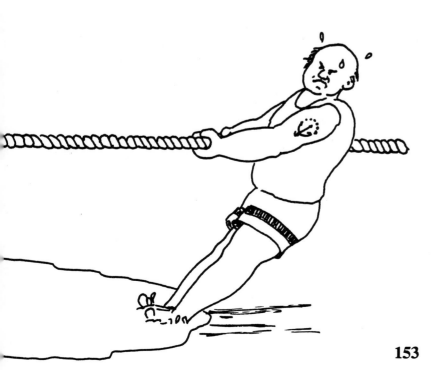

# Lesson #114: *Portraits*

When we draw someone's face, it is called a *portrait*. The human face can be wonderful subject matter for the art student, so do not be intimidated. It takes much practice and time before the student will produce a likeness to the face he or she is drawing. First, it is important to learn about *proportions*. Just as we learned about proportions for the human body, the same holds true for the human head.

There are basically three different positions for drawing a portrait: the front view (A), the three-quarters view (B), and the profile (C). For now we will concern ourselves with the front view. The first thing to do is draw an egg shape. Remember, go around lightly four or five times with your pencil. Then divide that shape into equal quarters, side to side and top to bottom (D). The eyes are located on the middle line separating the top half of the head from the bottom. Many students think the eyes are higher up on the head (E). To draw the eyes correctly, they should be one eye apart. Remember, the eys are in the center of the head.

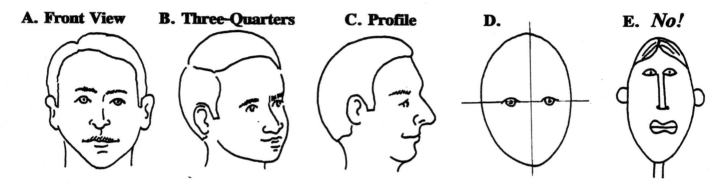

**A. Front View**   **B. Three-Quarters**   **C. Profile**   **D.**   **E. *No!***

Draw a horizontal line halfway down from the eye line (F). This is where the bottom of the nose sits. Next, draw the eyebrows slightly above the eyes and draw another horizontal line across the head at that point (G). The nose extends down from the eyebrows to line (F) for its base. A straight line down from the center of the eyes will give you the corners of the mouth (H). The ears extend from the eyebrow line to the nose line. A straight line down from the inside corners of the eyes will give you the width of the nose and nostrils (I). The hair is puffed up on the head and not flat, and the neck is almost as wide as the head (J). Again, look at the face in E to see some of the wrong ways some students draw facial features.

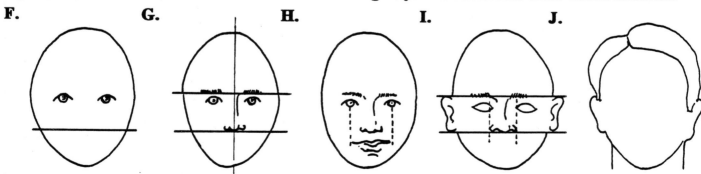

**F.**   **G.**   **H.**   **I.**   **J.**

Use a mirror and draw your self-portrait on the next page. Lightly lay in all of the guidelines for proper proportions before beginning. Date your drawing. Remember, this is your first self-portrait. It takes a lot of time and patience to learn how to draw portraits correctly. For now, just have fun! Go to the library and look at some of the portraits by Rembrandt van Rijn.

## A. Self-Portrait

Draw your self-portrait in figure box A. Select two pictures from a magazine of a three-quarters view and a profile of the human face, and draw them below (B and C). Lightly draw all three portraits with your yellow pencil and color when finished.

## B. Three-Quarters View

## C. Profile

**Pointer:** To learn more about how to draw portraits, model the human head out of clay. This will allow you to understand all of the different shapes and forms of the head.

# Lesson #115: *Nose, Lips, & Eyes*

It is helpful to learn little hints for drawing facial features such as the nose, lips, and eyes. Let's draw some facial features below.

As mentioned in Lesson #114, the nose is drawn down from the eyebrows, and not from the eyes! The nose is as wide as the corners of the eyes (A). At the bottom of the nose is a round shape which is connected on either side by the nostrils. Under this is a teardrop shape which connects the nose to the lips. Draw your nose below.

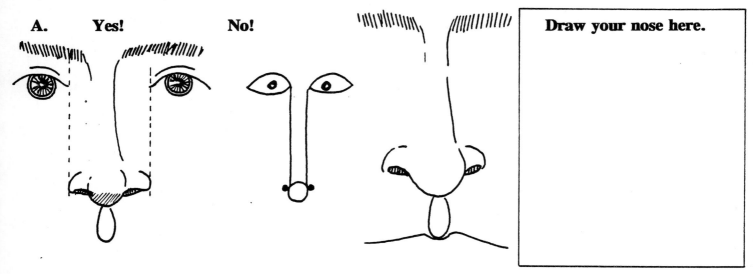

**A.  Yes!        No!                              Draw your nose here.**

The top lip is shaped like a wide "M", and the bottom lip like a wide "W". The teardrop from the nose sits directly in the wide "M" (B). Many students draw lips that look like a peanut (C). The only dark line for the lips is the center line for the mouth. This line has some curves to it, and should not be drawn as a straight line. The line for the top and bottom lips are drawn very lightly.

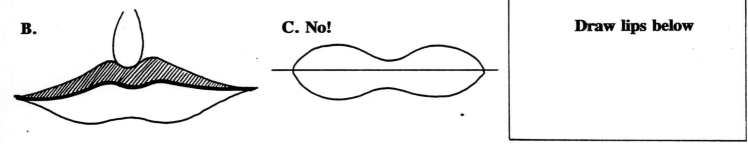

**B.                          C. No!                          Draw lips below**

The eye is a sphere or ball shape. It sits in the eye socket and is covered by the eyelids. The top lid comes over the eye and is drawn with a heavy dark line. The bottom lid is very light. The iris is the larger circle within the eye, and the pupil is the smaller darker circle. For now, you can draw the iris by using spoke-like lines that go in a circle (D). Leave a little highlight in your eyes, like a little white window.

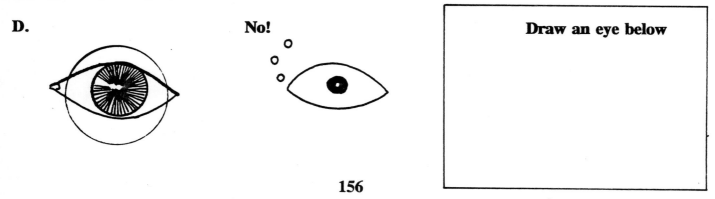

**D.                          No!                          Draw an eye below**

156

# Lesson #116: *Smiling Faces*

Can you draw a smiling face? Look at your face in the mirror and see how the mouth is shaped when you are smiling (A). When a person laughs, the mouth is open (B). Using your orange pencil, draw a smiling and laughing mouth below (C and D). Do not color the whites of the eyes and the teeth a bright white, but give them a very light color. Add a very light orange to the whites of the eyes so they will not stand out as much. Add just a touch of violet to the teeth to give them a faint color, and then blend with white. Also, lips are not red. They are a slightly darker skin color. Color your lips orange and white with a touch of brown. Do not outline them, but let the color be the outline.

| A. Smiling | B. Laughing | C. Smiling | D. Laughing |
|---|---|---|---|
|  |  | | |

Create some other facial expressions. How about a sad look, an angry look, or an expression of excitement? Find some pictures of faces with different expressions to copy. Use your orange pencil, and draw these expressions in the four figure boxes below. Finally, do a self-portrait of yourself looking in the mirror, and select one of the expressions to wear on your face. When you are finished, lightly color the portraits with colored pencils.

| Sad | Angry | Your Self-Portrait with Expression |
|---|---|---|
| | | |
| Excited | Perplexed | |

**This is me.**

# Lesson #117: *Funny Faces*

Let's create some funny faces. Find three objects around the house that will distort your image, such as a stainless steel soup ladle, a kettle, a teapot, or a large soup spoon. Hold them up to your face and draw your images below. Can you add expression to the pictures as you pose? Use your light blue pencil and color in the three self-portraits when finished.

**A. Me in a ladle.**  **B. Me in a kettle.**  **C. Me in a soup spoon.**

# Lesson #118: *Making a Collage*

A collage is a composition made up of different materials like cloth or paper. For today we are going to make a collage with cut paper. First, find some old magazines and cut out eyes, noses, mouths, and ears, and glue them on the face in A. See if you can make a complete face. Then draw the same face in figure box B and see what it looks like. On the bottom of the page, draw two large heads in the figure boxes (C and D). Cut out and add only half of the features in each: one eye, half a mouth, one ear, part of the nose and half of the hair. Then, see if you can draw the rest to make a matching face.

A.

B.

C.

D.

159

*"When you are out for a walk, see to it that you watch and consider men's postures and actions as they talk, argue, laugh or scuffle together; their own actions; and those of their supporters and onlookers; and make a note of these with a few strokes in your little book which you must always carry with you."*
                                                    **Leonardo Da Vinci**

## Lesson #119:  *Leonardo da Vinci*

Leonardo da Vinci was a Renaissance man.  Do you know what a *Renaissance man* is? It is someone who can do a lot of things in an excellent manner.  Da Vinci was a painter, scientist, inventor, sculptor, musician, and one of the most versatile men of the Renaissance. The Renaissance (1400-1600) was a period of revival in classical learning, especially in the arts. Among the many great things Da Vinci accomplished was his research in studying the human anatomy.  Go to the library and look at some of Leonardo's drawings of the human figure and draw several of them below.  Color in the figure boxes with light brown before beginning, and then complete the drawings with your dark brown and black pencils.

# Lesson #120: *Keeping a Journal*

Leonardo da Vinci was also noted for keeping some of the best art journals in the history of mankind. His journals were of the highest quality, and included excellent drawings of the human figure, nature, buildings, and inventions. His writings revealed much thought as he searched for elements of truth. Take a look at his journals, and then write a page in your own journal below. Include drawings of the things around you which filled your day.

Date: _____

Location: _____

_____
_____
_____
_____
_____
_____
_____
_____
_____
_____
_____
_____
_____
_____
_____
_____
_____
_____
_____

# Lesson #121: *ANATOMY & PORTRAIT EXAMINATION*

**I.  Fill in the blanks (5 points each):**

1.  The mature human figure stands _____ head lengths tall.
2.  The eyes are one _____ apart.
3.  The mid-section of the human figure is below the _____.
4.  The hands extends down _____ head lengths.
5.  The ear extends down from the eyebrow to the bottom of the _____.
6.  _____ _____ _____ was known as a Renaissance man because he could do many things in an excellent manner.
7.  Three views of the head for portrait drawing are:  _____, _____, and _____.
8.  When you do a drawing of yourself, it is called a _____ _____.
9.  The _____ (1470-1600) was known as a period of classical revival and a rebirth of the arts.
10. Rembrandt van Rijn was a great _____ artist.

**II.  Matching:  Match each part (number) on the body with the correct term (letter) in the right column.  Place the letter next to the number (3 points each).**

___ 1.
___ 2.
___ 3.
___ 4.
___ 5.
___ 6.
___ 7.
___ 8.
___ 9.
___ 10.

A.  Femur
B.  Pelvis
C.  Skull
D.  Clavicle
E.  Radius & Ulna
F.  Scapula
G.  Humerus
H.  Rib Cage
I.  Tibia & Fibula
J.  Patella

**(Answers on page 310)**

**III. Draw the human head in the figure box with all the proper proportions. Illustrate where the eyes, nose, ears, and mouth go by using guidelines. Complete the head by drawing the neck and hair (20 points.)**

# Nature

*"In every seed to breathe the flower,*
*In every drop of dew*
*To reverence a cloistered star*
*Within the distant blue;*
*To wait the promise of the bow*
*Despite the cloud between,*
*Is Faith - the fervid evidence*
*Of loveliness unseen."*

**John Banister**

*"Nature is the art of God."* **Dante**

# Nature

Nature studies can be a wonderful form of learning, especially for the young artist. We greatly encourage you to take your pencils and pad and go outdoors to study what God has created. There are many interesting and delightful things to observe: rock formations, insects, flowers, trees, birds, and clouds. Nature studies encourage us to draw from life. Going outside can open our eyes to light and the way it forms things with a brilliant array of colors. God's studio, the outdoors, can be much more rewarding than simply drawing at your desk or in the comfort of your own home.

Throughout *Feed My Sheep*, you will continually be encouraged to keep an art journal. As an art student, learn to draw the things which are around you. Nature studies are perfect for this: a branch with a few leaves, some pebbles, a distant tree, a running brook, weeds, thistles, and so on. The Orientals are noted for the simple studies they do from nature: one flower, a branch and a song bird, or a sunset.

There are several things you may want to take along when you go outside:

1. A hat to protect you from the sun.
2. Clips to hold your paper down when it is windy.
3. A comfortable chair.
4. Your art supplies.

*"It would not be right if in drawing from nature I took up too many details."*

Van Gogh

# Lesson #122: *Simple Nature Studies*

One of the biggest concerns students have is not knowing what to draw or paint. Nature will provide a wonderful wealth of subject matter to draw from. At first it will be rather difficult to comprehend nature in all her glorious attire, but after a while it will become a delightful studio for learning. How does one go about drawing a panoramic landscape, or a forest, or a mountain range? The key to studying nature is to start simple, learning to have a better understanding of how things are created.

Therefore, let's start by doing some simple studies. Go outside and collect three stones, some leaves, berries, and a few acorns (if available). Place your subject matter on a piece of dark paper. Shine a spotlight on it, or place your subject matter next to the light from a window. Color the three figure boxes on this page with your light brown pencil, and then use your light brown, dark brown, and black pencils to draw the nature studies. However, add a little blue for the stones, a little dark green for the leaves, and a little orange for the acorns.

**Leaves & Berries**

**Three Stones or Pebbles**

**A Few Acorns**

165

# Lesson #123: *Drawing a Flower*

There are a few simple rules to follow when drawing a flower. For one thing, most flowers are round. You either see them as a circle (A) or on an angle as an ellipse (B). Therefore, draw a circle or an ellipse to represent the flower. Secondly, all of the petals come out of the center like spokes on a wheel and the center of the flower goes down into the stem. For this assignment, find a flower and draw it at different angles with your yellow pencil. Use ellipses or circles and have the petals go to the center, connecting everything to the stem. Color your flowers when finished. Finally, research the definition of a flower. Then locate and identify these parts of the flower: the pistil, the stamen, the corolla, and the calyx.

# Lesson #124: *Foreshortening*

    *Foreshortening* is a term used in drawing to show perspective, or depth, by making certain areas larger or smaller. For instance, when drawing a flower at a certain angle (A), the petals in the foreground will be drawn much larger than the petals on the far side of the flower. Draw a flower below in C, showing foreshortening by making the petals in the foreground larger. Use your violet pencil, and when finished, color it with cool colors. Notice the flowers in B have two layers of petals that connect to the center. The first layer goes around in one circle, and the second layer of petals follows in another circle, all connecting in the center. Draw the flower below in D with an orange pencil, and color it with warm colors when finished.

A.

B.

C.

D.

167

# Lesson #125: *Pinecones*

For this assignment, we are going to draw pinecones. Pinecones can be found just about anywhere. We live in the Florida Keys and there are even pinecones there! Pinecones are a wonderful subject matter to study. If you look closely, you will see some of God's patterns of creativity at work. First, just like the flower, there is a center which the stems come out from (A). Second, there is a pattern similar to the way we drew bricks in Lesson #51, as one layer goes around, and then another layer starts in the center of the first layer (B). Finally, some of the stems come out at angles. You can draw some of them the same way as the flower petals, using foreshortening (C). Other stems can be drawn at different angles to show the curves. Remember, even though they come out at angles, they are still drawn to the center of the cone (D). For this assignment, find some pinecones to draw on the next page, placing one in each of the figure boxes. In one, draw the pinecone with pencil. In another, use your light brown, dark brown, and black pencils, toning the background with your light brown pencil. In another, use your dark brown, black, and white pencils. Finally, in the last one, use any colors you like.

A.

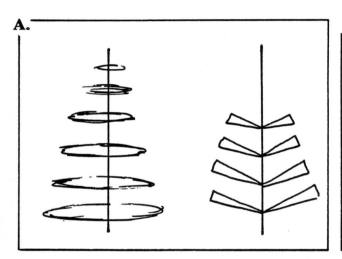

B.

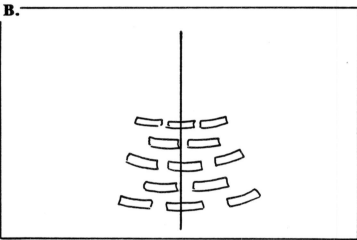

C.

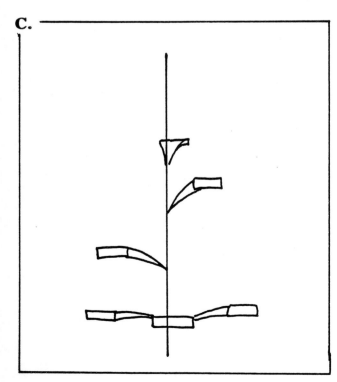

D.

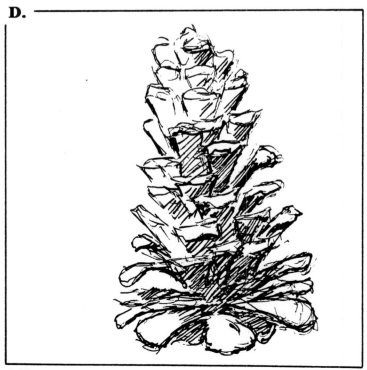

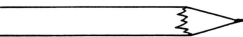

**Pointer:** While I was teaching in the public schools, one of my students drew a pinecone and received first prize in the county for her artwork. It is not *what* we draw that makes it good, but the *quality*, or degree of excellence of the drawing.

# Lesson #126: *Designing Floral Patterns*

There are many different ways of drawing the same things. Let's draw some more flowers. This time we will draw them with a sense of design, trying to create an interesting pattern. One approach is to draw flowers as though they were stained glass or a mosaic, breaking up each flower with segmented patterns (A). Another way is by doing a contour drawing, allowing your pencil to freely flow with floral patterns and designs (B), as in Lesson #46. In the bottom figure boxes, experiment with each drawing. Color one with warm colors, and the other with cool colors. Be creative with your colors!

**A.**

**B.**

**Mosaic with Warm Colors**

**Contour with Cool Colors**

# Lesson #127: *Let There Be Light!*

Place faces on the
suns.  Can you also draw beams
around their faces?  Color the sun at
the top yellow and white.  Color the next two (one on
each side) yellow.  Then the next two yellow with some orange.
Finally, color the last two yellow and red and orange.

Shade the trees.  Notice where the sun is in each
picture.  Which side will be in sunlight and which side
will be in shade?  Color the sunny side of your tree
and the grass below it with yellow and a little light
green.  Color the shaded side and the grass in the
shade with light green, dark green, and dark blue.

**Put shining faces on the suns above.**

# Lesson #128: *How to Draw a Tree*

Trees make good outdoor studies. There is such a variety to choose from, and you can draw them in their different seasonal attire: summer, autumn, winter, and spring. However, trees are difficult to draw. It might take some time to learn how to draw a tree in a pleasing manner.

A.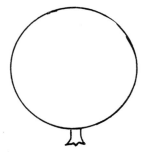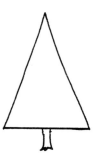

 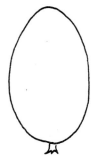

The first thing to do when drawing a tree is decide whether it is long or wide (A). If it is a long tree, then hold your paper vertically. If it is a wide tree, hold your paper horizontally.

After you have figured out how you are going to place the tree on your paper, take a pencil and lightly sketch it in. You want to do this in a few seconds, just to see how the tree will be situated on your paper and to show the overall shape of the tree (B). Does it have a round shape? Is it cone shaped? Is it shaped like a long ellipse or a wide ellipse?

B.

C.

On the next page, draw and color a tree without leaves. It is best to do this outdoors, but if it is not the season, then you can find a picture to copy. Again, is it long or wide? What is its basic shape? When drawing trunks or limbs, they are always thickest near the base, and thinner as they extend out (C), like tributaries of a river. Draw some other things in your landscape along with the tree, and color it in when finished.

**Pointer:** Remember, the first thing you always want to do is figure out if your composition is long or wide, and turn your paper the proper way to achieve a pleasing composition. When we do not take this into consideration, we have a tendency to *scrunch* our subject matter into the picture, especially trees.

# Lesson #129: *Name that Tree*

Below are some of the many trees which God has created. Can you identify different trees? Draw them in the figure boxes on the next page. Notice the figure boxes are rather small. Learn how to draw things large and small. Today, we will draw them very *small*. Lightly draw the shape of each tree, and then add the details with darker values. Use your colored pencils. Finally, letter each tree's name underneath your drawings.

**Balsam Fir**

**Common Cottonwood**

**Sugar Maple**

**Northern White Cedar**

**White Oak**

**Lombardy Poplar**

**Lesson #130:** On a 22" x 28" sheet of white poster board, lightly draw a tree with one of your pencils. Make sure to draw the tree lengthwise on the poster board. When you are finished, color everything in with colored markers.

# Lesson #131: *Learning about Leaves*

For this assignment, go outside and find some leaves. Draw five different types on the next page. First, lightly draw the overall shape of the leaf, and then start changing the form and adding detail. Use thick and thin lines to draw the veins in each leaf. Use your light brown pencil to color in the background, and then color each leaf with an assortment of colors. Practice making a variety of greens in the leaves below, and see if you can color them their exact colors.

**Cone Birch**

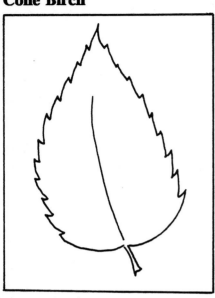

**White Birch**

**Common Cottonwood**

**Hickory**

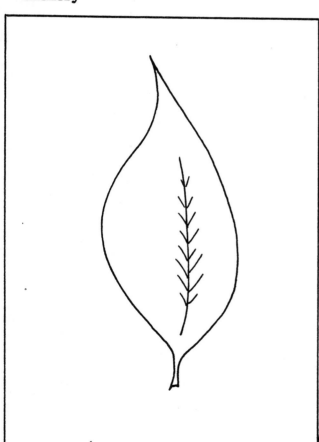

**Maple**

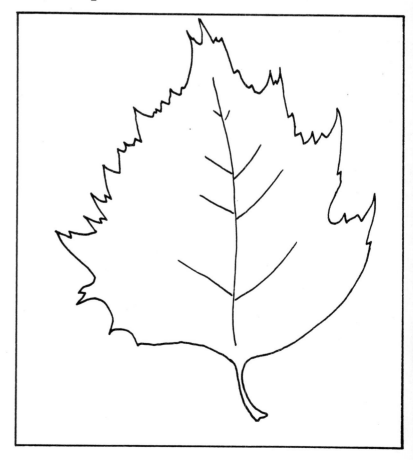

176

*"She bid me take love easy, as the leaves grow on the tree...."* **William Yeats**

# Lesson #132: *Finding the Missing Clue*

For this assignment, go outside and find clues that identify different trees. Trees will let you know who they are by what they drop under their boughs: acorns, pinecones, leaves, needles, branches, and so forth. Gather and draw evidence for two trees on the next page. Also, do a small drawing of each tree. You may want to draw an acorn and a leaf from the tree, or a part of a branch and a pinecone that identify it. Use your colored pencils.

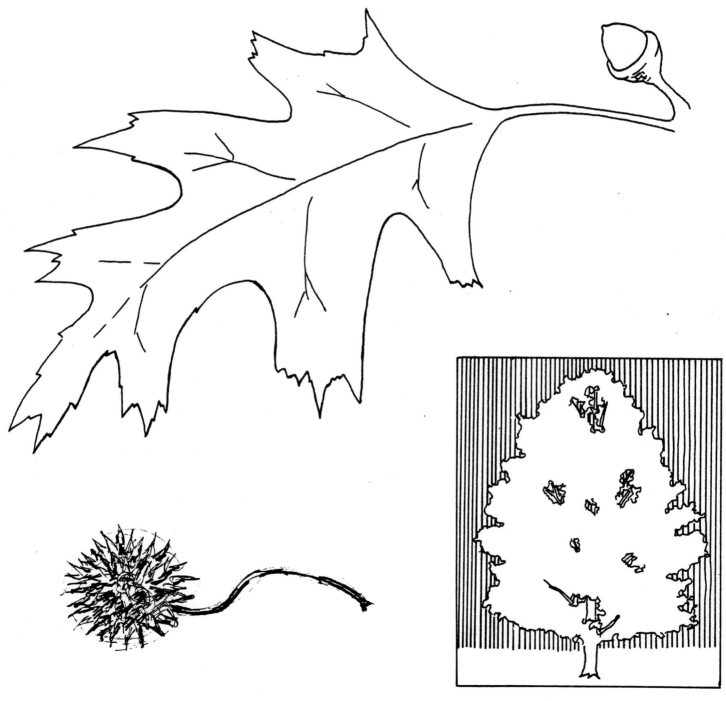

*"A free mind is a great thing, no doubt, but loftiness of heart, belief in goodness, capacity for enthusiasm and devotion, the thirst after perfection and holiness, are greater things still."*

Amiel

**Tree #1**                    **Evidence**

**Tree #2**                    **Evidence**

# Lesson #133: *Putting the Limbs to the Trunk*

There are several things to know about drawing trees. First, it is good to draw trees with thick and thin lines. This will allow light to come into your tree, and also make the branches more delicate (A). Second, do not draw wavy limbs (B). The best way to start your tree is by using angles to show its form (C). Bark is drawn the same way we drew the grain in wood, using thick and thin lines. Always draw more bark on the shaded side of the tree, and less on the side where the light is shining (D). Leaves are drawn with thick and thin lines (E). Try drawing the tree below (C) on the bottom of the next page. Then, draw several leaves and another tree, using contour lines for both. Draw them in the remaining figure boxes on the next page. Remember, a contour line is one continuous line drawn without lifting your pencil from the paper (F and G). Look at another example on the top of page 181. Finally, use colors other than brown to color your tree trunks and limbs. You may want to use different combinations of red, blue, yellow, and green. See what colors you can create in the four tree trunks below (H).

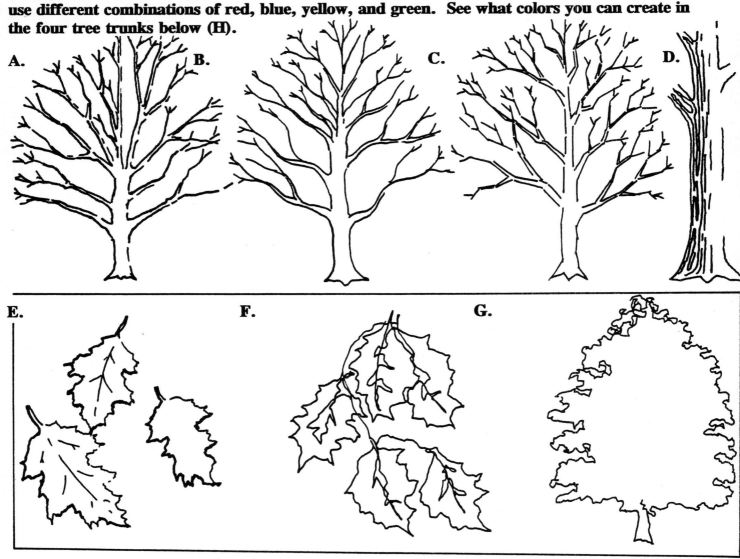

A.    B.    C.    D.

E.    F.    G.

## H. Mixing different browns

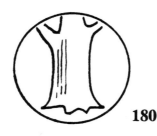

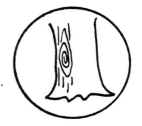

*"Poems are made by fools like me, but only God can make a tree."* Joyce Kilmer

**Tree with Contour Line**

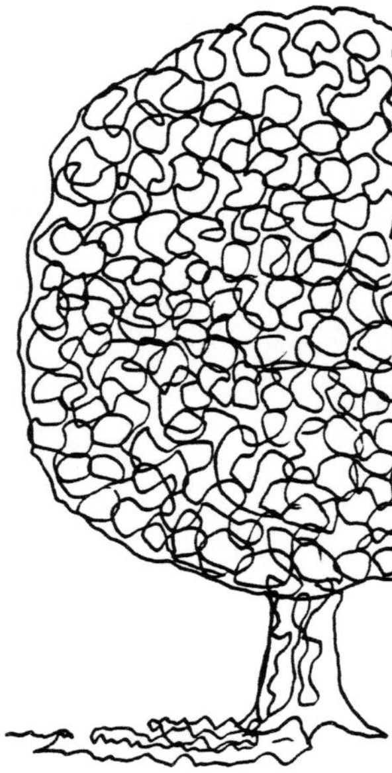

**Tree with Contour Line**

**Leaves with Contour Line**

**Winter Tree**

# Lesson #134: *How to Draw an Iris*

Students will learn many of God's principles about patterns and designs when drawing from nature. For instance, a pineapple (A) has the pattern of diamond shapes (Lesson #62), the flower (B) has all of the petals coming out of the center (Lesson #123), and the pinecone has layers of stems that overlap (C), one row on top of the next, like layers of bricks (Lessons #81 and #125).

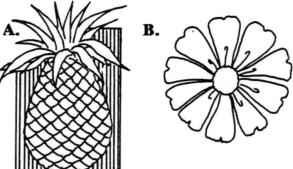

A.

B.

C.

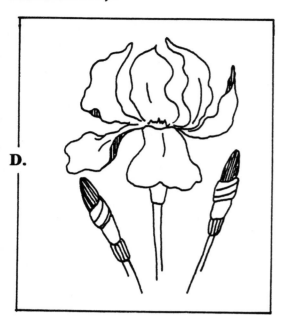

D.

Now, let's look at the iris (D), a beautiful flower that artists love to draw and paint. (If you do not have an iris to study, you may use a picture.) Look at the way the iris is constructed. God has done a marvelous job in creating this delicate flower and it should be observed closely to understand its design.

Just as with the tree, the first thing we need to see is the overall shape. For an iris, it is a circle (E). The iris has three large petals that go down, and three large petals that go up, looking as though they are covering a lovely, shy face (F). Notice how the petals curve (G). The stem comes down from the center of the flower, and is drawn with two parallel, controlled lines. The best way to draw an iris is by using thick and thin lines to show its delicacy. For this assignment, draw two more irises on the next page. Lightly draw the irises using your light blue pencil. Then, color them with light blue, violet, and white. Color your stems and leaves a pale green by combining yellow, white, and light blue. Go to the library and see the irises painted by Vincent Van Gogh.

E.

F.

G.

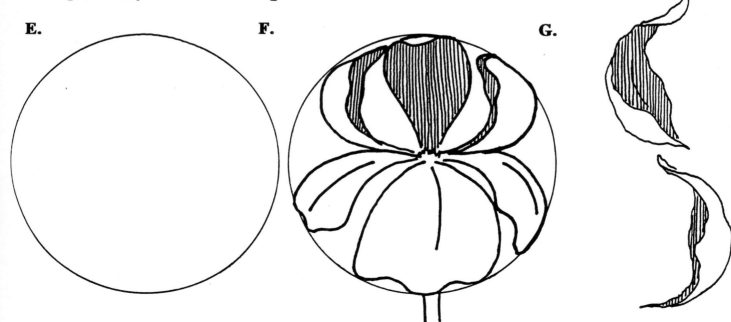

**Pointer:** Before starting your final drawing, it is always good to practice on another piece of paper. This will solve many of your drawing problems before beginning. It is also good to do a color study to figure out which colors you are going to use.

**A.**

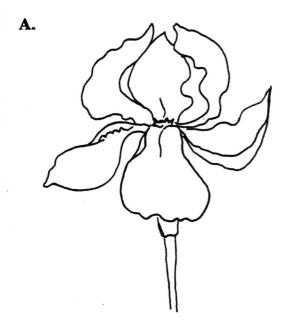

## Lesson #135: *Irises & Contours*

Students love to draw and color flowers. Studies like these will teach you much about drawing and color theory. Let's draw the iris again. There are many different approaches to drawing the same thing. For today's lesson, we will do two contour drawings of the iris (A). In the first contour drawing, we will keep our eyes on the flower and not look down at what we are drawing. Remember, a contour drawing is one continuous line going in and out, over and around. Do not lift your pencil from the paper. Then, in the second contour drawing, you may look down at what you are drawing. Do both drawings lightly with your violet pencil. When you are finished, go over your flowers with darker lines and see if you can create a more interesting design. Color one by blending red, orange, and white, and the other by blending light blue, violet, and white.

**Not Looking at Your Drawing**

**Looking at Your Drawing**

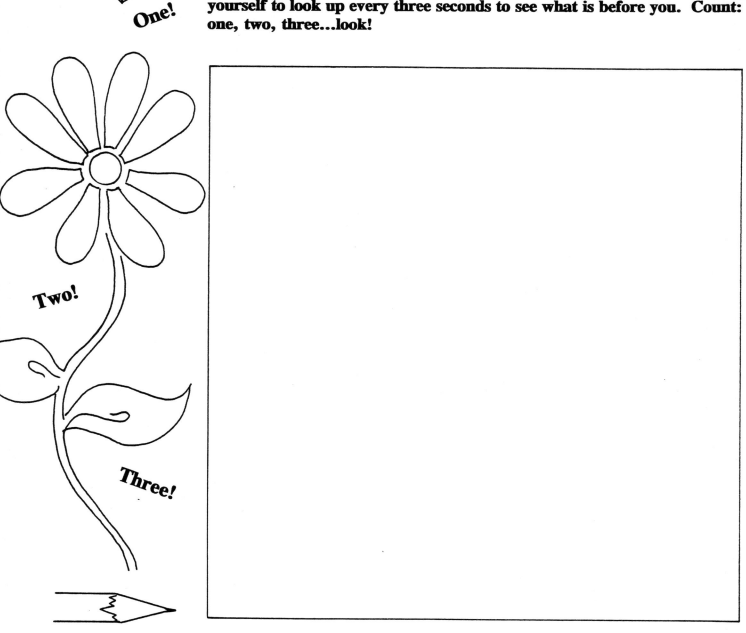

## Lesson #136: *Count: One, Two, Three...Look*

Let's draw another flower. Try to find a flower outside, but if you do not have a live flower, use an artificial one. Set it up in front of you and draw it from life. Learn to *look up* at what you are drawing. Most students become so preoccupied with their drawing that they forget to look up at their subject matter. A general rule is to look up every three seconds to see what you are drawing. If you do not, your mind will forget what it has seen and your pencil will begin to wander, doing what it pleases, and not drawing exactly what it sees. For this exercise, remind yourself to look up every three seconds to see what is before you. Count: one, two, three...look!

**One!**

**Two!**

**Three!**

**Pointer:** Before drawing, arrange your subject matter just the way you want it. Most students simply place something in front of them and begin to draw. You will be surprised at how much more interesting even a single flower is when you place it at just the right angle, at just the right height, with just the right light.

185

# Lesson #137: *A Bouquet of Flowers*

Let's draw a bouquet of flowers. In this bouquet, sketch flowers at different angles. Also, some will be overlapping, or in front of others. There is always much activity, or detail around flowers, such as the stems and leaves. In Lesson #124, we showed flowers at different angles (A). You will probably have some of these in your bouquet. It is important to overlap of your flowers (B), which shows depth, and makes your bouquet more realistic. Likewise, most of the flowers you draw will not be flat, but will have the shape of a small cup. Some will have deep centers (C). Draw the cup first, and then fashion the flower around it. When drawing the leaves and stems, you do not have to draw every detail. It may be better to just *suggest* the stems and leaves (D). If you are coloring a white flower, you can make it more pronounced by drawing and coloring the activity around it (E). Finally, if you do not have a live bouquet, find a picture to copy from, and draw your bouquet of flowers on the next page using your colored pencils.

*"Insomuch as love grows in you and so in you beauty grows.  For love is the beauty of the soul."*

St. Augustine

# Lesson #138: *Let's Go Outside!*

This can be a fun assignment, and also a very creative one. Take a pencil and your sketch pad outside and draw a landscape. A landscape is a wide range of natural scenery that can be viewed at one time, such as trees, mountains, valleys, barns, and pastures. Do your drawing in pencil on a plain piece of paper, putting as much detail in it as possible. Make notes on your drawing as to what colors you see in different areas (A). Really study what you are drawing to see colors the average eye would not see. When you are finished, take your drawing home and copy it in B, using your colored pencils. Be creative!

**A.**

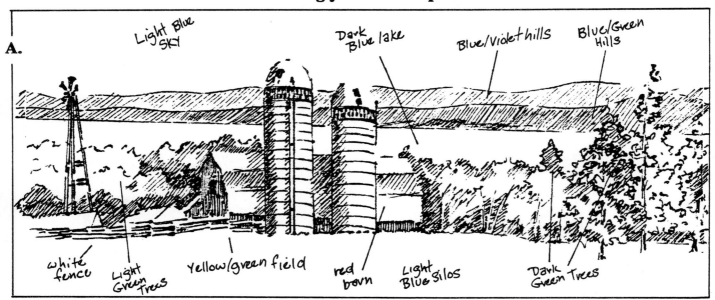

**B.**

# Lesson #139: *Foreground, Middle Ground, Background*

When drawing and coloring a landscape, there are three areas to take into consideration: foreground, middle ground, and background. The foreground is the part of the landscape closest to you. Things in the foreground will have the most detail, the darkest values, and the most color. The middle ground is the area in a landscape between the foreground and the distant horizon. This area has some detail and color, but not as much as the foreground. Finally, there is the background. There is little color in the background and no detail. Things in the background are simply *suggested*. However, things in the distance have *atmospheric perspective*, a slightly bluish color like the sky. Therefore, distant trees and mountains will have very little detail or color, and a slightly bluish color to them. Copy the picture below, putting the most detail and color in the foreground.

# Lesson #140: *Adding Colorful Colors*

Let's add some colors to our landscape. Many times you can make a picture look even better if you add colors that are not there. That's part of the fun of being an artist, you can do anything you like! For this assignment, color the picture below using colorful colors. First, combine different colors, and see what you come up with. Do you remember the different greens that you created by blending colors? See if you can create more greens in the circles below, by mixing yellow and blue; yellow, blue, and green; light green and yellow; dark green and dark blue; dark green and its complement - red, and so forth. Then, make two pinks by blending red with a little orange and white. Finally, create two violets by blending violet with light blue and white, and red, dark blue, and white. Under each color, letter the colors you blended together. After creating your new colors, color the road pink; the shadows on the tree and ground blue/green; the grass in the foreground yellow with a touch of light green; the tree trunk pink or violet; the grass in the middle ground dark green with yellow; the distant mountains violet, blue, and white; and the sky light blue, violet, and white.

**Greens**                                    **Pinks**                    **Violets**

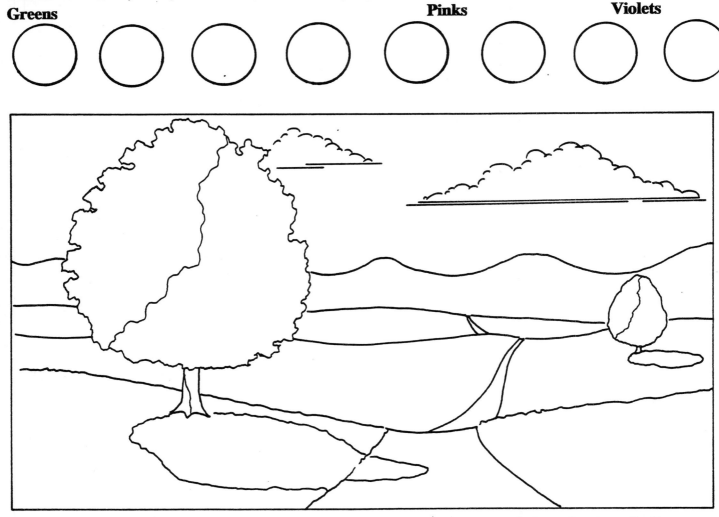

**Pointer:** When mixing and blending colors, sometimes it is easier to code them. For example, light blue can be Lt Bl, dark blue is Dk Bl, yellow is Y, red is R, orange is Or or O, violet is V, light green is Lt Gr, dark green is Dk Gr, brown is Br, and black is Blk. Always start with the color you use the most, and end with the color you use the least. Using Lt Gr + Y + B, we would add a little yellow to light green, and add a touch of blue.

# Lesson 141: *Moving Things in Nature*

Did you know that you do not have to draw everything in front of you? You can leave things out of your picture, or put things in. When you are drawing and painting, remember, if you feel that a tree or a sign is in the wrong place, you can draw it in another area of your picture to create a more pleasing composition. As an artist, you have the liberty to move things around, color them differently, add things, or take things away. For this assignment, rearrange the drawing below into a more pleasing composition. Add, take away, and move things around in your picture. Do three studies in the small figure boxes below (B). These are called *thumbnail sketches*, and will help you in formulating ideas for your finished artwork. Take your best study, and draw it in the large figure box below (C) with your light green pencil. Color your completed work.

A.

B.

C.

## Lesson #142: *The Birds & The Bees*

Draw the bird and bee on the bottom of the page. Remember to draw things going *around* to show form: the bird's feet go around the branch, the bee's stripes go around its lower body, etc. Draw and color the bird with warm colors. The honeybee will be yellow, brown, and black. Make your browns and blacks by mixing colors. Try Y + Or + V for brown, and R + Dk Bl + a touch of Y for black.

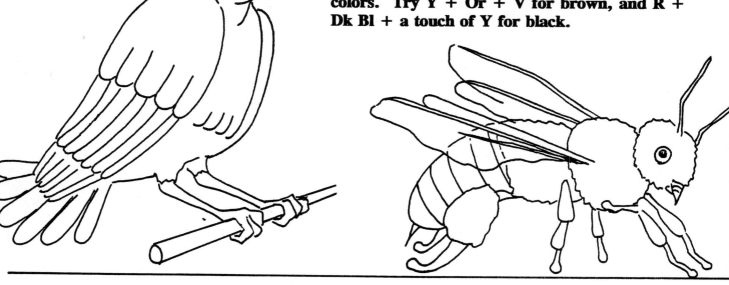

# Lesson #143: *Drawing a Bird*

A.

B.

C.

D.

Let's draw another bird. This time we will draw it step by step. First, draw a circle for the head (A). Then, add a long round body (B). Add the details to the head, tail, wings, legs, and feet (C). Notice how the feathers are long and straight? Do you remember how to draw long controlled lines (Lesson #25)? Draw the bird below, and color with cool colors when finished. However, you may want to use yellow and orange for the feet, beak, and eye. Can you show the feet going around a pole (D).

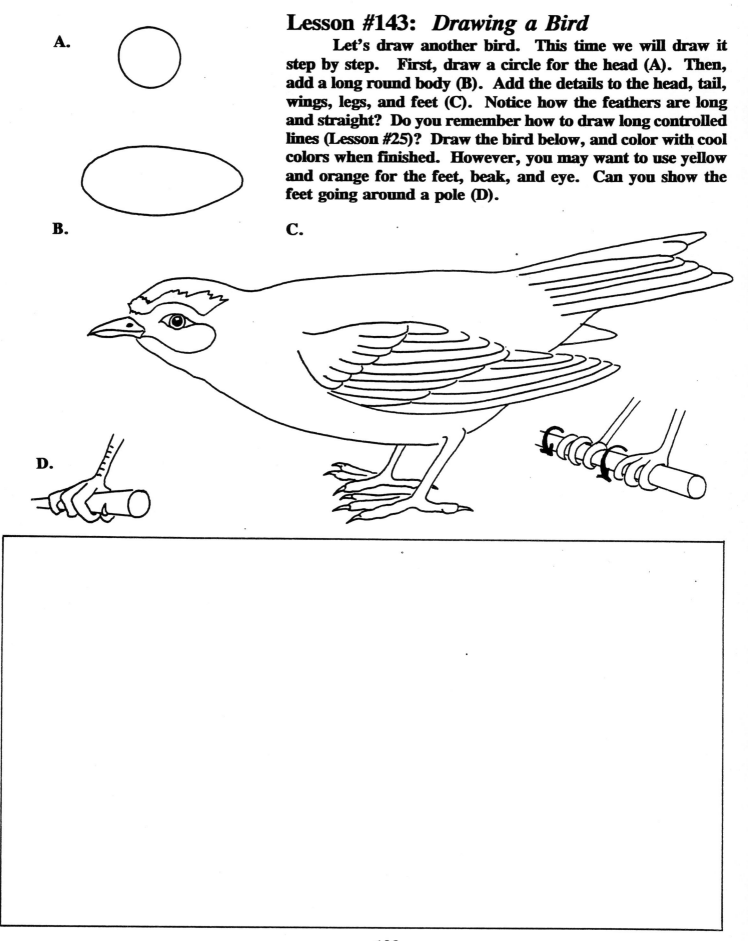

## Lesson #144: *Baby Birds in the Nest*

**A.**

**B.**

**C.**

Mama bird is watching over her nest. Can you place some more birds on the line above, and add some more musical notes? Color them with cool colors. Also, draw a mama bird, baby birds, and nest in the figure box below. A bird's nest is drawn like a bowl. Start with ellipses that go around (A). Finish the bowl, and then add texture by drawing the straw and branches that make up the nest (B). Make your straw and branches a little thicker by using a double line (C). Finally, draw some baby birds in the nest, and color your picture when finished.

**Mama Bird & Baby Birds**

# Lesson #145: *Polly Wants a Cracker*

**Red/Orange**

**Yellow/White**

**Black**

**Yellow**

**Light Blue**

**Red**

For this assignment, draw and color the parrot in the area below. Start with your yellow pencil, drawing everything in exactly how you want it. Notice the feathers are shaped and patterned the same way as layers of bricks. Draw one row, and then start the next row in the center of the first row, etc. Use long, controlled lines to draw and color your parrot. Color with the colors recommended.

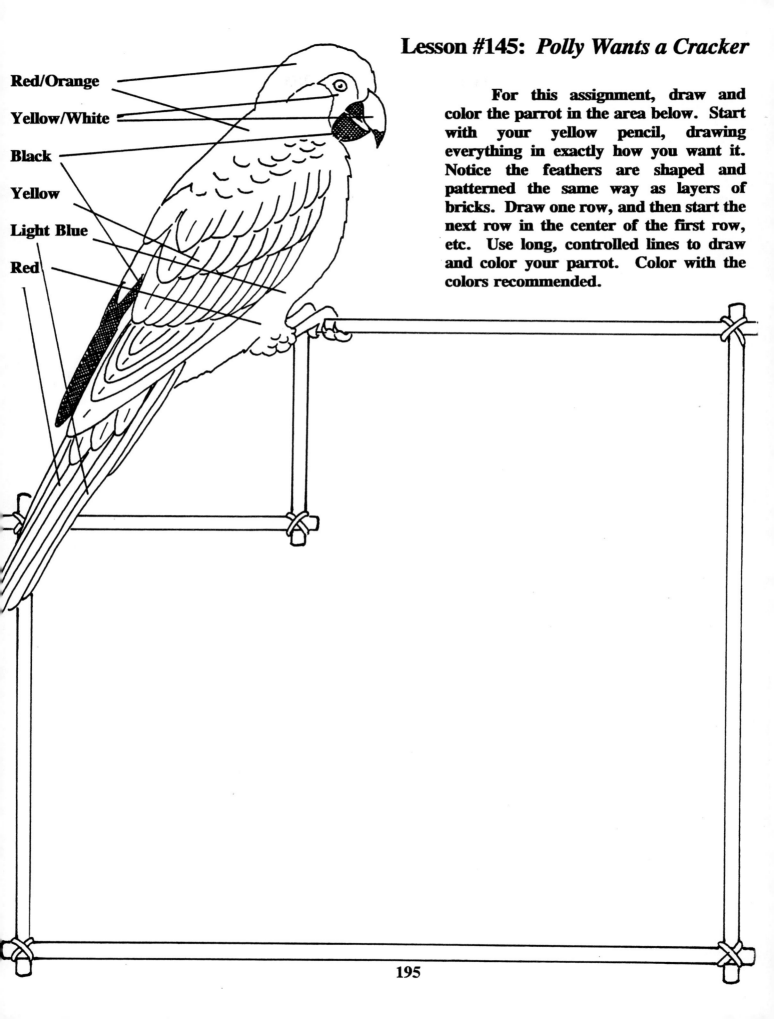

## Lesson #146: *Entomology*

A.

*Entomology* is the study of insects. For this assignment, gather some insects, and draw and color them. Draw them realistically and larger than they really are. Color them when finished, but use colors other than black and brown. When drawing their legs, make sure to use two parallel lines to show the thickness (A).

# Lesson #147: *Comical Critters*

Let's take the same insects and make them a little more comical. Give them larger eyes and more color. Draw some of your new *critters* below.

# Lesson #148: *Keeping a Journal*

Let's add another day to your journal. Leonardo Da Vinci did many studies about nature in his journals. So, today, go outdoors, and write and draw about your findings. What are your thoughts? How is your day? What are you learning from nature? Use colored pencils and be a studious observer of nature.

Date:_____

Location:_____

_____
_____
_____
_____
_____
_____
_____
_____
_____
_____
_____
_____
_____
_____

# Penmanship

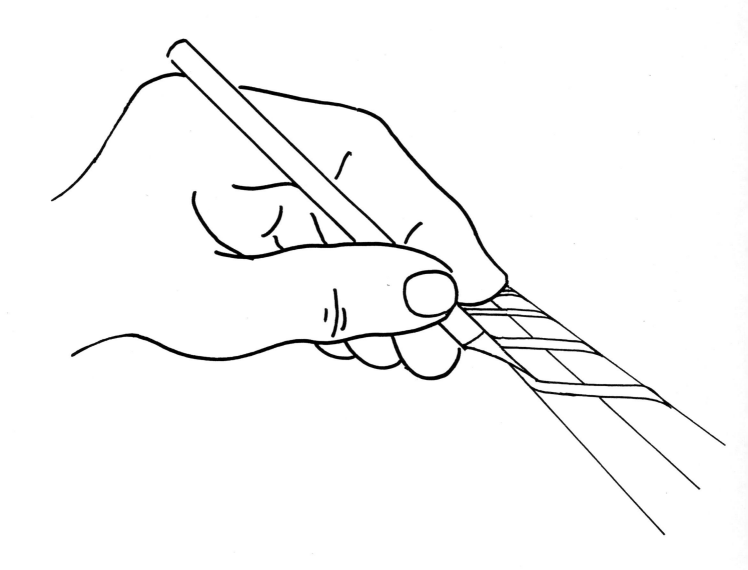

*"We write this to make our joy complete."*  I John 1:4

a b c d e f g h i j k l m n o p q r s t u v w x y z

# Penmanship

Drawing and writing have many things in common.  First of all, you start with a blank piece of paper for both, and regardless of how your work looks when finished, it is your own style.  Secondly, both drawing and writing are *learned disciplines*.  You must learn to develop both of them.  In tennis, the more you hit the ball, the better you will become; the same goes for writing and drawing.

Why is there a chapter on penmanship in an art book?  Because the two go hand in hand.  You are developing the same area of the mind.  When you, as a young artist, develop your writing skills, you will find as much creative pleasure as you do with your artwork!  Did you know that your drawings have your personality in them?  No two people draw exactly alike.  The same is true with writing.  Each of us has a unique style.  Your handwriting can be developed to a high state of eloquence in design and beauty, with calligraphy being the most beautiful form of penmanship.

Many oriental artists write poetic statements directly on their paintings; their art and writing become one.  Each letter and word has its own beauty in stroke and form, and the artwork becomes further enriched by the meaning of the words.  As an artist, you may be called upon to write and illustrate a children's story, or to create a poem and do some creative artwork to surround the words.

Likewise, penmanship is essential for corresponding with friends, writing reports for school, or producing important letters for business.  We, as students of higher learning, are incomplete if we do not nurture our ability to write.

Remember, as an art student, your writings are very important.  Vincent Van Gogh's letters to his brother Theo give us much insight into his life.  Michelangelo was a poet, along with being a sculptor and a painter.  Leonardo Da Vinci kept remarkable journals, which almost 500 years later, are still a wealth of enlightening information.  The term *Renaissance man* originated with Da Vinci because he was so well-rounded.  His ability to write well was part of his greatness.

In this chapter, we are going to cover a broad area of penmanship.  We will learn basic lettering, prose, poetry, design, keeping a journal, greeting cards, and creative stories.  Hopefully, this chapter will reveal to you the breadth and scope of penmanship, and assist you in learning to enjoy this wonderfully creative form of expression.

# Lesson #149: *Creating a Logo*

A *logo* is a statement that identifies something. There are many logos in business, and you will find brand name products usually carry an image, design, or word to identify them. As an artist, your signature identifies you as the creator of the work. Your *artistic signature* is very important, so take this into consideration when you sign your artwork. Notice how masterful signatures of the great artists are. Your artistic signature should be handled with the utmost care. It should not be too bold or large and should blend softly with the rest of your picture. Your signature should also have a nice sense of design and penmanship to it.

There are many ways you can sign your name to a picture, such as vertically, diagonally, or horizontally (A). Vincent Van Gogh signed his work with the letters of his first name, *Vincent*. Albrecht Durer signed his artwork with his initials "A" and "D". Claude Monet lettered his last name, *Monet*, while Norman Rockwell created a beautiful logo by stylizing his first and last name (B). Remember, you can print, write, or design your entire name, or just your last or first name. You can even sign your artwork anywhere on the picture you like. However, the most proper place is the bottom right corner.

Years ago, I spent many days experimenting with my artistic signature. After much deliberation, I finally came up with my logo, *Stebbing*, with a long line crossing the "t". Below are some of the experiments I had with my name before being satisfied with the one on the very bottom of C. Practice your logo on scrap paper for a few days, and then place the designs you like best in figure box D.

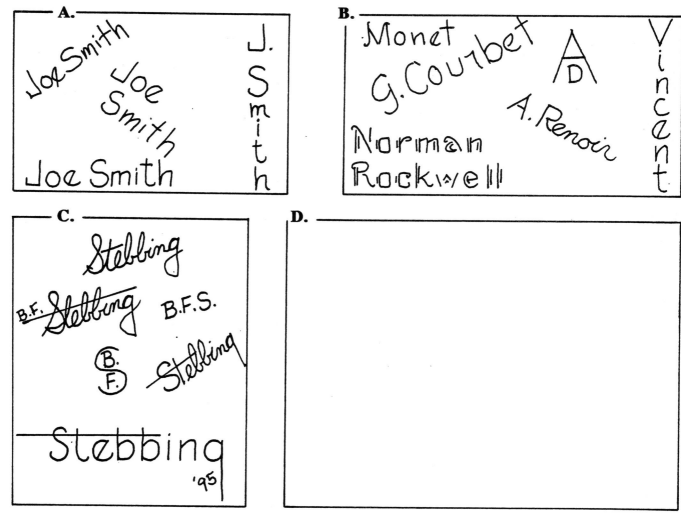

# Lesson #150: *Designing Letters*

For this assignment, design six different letters and place them in the squares below. Be creative with your designs (A) and make some interesting patterns around each letter when you have finished. Practice your designs for several letters on a piece of paper, and then draw and color your final patterned designs with colored pencils below (B). You may want to use a ruler for parts of this exercise.

A.

B.

**Pointer:** The art student should have a collection of *source materials*. Source materials are pictures and ideas that can assist you in future artwork. For example, you may want to cut out pictures of different designs for letters of the alphabet, or pictures of trees, children, animals, etc., to have on hand when you need them.

# Lesson #151:  *Letters with Meaning*

Let's make letters that say something about the word.  For example, B is for ball, S is for swan, and H is for happy (A).  Design five letters that say something about the word they represent, and write the word underneath each (B).  Color with colored pencils.

A.

B.

# Lesson #152: *Poetry*

Read the poems on this page, and page 205. Below, write 25 words or more comparing the two poems, and explain which one you liked best, and why. Then draw illustrations or designs around each of the poems. Color your pictures when finished.

**Trees**

*"I think that I shall never see*
*A poem lovely as a tree.*
*A tree whose hungry mouth is pressed*
*Against the earth's sweet flowing breast;*
*A tree that looks at God all day*
*And lifts her leafy arms to pray;*
*A tree that may in summer wear*
*A nest of robins in her hair;*
*Upon whose bosom snow has lain;*
*Who intimately live with rain.*
*Poems are made by fools like me,*
*But only God can make a tree."*

Joyce Kilmer

**Summary of Poems:**

_____

_____

_____

_____

_____

_____

_____

_____

## Flowers

*"All the names I know from nurse:*
*Gardener's garters, shepherd's purse;*
*Bachelor's buttons, lady's smock,*
*And the lady hollyhock.*

*Fairy places, fairy things,*
*Fairy woods where the wild bee wings,*
*Tiny trees for tiny dames -*
*These must all be fairy names!*

*Fair are grown-up people's trees,*
*But the forest woods are these.*
*Where, if I were not so tall,*
*I should like for good and all."*

Robert Louis Stevenson

# Lesson #153: *Rhyming Words*

**See how many words you can rhyme with the five words below. Write a list under each. Then, create a poem using some of the rhyming words from two of the columns. In your poem, the last word in the first and third lines should rhyme, and the last word in the second and fourth lines should rhyme. Write your poem below. Draw and color a nice design around it. Use guidelines for your lettering.**

| pray | tree | flew | bow | run |
|------|------|------|-----|-----|
|      |      |      |     |     |

## My Poem
### by
_____

_____

_____

_____

_____

_____

_____

_____

_____

*"If I can stop one heart from breaking,*
*I shall not live in vain;*
*If I can ease one life from aching,*
*Or cod one pain,*
*Or help one fainting robin*
*Unto his nest again,*
*I shall not live in vain."*

Emily Dickinson

## Lesson #154:  *Patterns & Poetry*

Let's make another poem, but this time we will have the last word in the first and second line rhyme, and the last word in the third and fourth line will rhyme (A).  You may select from your lists on the previous page.

**A.**

*"Roses are red,*
*and so they've said.*
*violets are blue,*
*you knew that too!"*

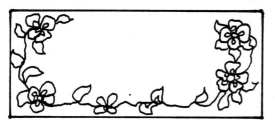

**B.**

**C.**

Write your poem below.  You may want to practice on a piece of paper first.  Give your poem a theme, telling a little story.  Use your best handwriting for your finished poem. Does it have a title?

When you are finished, create an interesting design, or pattern, around your poem. You can do this with contour line by drawing with one continuous line (B), or you can design little patterns like stained glass to go around the poem (C).

**Title:** _____

**by:** _____

_____
_____
_____
_____
_____
_____
_____
_____
_____
_____
_____
_____
_____

# Lesson #155: *Centering Your Composition*

A.

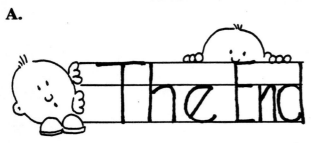

As in drawing, when creating prose, it is important to have a pleasing composition. Have you ever lettered something and could not squeeze it all on the paper? It often happens that students invest much time in doing a poster, and then run out of space. The letters often become smaller, thinner, and crunched, bumping into one another (A).

It is important to learn how to *center* each line of lettering to create balance, and give the reader a pleasing composition. Using your best penmanship, letter part of Psalm 23 below, centering the entire verse. Lightly draw in your guidelines with a ruler and pencil. A good size may be 1/4" for your lower-case letters, and another 1/8" above that for your capitals. Then, draw a vertical line directly down the center of your page. Take one line at a time, and count the number of letters and spaces. Divide that number by two to determine the center of the line (C). With your pencil, lightly letter the second half of the line from the center, *"my shepherd"* (D). Then, lightly letter the first half, going backwards from the center line, *"The Lord is"* (B). After you have a rough outline, go over it with your best handwriting. Use your black marker pen, and erase the pencil guidelines when finished.

B.      C.      D.

Psalm 23

# Lesson #156: *A Beautiful Story*

There are some wonderful stories about the lives of poets and writers. Did you ever hear of Elizabeth Barrett Browning? She was a poet who married another poet, Robert Browning. Using an encyclopedia, research the story of their lives, their poetry, and their time together in Italy. Write a short essay about them on the bottom of page 210.

Copy a favorite poem by Elizabeth Barrett Browning below. Make sure to use guidelines and center each line of verse. To make parallel guidelines, start with the straight edge at the top of the paper. Mark off equidistant points from the top, and connect these points for parallel guidelines (A). Let's also make guidelines for the upper-case (capital) letters, and lower-case letters (B). When you have your lettering just right, go over each letter with your black marker. In the square to the upper left of the poem (C), draw a portrait of Elizabeth Barrett Browning. Finally, create a floral decoration to go around the poem, using colored pencils.

**A.**

**B.**

*Elizabeth Barrett Browning*

**C.**

**Title:**_____

*by*
***Elizabeth Barrett Browning***

*"...and that you aspire to lead a quiet life, to mind your own business and to work with your own hands.."*

1 Thessalonians 4:11

**Summary:**_____
_____
_____
_____
_____
_____
_____
_____
_____
_____
_____

In the large figure box above, copy a favorite poem by Robert Browning. Make sure to use guidelines and to center the verse. Lightly letter with pencil, and after you have it lettered properly, ink in the poem. *Use your best penmanship.* Draw a portrait of the poet in the small square to the upper left. Create a floral design or pattern to frame the work, and color when complete. You may find some nice floral patterns in books or magazines. Finally, write a summary of the life that Robert and Elizabeth had together.

*"How beautiful on the mountains are the feet of those who bring good news."*

Isaiah 52:7

## Lesson #157: *Writing a Friend*

Doesn't it feel good to receive a letter from a friend? However, many times we do not write back. Why? Because we do not take the time to reply, or it is easier to call on the telephone. Everyone should develop the art of letter writing; it is a means of communicating that cannot be expressed in any other way. Sometimes when I have something special to say to someone, telling them in person or calling on the telephone will not make the same impression as writing a letter. Letter writing is quality time; a time when we put everything else aside and dedicate special moments to find the words we want to share with friends. Letter writing should be more creative than just sentiments like, *"How are you?"* or *"What is the weather like?"* Corresponding is a good way to practice *penmanship.* Webster's dictionary sums up penmanship as: *"The art or practice of writing with the pen. Quality or style of handwriting."* I believe beautiful handwriting is the same as beautiful drawing, and that our penmanship can influence others. Again, Webster's says: the "*art* or *practice* of writing", so it is both an art and something we should practice. Corresponding will become an enjoyable sidenote to your daily life as you mail a letter and wait for a reply.

When practicing *penmanship,* use guidelines to create uniform letters (A). Make sure all the words are slanted on the same angle (B). Take your time, and develop your own personal style. Allow the beauty of your words to flow across the paper (C).

A.                              B.                              C.

Dear Hannah;    Greetings in

Charles Russell was an American artist who lived in the old West before the turn of the century. He spent a great deal of time with the Indians and was able to capture their way of life in his paintings and drawings. Go to the library and study him. When Charles Russell wrote his closest friends, he drew little pictures on the letters and envelopes. His friends truly cherished these letters. For this assignment, practice your penmanship by writing a letter to a friend on the next page. Include some drawings of things around you on the letter and envelope. Be creative with what you write and make it enjoyable reading.

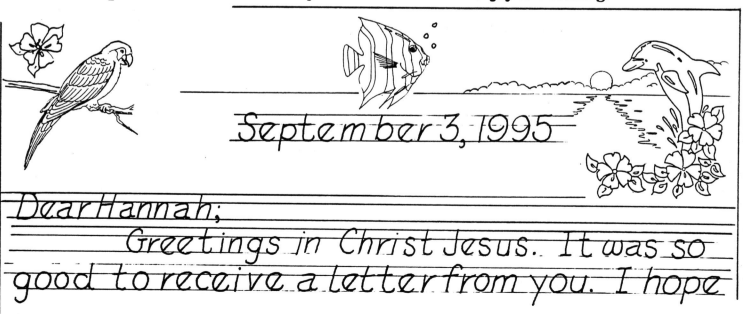

September 3, 1995

Dear Hannah;
    Greetings in Christ Jesus. It was so good to receive a letter from you. I hope

_____

_____

_____

_____

_____

_____

_____

_____

_____

_____

_____

_____

_____

_____

_____

_____

_____

_____

_____

_____

_____

_____

_____

_____

**Write to a friend in the space above.  Place the date in the upper right corner.  Use guidelines for your letters and practice good penmanship.  Be creative in what you write about. Do some drawings near the top of your letter, the way Charles Russell did.  You may want to use colored pencils for your drawings.**

# Lesson #158: *Lettering*

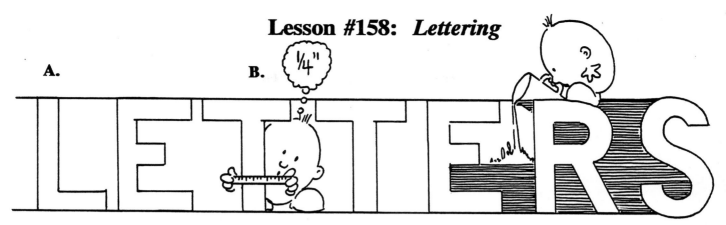

**A.**     **B.**

Lettering is important in art and is practical to know throughout your life. For instance, what if you have to make a poster for a church dinner, or your family has a yard sale, or you have lost your kitten, or you have to make a science project? Let's learn a few of the basic rules for lettering:

1. Always use guidelines for the tops and bottoms of your letters (A).
2. Try to make your letters the same thickness (B).
3. Space your letters correctly. Generally speaking, most letters are the same distance apart. If you filled the spaces between the letters with water, they would hold the same amount.

Print the word LETTERS below (C), using guidelines for the top and bottom of each letter. Make sure to have all the letters the same thickness. Space them correctly and use your ruler for making straight lines. Draw with your orange pencil, and color each letter with warm colors, using vertical lines.

**C.** _____

_____

Finally, create another set of guidelines below (D). Make sure they are perfectly horizontal and parallel. Place your guidelines 1 1/2" apart from top to bottom, and letter your first name with block letters (see above). Try to make each letter the same thickness and distance apart. If you do not have enough space to do it below, use another sheet of paper.

**D.**

# Lesson #159: *Letters with Pizazz!*

For this assignment, we are going to create some new, fanciful designs for letters. Give your letters more curves and vitality. Practice drawing several letters on another sheet of paper, and then draw your best designs in the boxes below with colored pencils. Create some patterns or designs around each letter when you have finished.

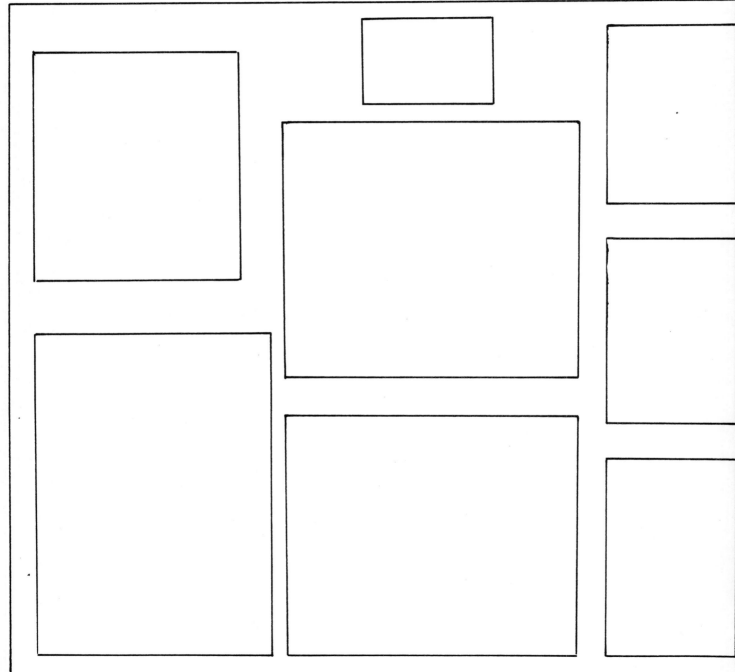

**A.**

# Lesson #160: *Frames with Decorative Design*

We have discussed several ways of placing designs and patterns around your lettering, writing, or prose. You can find interesting subject matter in magazines and books to incorporate into your own designs. You can also doodle and experiment to see what interesting patterns you can create. Most important, remember to work with controlled lines.

Patterns and designs are not *sketchy* like some of the other drawings we do. They should be done with precision. For instance, look at the stem of the flower (A). Notice the controlled lines for both sides of the stem and the line that goes into the leaves.

**B.**

Another way to create nice designs is to do a contour drawing. Place your pencil on the paper, and let it go in and out without lifting it off the paper. Consider a flower garden, and see what happens by suggesting it with one long, continuous line (B).

Detail is great for decorative frames and offers an opportunity to make some interesting designs (C). An extra fine black marker gives a nice line and works well for detailing. Design a floral archway on the top of the next page. Use this to frame one of your favorite scriptures or other writings. By photocopying your archway, you will be able to use it again with other writing assignments. Place your scripture or phrase in the center and color the archway with colored pencils after you have inked it in (D).

**C.**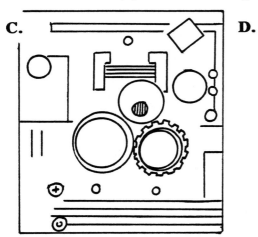

**D.**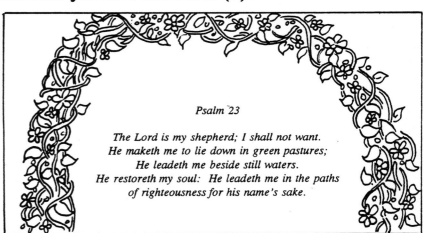

*Psalm 23*

*The Lord is my shepherd; I shall not want.*
*He maketh me to lie down in green pastures;*
*He leadeth me beside still waters.*
*He restoreth my soul: He leadeth me in the paths*
*of righteousness for his name's sake.*

On the bottom of the next page, design three letters with different colored pencils. Use your ruler to make light guidelines. See how creative you can be by placing detailed designs within each letters (E).

**E.**

On the top of the page, design a floral archway using your yellow colored pencil. Draw a lot of detail and leave a large enough opening for your writings, scripture, or prose. When you have placed all the details in your archway, go over it with your black pen. On the bottom of the page, design a letter in each of the squares. Place detailed design in or around each letter with colored pencils. Color one with cool colors, one with warm colors, and one with complementary colors.

# Lesson #161: *Writing with a Slant*

Earlier, we discussed having the same slant, or angle, for all your letters (A). A good slant is a slight tilt from the left to right (B). Practice several letters in the rows below (C), like *"l"*, *"b"*, *"h"*, *"m"*, *"d"*, and *"f"*. Practicing these letters will help you to develop the proper stroke and slant. Using your best penmanship, find a scripture that you like, and write it on the bottom of the page (D). A calligraphy pen would be good for this assignment, but a marker pen will do. Place a design around your verse when complete.

A.

B.

C.

D.

# Lesson #162: *Writing Your Congressman*

There are times when you will be called to write an important letter to someone. As a citizen of this country, you have the liberty to write your Congressman, Senator, or even the President, stating your concerns about political matters. Your voice through letter writing is very important, and your letter will make a much better impression if it is written with excellence in both content and penmanship.

The first part, or heading, of an important letter is placed about an inch from the top of the page on the left margin. This would include your complete address and the date.

Next, the inside address is placed approximately four to seven lines spaces below the heading. It includes the name and address of the person and/or company the letter is being sent to.

The greeting, or salutation, starts a few line spaces under the inside address. If you are writing to an individual, you should address him or her as *Dear Mr. President....,* or *Dear Mrs.....* The most common salutations to a company are *Gentlemen:, Dear Sirs:,* or *Dear (Company Name).*

The body of the letter expresses the purpose of the letter, and the closing customarily is *Sincerely,* or *Respectfully yours.*

End with your handwritten signature. If an enclosure is sent with the letter, place the word *Enclosure(s)* or *Enc.* below the signature.

Select an issue that concerns you and voice your opinion to your federal, state, or local representative. Using a nice piece of stationary, write legibly, let your thoughts be clear, and use your very best penmanship. Practice writing the heading, inside address, and greeting below, along with the opening sentence of your letter.

_____

_____

_____

_____

_____

_____

_____

_____

_____

_____

_____

_____

_____

_____

_____

_____

_____

_____

# Lesson #163: *Greeting Cards*

Handmade cards are always special to receive. People cherish the originality of the artwork and the extra time taken to create it. Do you know the difference between a greeting card and a note card? A greeting card has a verse or message inside, and a note card has blank space inside for writing. Today we are going to make a greeting card. There are many types of greeting cards for different occasions. We will make a general, or *all occasion* card. All occasion cards are practical to send to almost anyone for any occassion.

To create a design, or illustration, for the front of a greeting card, it is a good idea to first do *thumbnail sketches*. Thumbnail sketches are small drawings that are done to help decide which idea we like best. Do several thumbnail sketches below for your greeting card (A). Select the best one and place it in the large figure box (B). You may want to use colored pencils. Decide what type of greeting you want to place inside your card. Will it be something from the heart, a verse from Scripture, or a few lines from a nice poem? Practice your greeting on the lines provided (C).

**A. Thumbnail Sketches**

**B.**

**C. Practice Your Greeting Here**

# Lesson #164: *Keeping an ART Journal*

The importance of both keeping an art journal and penmanship are mentioned throughout this text. An art journal is a combination of a diary and a sketchbook. While an art journal includes sketches of the world around us and records the writer's thoughts, a diary contains writings of a more personal nature. Research the journals of Leonardo Da Vinci and read some of his observations.

Remember, an art journal is a combination of drawing things around you that make up each day and practicing penmanship. Your drawing studies could be of a candle, a book, a pet, or a scene from a window. Whatever you draw in your journal becomes a part of that day.

Your writings may include such things as the date, what the weather is like, what you are learning, or the experiences you had during the day. You may also want to tape things to the pages such as: leaves, small flowers, tickets from the zoo or movies, postcards from friends, or even pictures from a magazine that you like. Most importantly, *write* and *draw*.

Do journal entrees on the bottom of this page and the next page. You may want to do one today and the other next week. Be patient with keeping a journal; the more you do it, the more you will enjoy it. You may want to obtain a sketchbook, or a hardbound journal, and start working in it on a daily or weekly basis.

Date:_____

_____
_____
_____
_____
_____
_____
_____
_____
_____
_____
_____
_____
_____
_____

# My Journal

Date: _____

_____

_____

_____

_____

_____

_____

_____

_____

_____

_____

_____

_____

_____

_____

_____

_____

*"Be like the bird, who*
*Halting in his flight*
*On limb too slight*
*Feels it give way beneath him,*
*Yet sings*
*Knowing he hath wings."*

**Victor Hugo**

**Complete the picture above and color it with your colored pencils.**

# Art Appreciation

*"Copy and re-copy the masters."* **Edgar Degas**

# Art Appreciation

There are many ways to appreciate art and the great masters of the past. Our purpose in *Feed My Sheep* is to make art appreciation as simple and practical as possible.

Over the years, I have found that encyclopedias and public libraries offer everything needed to have a deeper appreciation of artists, their times, and their styles. Photographs and prints were not made available to man until more recent times; past generations had to go to see artwork in person. We now have easy access to see great pieces of art, along with comprehensive written information about the lifestyles of the artists. We are a very blessed generation to have local libraries and color reproductions at our disposal.

Let's use the public libraries as a means of studying different time periods of art, such as: Egyptian, Greek, Roman, Early Christian, Renaissance, Baroque, Neo-Classical, Pre-Raphaelite, Impressionism, and 20th Century art. With each period of time, you will be required to write a summary about that style of art in approximately 100 words. The encyclopedia is a good resource for a concise explanation of these periods and the artists. There is a large figure box on each page for the student to draw and color a piece of artwork from that period of time. A smaller figure box is also provided for the student to draw the artist's portrait.

In the second portion of "Art Appreciation", the student will be asked to research two artists for each lesson. The assignment will be to write approximately 100 words comparing the artists and to draw their portraits in the small figure boxes provided in the upper left and right of each page (A & C). Then, in the larger figure box (B), draw and color a piece of artwork by one of the two artists. Place the title of the artwork under the picture (D). Finally, research the way each artist signed his work (if you can), and copy it where it says, *"Artist's Signature"*(E).

A.

Name: Jean Millet

C.

Name: Gustave Courbet

D. Title: "The Walk to Work"

E. Artist's Signature: Millet

Artist's Signature: G. Caurbet.

Essay: _____
_____
_____
_____

# Lesson #165: *God & Creation*

Our first lesson in art appreciation will be to study the greatest artist in the history of the universe - God. When we think about what God has created, it will give us a much better sense of who we are and what our purpose is.

There have been many drawings, paintings, and sculptures done of Jesus, but have you ever seen a picture of God? One of the few pictures I have seen of God was done by Michelangelo on the Sistine Chapel ceiling. God is holding out His hand to touch Adam.

Draw a picture of what you think God looks like in A and then draw and color something beautiful that He has created in B. You can start with the book of Genesis, where God began creation. What a great Artist! On the bottom of the page, write a short essay about God as an Artist. Describe some of His masterpieces, His lifestyle, and what you feel His greatest pieces of art are.

A.

B.

C.

_____
_____
_____
_____
_____
_____
_____
_____
_____
_____
_____
_____
_____
_____
_____
_____
_____
_____
_____

# Lesson #166: *Egyptian Art*

Research Egyptian art in the encyclopedia and library. Draw a picture of one of the pharaohs in figure box A. Write the dates of the Egyptian art period and find a picture or painting to copy in the large figure box (B). Below, write an essay describing Egyptian art and explaining its style. Do you like the artwork? Is it colorful? Realistic? What surface was it painted on?

**A.**

**B.**

Dates: _____

Title: _____

_____
_____
_____
_____
_____
_____
_____
_____
_____
_____
_____
_____
_____
_____
_____
_____
_____
_____
_____
_____
_____
_____

# Lesson #167: *Greek Art*

Find some information about ancient Greek art. Draw the head of a Greek statue in figure box A. Write the dates for the period of time when Greek art was flourishing in the world. Then, find a picture of Greek art and draw and color it in figure box B. Finally, write an essay describing Greek art and what you think of it. What does "Hellenistic" mean?

A.

B.

Dates: _____

Title: _____

_____
_____
_____
_____
_____
_____
_____
_____
_____
_____
_____
_____
_____
_____
_____
_____
_____
_____
_____
_____
_____
_____
_____

# Lesson #168: *Roman Art*

Research Roman art in the encyclopedia and library. Draw a head from a Roman statue in figure box A and then a piece of sculpture or painting from that time period in figure box B. Finally, write an essay describing Roman art. Compare Roman with Hellenistic art and explain the differences and the similarities. How was Roman art influenced by the Greeks?

A.

B.

Dates: _____

Title: _____

# Lesson #169: *Early Christian Art*

Research Early Christian art in the encyclopedia and library. Draw a head from one of the mosaics in figure box A and do another drawing of a picture or painting in figure box B. If it is a mosaic, you may want to use your colored pencils. Finally, write an essay describing Early Christian art. What are some of the differences between Roman and Early Christian art? What does *Byzantine art* mean?

**A.**

**B.**

**Dates:** _____

**Title:** _____

_____
_____
_____
_____
_____
_____
_____
_____
_____
_____
_____
_____
_____
_____
_____
_____
_____
_____
_____
_____
_____
_____

# Lesson #170: *The Early Renaissance Art*

Research Early Renaissance art in the encyclopedia and library, particularly the artwork of Giovanni Cimabue and Giotto di Bondone. In figure box A, draw a portrait of one of them, or a portrait of another artist from that time period. Then, copy a piece of artwork from the Early Renaissance period in figure box B. If it is in color, copy it with your colored pencils. Finally, write an essay describing the Early Renaissance period below.

A.

B.

Name: _____

Dates: _____

Title: _____

_____
_____
_____
_____
_____
_____
_____
_____
_____
_____
_____
_____
_____
_____
_____
_____
_____
_____
_____
_____
_____

# Lesson #171: *The High Renaissance*

Research the High Renaissance in the encyclopedia and library, particularly the artwork of Leonardo da Vinci, Michelangelo, and Raphael. Draw a portrait of one of the three great artists in figure box A. Copy a painting from the High Renaissance in figure box B. If it is in color, use your colored pencils. Finally, write an essay about the High Renaissance below.

A.          B.

Name: _____

Dates: _____          Title: _____

_____
_____
_____
_____
_____
_____
_____
_____
_____
_____
_____
_____
_____
_____
_____
_____
_____
_____
_____
_____
_____
_____
_____

# Lesson #172: *The Baroque Period*

Research Baroque art in the encyclopedia and library, particularly the works of Rembrandt, Caravaggio, Bernini, and Vermeer. Draw a portrait of one of the artists in figure box A, and then copy a painting from this period in figure box B. Finally, write an essay about this period of art explaining your likes and dislikes.

A.    B.

Name: _____

Dates: _____        Title: _____

_____
_____
_____
_____
_____
_____
_____
_____
_____
_____
_____
_____
_____
_____
_____
_____
_____
_____
_____
_____
_____
_____
_____
_____

# Lesson #173: *The Neo-Classical Period*

Research the Neo-Classical period of art in the encyclopedia and library, particularly the works of Jacques Louis David, and Jean Auguste Dominique Ingres. Draw a portrait of one of them in figure box A, and then copy a piece of artwork from that time period in figure box B using colored pencils. Finally, write an essay about the Neo-Classical period of time below.

A.

B.

Name: _____

Dates: _____

Title: _____

_____
_____
_____
_____
_____
_____
_____
_____
_____
_____
_____
_____
_____
_____
_____
_____
_____
_____
_____
_____
_____
_____
_____
_____
_____
_____
_____

# Lesson #174: *The Pre-Raphaelites*

Research the Pre-Raphaelite period in the encyclopedia and library. Draw a portrait of one of the artists in figure box A. Then, copy one of their paintings or drawings in figure box B. Finally, write an essay about this period. What Pre-Raphaelite artist is your favorite? Why? Did any of them have a Christian motive?

A. _____  B.

Name: _____

Dates: _____   Title: _____

_____
_____
_____
_____
_____
_____
_____
_____
_____
_____
_____
_____
_____
_____
_____
_____
_____
_____
_____
_____
_____
_____
_____
_____

# Lesson #175: *Impressionism*

Research the Impressionists in the encyclopedia and library. Draw a portrait of one of the artists in figure box A, and copy one of their paintings in figure box B, using colored pencils. Finally, write an essay about the period. Do you like the artwork? Why? Who is your favorite Impressionist?

A. ⎯⎯⎯

B.

Name: _____

Dates:_____

Title: _____

_____

_____

_____

_____

_____

_____

_____

_____

_____

_____

_____

_____

_____

_____

_____

_____

_____

_____

_____

_____

_____

_____

_____

_____

_____

# Lesson #176: *20th Century Art*

This period covers a wide range of styles of art including Fauvism, Cubism, Expressionism, and Surrealism, and is often called *Modern Art*. Is there a particular artist that you like from this period? You may want to do a study on *Fauvism*, and the artist George Rouault. Draw a portrait of a 20th century artist in figure box A and then copy a painting and color it in figure box B. Finally, write an essay about this period.

A.

Name: _____

B.

Dates: _____

Title: _____

_____
_____
_____
_____
_____
_____
_____
_____
_____
_____
_____
_____
_____
_____
_____
_____
_____
_____
_____
_____
_____
_____
_____
_____
_____
_____

# *Art & Artists*

In this section, you are going to look at different artists who lived around the same time, comparing their styles of art, and what you like and dislike about their work. You will be asked to draw a small portrait of both artists in the small figure boxes provided on each page and to copy one of your favorite pieces of artwork in the larger figure box. Write the title of the artwork and the signatures of the artists on the proper lines below (see p. 224). Finally, write a short essay comparing the artists and their works. Start below by comparing any two artist that you like. A good study might be Raphael and Carravaggio.

**Artist's Signature:**

**Artist's Signature:**

**Title:** _____

# Lesson #177: *Leonardo Da Vinci & Michelangelo Buonarroti*

Compare these two great artists from the Italian Renaissance by drawing their portraits, signing their signatures, and copying one of your favorite pieces of their artwork. Below, write an essay comparing these two.

**Artist's Signature:**

**Artist's Signature:**

**Title:** _____

# Lesson #178: *Rembrandt & Vermeer*

**Compare Rembrandt and Vermeer below, drawing a portrait of each in the figure boxes. Copy and color one of your favorite paintings by these two great Dutch masters in the larger figure box. Write an essay comparing these two. Which artist do you like best? Why? What is your favorite piece of artwork? Why?**

**Artist's Signature:**

**Artist's Signature:**

**Title:** _____

239

# Lesson #179: *Constable & Turner*

Compare the works of these two great English artists. Draw a portrait of each, and try to sign the signatures they used on their paintings. Learning their signatures will teach you the importance of a good artistic signature. Copy and color a favorite painting by one of the artists below. Which artist do you like best? Why?

Artist's Signature: _____

Artist's Signature: _____

Title: _____

_____
_____
_____
_____
_____
_____
_____
_____
_____
_____
_____
_____
_____
_____
_____
_____
_____
_____
_____
_____
_____
_____
_____

# Lesson #180: *Charles Russell & Frederic Remington*

**Compare the artwork of these great American Old West artists. What was the difference in their lifestyles? How about their backgrounds? Which artist do you like best? Why?**

Artist's Signature: _____

_____

Artist's Signature: _____

_____

**Title:** _____

_____
_____
_____
_____
_____
_____
_____
_____
_____
_____
_____
_____
_____
_____
_____
_____
_____
_____
_____
_____
_____
_____
_____
_____

# Lesson #181: *Winslow Homer & James McNeill Whistler*

**Research the lives and works of these late 19th century American artists. Compare their artwork, and write about their styles below.**

Artist's Signature:

_____

Artist's Signature:

_____

Title: _____

_____

_____

_____

_____

_____

_____

_____

_____

_____

_____

_____

_____

_____

_____

_____

_____

_____

_____

_____

_____

_____

_____

_____

_____

_____

_____

# Lesson #182:  *Claude Monet & Vincent Van Gogh*

**Compare the works of the Impressionists, Claude Monet and Vincent Van Gogh.  What is the difference in their styles?  What was their theory on color?  What does Impressionism mean?  Complete the assignment below.**

**Artist's Signature:**

**Artist's Signature**

**Title:** _____

_____
_____
_____
_____
_____
_____
_____
_____
_____
_____
_____
_____
_____
_____
_____
_____
_____
_____
_____
_____
_____
_____

# Lesson #183: *Christian Artists*

For the final assignment in this section, let's research an artist and see what his Christian commitment was in his artwork. Michelangelo, El Greco and Rembrandt did extensive series of Biblical paintings. Bernini created elegant human forms out of marble. Carl Bloch and Rien Poortvielt did wonderful artwork portraying the story of Christ. George Rouault, a 20th century artist, also committed his works to God. Select one of these artists and do a study of his life, his commitment to God, and his artwork below.

**Artist:**

_____

**Title:** _____

**Dates:** _____

_____
_____
_____
_____
_____
_____
_____
_____
_____
_____
_____
_____
_____
_____
_____
_____
_____
_____
_____
_____

# Lesson #184:  *Art History Poster*

For this assignment, take a large sheet of white poster board (22" x 28") and do a poster from any period of art.  It can be Impressionism, the Renaissance, or even 20th century art.  Include a variety of ideas, artwork, and artists from that period.  Place a title on your poster using guidelines for your lettering.  Be creative with your composition.  You may want to do a series of thumbnail sketches before starting.  When finished, color your poster with colored markers or paint.

# Vincent Van Gogh 1853-90

# Impressionism

Note:  Other artists you may want to research and compare:
- *John Singer Sergeant & Thomas Eakins*
- *Millet & Corot*
- *Norman Rockwell & Andrew Wyeth*
- *Edgar Degas & Paul Cezanne*

Name: _____          Date:_____

# Lesson #185: Art Appreciation Examination

**I. Matching:** Match each word with its definition by placing the letter next to the correct number (3 points each).

1. Vincent Van Gogh
2. Renaissance
3. Charles Russell
4. Jacques Louis David
5. Michelangelo
6. Impressionism
7. Giotto
8. Modern art
9. Turner
10. George Rouault

A. Great artist of the High Renaissance
B. Art concerned with light and color
C. Early Renaissance artist
D. American Western artist
E. 20th century art
F. Great English painter.
G. Great Impressionist
H. A rebirth in classical art in Italy
I. Christian artist who lived in France
J. French Neo-classical master

**II. Fill in the blanks (5 points each).**

1. Michelangelo, Leonardo Da Vinci, and _____ were the three great artists of the High Renaissance.
2. Charles Russell and _____ were two great American Western artists.
3. _____ is another name for Early Christian art.
4. Another name for ancient Greek art is _____ art.
5. Two great American artists of the 20th century are Norman Rockwell and

_____.

**III. Summary:** In 100 words or more, compare the artwork from the Renaissance period and French Impressionism. What are the differences between the two periods? What style of art do you like best? Who were some of the great masters of each period? (45 points).

_____
_____
_____
_____
_____
_____
_____
_____
_____
_____
_____
_____
_____
_____

(Answers on Page 310)

# Academia

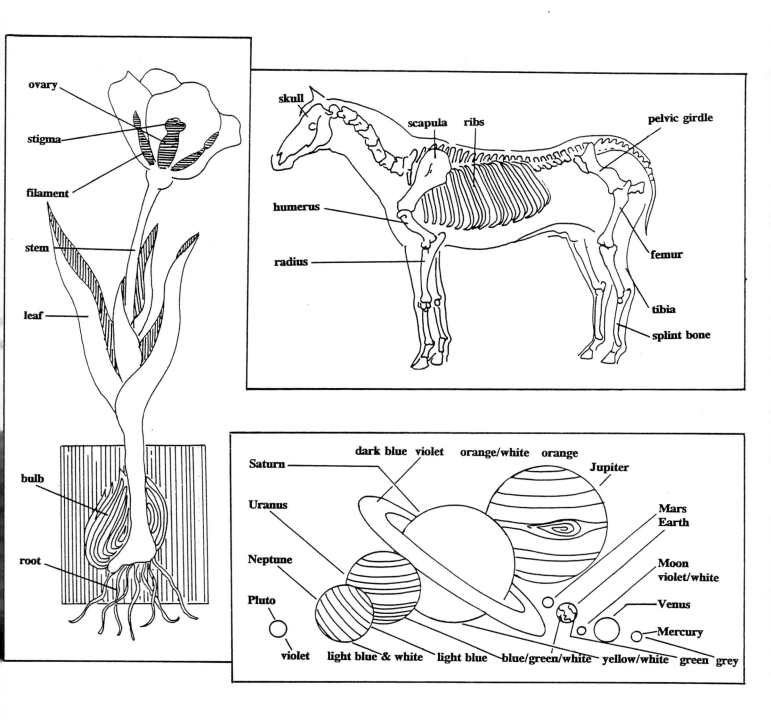

ovary
stigma
filament
stem
leaf
bulb
root

skull
scapula
ribs
pelvic girdle
humerus
radius
femur
tibia
splint bone

Saturn
dark blue    violet    orange/white    orange
Jupiter
Uranus
Mars
Earth
Neptune
Moon
violet/white
Pluto
Venus
Mercury
violet    light blue & white    light blue    blue/green/white    yellow/white    green    grey

*"Pleasure must be found in study."* Cezanne

*"I don't know a better definition of an artist than one who is eternally curious."*
Charles Hawthorne

## Academia

Every artist is a student of higher learning in one way or another. Just the act of mixing colors can, and should be, very scientific. The artist studies nature to see how God created everything. The artist studies the anatomy of man, his skeleton and muscles, in order to draw the human figure better. Students of art want to learn about perspective, design, composition, and so on. They want to learn how to use pencils, crayons, chalks, markers, and paint. In other words, artists are *"eternally curious"*.

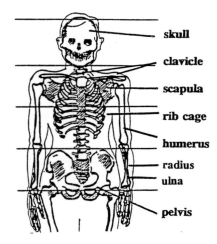

This chapter on *Academia* is a combination of science, biology, geography, astronomy, and other areas of higher learning. However, we will continue to learn more of the fundamentals of art through drawing and color theory. Again, the greatest scientist/artist that ever lived was Leonardo Da Vinci. His curiosity carried his studies into architecture, inventions, music, painting, sculpture, anatomy, and science. That is why he was called a *Renaissance man*, because he could do a lot of things in an excellent manner. Hopefully, this section will inspire you to broaden your breadth and scope of learning and assist you in applying much of it to your artwork.

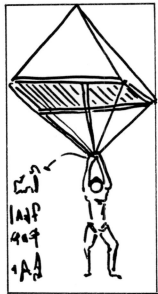

# Lesson #186: *Entomology*

**Entomology:** *A branch of zoology that deals with the study of insects.*

For this assignment, draw a series of insects below. Letter the names underneath each insect. Copy insects from an encyclopedia, dictionary, or other source material, and draw as much detail as possible. Draw each insect lightly, and then go over them with your fine black marker and colored pencils.

**Stag Beetle**      **Ailanthus Silk-Worm**      **Dragon Fly**

**Cockroach**

**Flea**

**Blow-Fly**

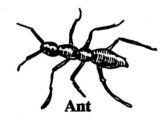

**Ant**

249

# Lesson #187: *Becoming an Entomologist*

In previous assignments, we drew and colored a variety of insects. For today's lesson, we are going to start a butterfly collection. Select one of the butterflies below, and draw and color it in the bottom figure box. Write the name of the butterfly underneath.

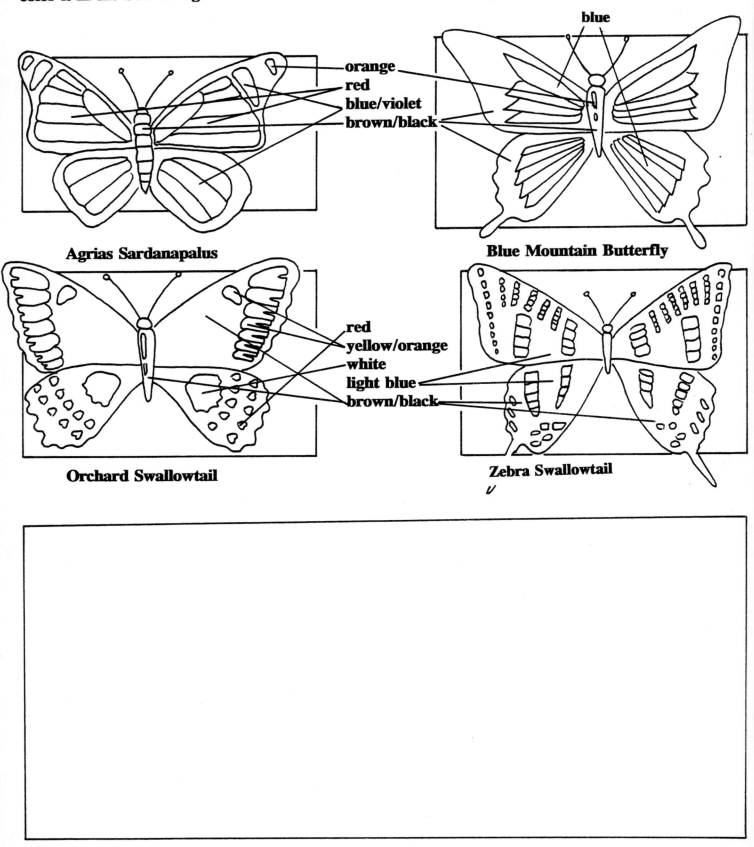

Agrias Sardanapalus

Blue Mountain Butterfly

Orchard Swallowtail

Zebra Swallowtail

# Lesson #188: *Astronomy*

**Astronomy:** *The study of objects and matter outside the earth's atmosphere.*
    Do you remember how to make circles, as instructed in Lesson #25? For this assignment, draw the solar system, and color the different planets with the appropriate colors. Do you remember how to draw *ellipses*? Ellipses are circles seen on an angle. Look at the ellipses that go around Saturn, and the stripes that go around Neptune, Uranus, and Jupiter. Draw each planet below, showing that they go *around*, and that some *overlap*. When you have finished, color the space behind the planets with your dark blue and violet pencils.

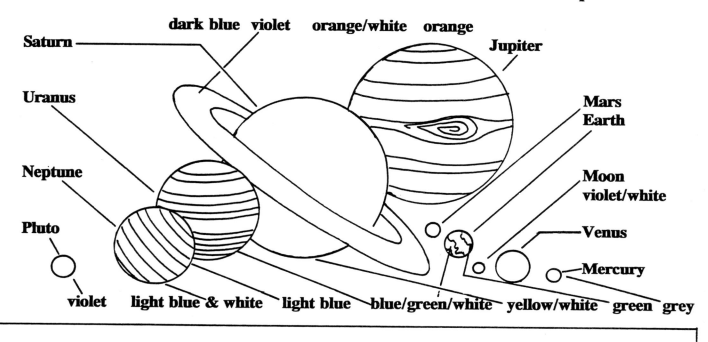

# Lesson #189: *Studying Tulips*

**Botany:** *A branch of biology dealing with plant life.*
In the chapter on anatomy, you learned different parts of the body and how to label them. The same is true with everything we study in art: the more you learn about the parts and their proportions, the easier it will be to draw the entire object. For this assignment, draw the tulip (A) in B, label the parts, and color them in when finished.

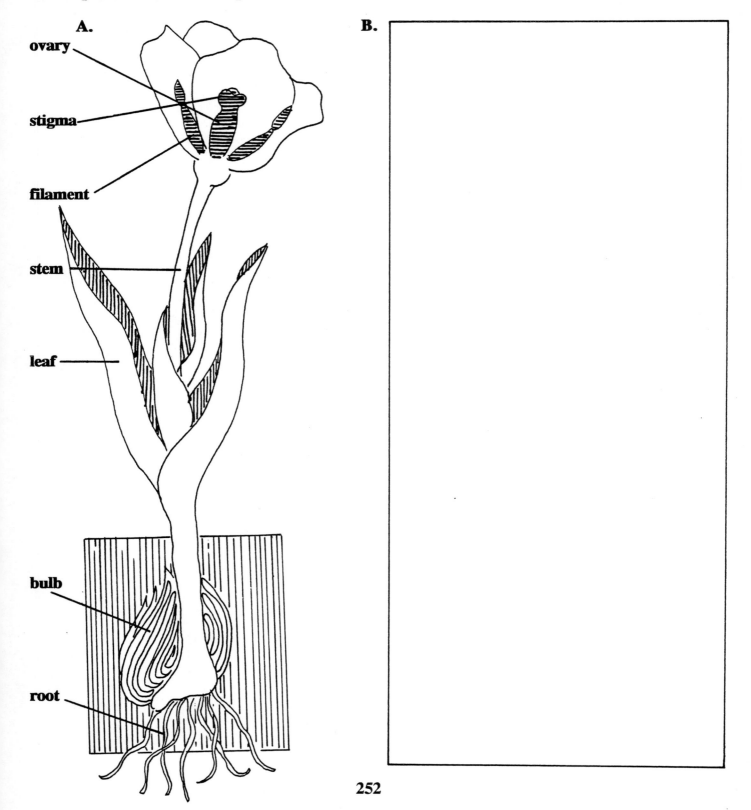

**A.**

ovary

stigma

filament

stem

leaf

bulb

root

**B.**

*"I study with the birds, flowers, God, and myself."* Antonin Dvorak

## Lesson #190: *Parts of a Tree*

**Botany also includes the study of trees. There are several major components of a tree: the crown (head of foliage), the limbs, the trunk, the tap roots, and the minuscule root-hair zone at the ends of the roots. Draw the tree (A) below in B, making sure to show half of it without foliage, and half with foilage. Color when finished.**

**A.**

**B.**

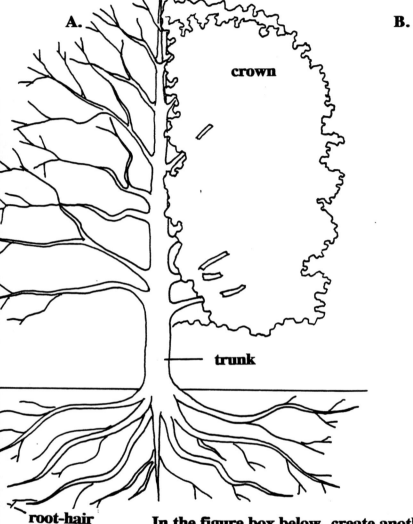

crown

trunk

root-hair

**In the figure box below, create another leaf pattern with contour line. Use your dark green pencil, making your drawing with one continuous line. Color with autumn colors: orange, yellow, light brown, dark brown, green, and a little red.**

# Lesson #191: *Cat Studies*

**Zoology:** *A branch of biology dealing with the study of animals.*

Find a photo or a picture of a cat to draw below. First, practice drawing the simple shapes (A): a circle for the head, a square for the body, and a larger circle for the back. Make sure all the shapes are the correct size. Do not make the head too large, or the body too small. Use lines to measure for proper proportions. For my cat, I drew a straight line across the top of the head and back (B). This horizontal line shows that the head and arch of the back are the same height. Lines like these are called *plumb lines*. Notice the space around the outline of the cat. This is called *negative space*. When you see negative space, it will help you draw your subject more accurately (C). Below, do two studies from a cat picture (D & E). Then, draw your complete cat in F. Draw lightly, and make sure to add detail and texture (refer to Lessons #35 & #36).

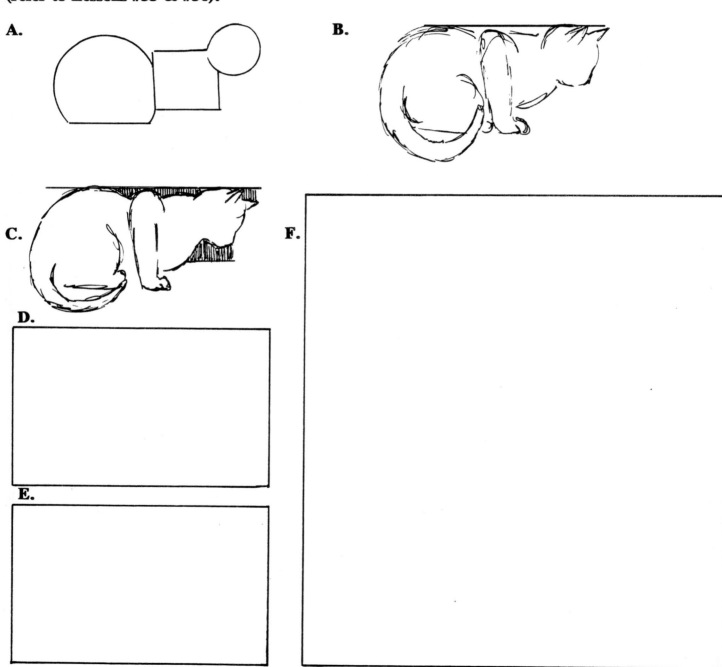

A.

B.

C.

D.

E.

F.

# Lesson #192: *Horse Studies*

There are many approaches to learning how to draw a horse. One is to draw from memory, another is to copy from pictures or photographs, and a third way is to draw horses from life. In the beginning, it is probably best to work from pictures and photographs. Drawing from life is difficult because horses will move as you try to sketch them. However, another way to draw horses is to have an understanding of their skeleton, just as you did with the human figure in Lesson #97. Notice that many parts of a horse's anatomy have the same names as the human skeleton. For this assignment, draw the skeleton of the horse (A), and label the parts in B.

A.

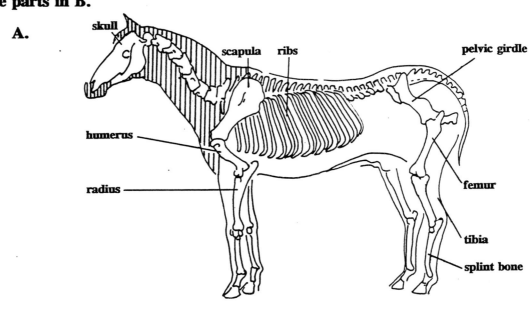

B.

# Lesson #193: *Aquatic Invertebrate*

Aquatic invertebrates are sea creatures that do not have a backbone. Over 95 percent of the known species of the animal world are invertebrates.

The giant squid, which can grow to be over 60 feet long (including tentacles), is an aquatic invertebrate. Draw the squid in the figure box below. Make him playful. Draw a baseball and a bat in two of his tentacles, making sure to show how the tentacles go around the objects. Color your squid a light yellow/brown, leaving the bottom part of each tentacle white. Finally, create a nice environment for your invertebrate friend by drawing and coloring coral and sea life around him. You may need some pictures to do this.

## Lesson #194: *Around They Go*

Complete the circle of bottle-nosed dolphins by adding two more dolphins to the loop. Color them light blue and light brown, leaving their underbellies white. Before beginning, practice drawing them in the aquarium below.

# Lesson #195: Creating a Color-Coded Chart of America

**Geography:** *The study of the physical descriptions of the earth's surface.*

Color in the fifty states, using a different color for each. Can you make 50 colors out of your set of 12 colored pencils? Place a color in the square above the name of the state, and color the state on the map with the same color. Use lines or blending to create each color.

| | | | | | | |
|---|---|---|---|---|---|---|
| ☐ | ☐ | ☐ | ☐ | ☐ | ☐ | ☐ |
| Alabama | Alaska | Arizona | Arkansas | California | Colorado | Connecticut |

| | | | | | | | |
|---|---|---|---|---|---|---|---|
| ☐ | ☐ | ☐ | ☐ | ☐ | ☐ | ☐ | ☐ |
| Delaware | Florida | Georgia | Hawaii | Idaho | Illinois | Indiana | Iowa |

| | | | | | | |
|---|---|---|---|---|---|---|
| ☐ | ☐ | ☐ | ☐ | ☐ | ☐ | ☐ |
| Kansas | Kentucky | Louisiana | Maine | Maryland | Massachusetts | Michigan |

| | | | | | | |
|---|---|---|---|---|---|---|
| ☐ | ☐ | ☐ | ☐ | ☐ | ☐ | ☐ |
| Nevada | Minnesota | Mississippi | Missouri | Montana | Nebraska | New Hampshire |

| | | | | | | |
|---|---|---|---|---|---|---|
| ☐ | ☐ | ☐ | ☐ | ☐ | ☐ | ☐ |
| Ohio | Oregon | New Jersey | New Mexico | New York | N. Carolina | N. Dakota |

| | | | | | | | |
|---|---|---|---|---|---|---|---|
| ☐ | ☐ | ☐ | ☐ | ☐ | ☐ | ☐ | ☐ |
| Oklahoma | Pennsylvania | Texas | Rhode Island | S. Carolina | S. Dakota | Tennessee | Utah |

☐
Vermont

☐
Virginia

☐
Wyoming

☐
Washington

☐
W. Virginia

☐
Wisconsin

258

# Lesson #196:  *Designing a New State Flag*

Let's pretend that the United States is about to annex another state, which would be the 51st state.  You are appointed to design a new state flag.  Take a look at the California state flag (A) to give you an example.  You may want to do some thumbnail sketches first (B), to help formulate ideas.  Create a name for the state.  Give the date for statehood, and list the state tree and state flower.  Finally, draw and color your best flag design below (C).

**A.**

CALIFORNIA REPUBLIC

**California**
**Statehood:  September 9, 1850**
**State Tree: California Redwood**
**State Flower:  Golden Poppy**

**B. Thumbnail Sketches**

**Name:** _____     **State Tree:** _____     **State Flower:** _____

**C.**

## Lesson #197:  *Numismatics*

**Numismatics:**  *The study or collection of coins, tokens, and paper money.*

Today we are going to draw some currency.  First, take a dime, penny, nickel, and quarter, and draw the front and back of each in the circles below (A).  Then, place the coins on the table, and see if you can draw them, making sure to show their thickness (B).  Finally, design a new $7.00 bill (C).  After all, that is God's perfect number!  This will be a technical drawing, so use your ruler to draw it.

**Front**

A.

**Back**

B.

C.

# Lesson #198: *The Revolutionary War*

## History: *A record of significant events.*

The Revolutionary War was the war of American independence, 1775-1781. There were many different soldiers, and various armies during this war. Some of the soldiers in the American, or Continental army, wore the uniform below (A). Using a ruler, lightly draw the 9 guidelines across the page from A to B. Then copy the American Revolutionary soldier to the right (B). Remember, the human figure is 8 head lengths tall, and the hands extend down 5 head lengths (see Lesson #97).

A.                                                                          B.

# Lesson #199:  *Philatelist*

## Philatelist:  *One who collects or studies stamps.*

Many artists have been awarded great sums of money for winning stamp designs.  For this assignment, you are going to design three stamps.  One will be a *Christmas Stamp,* another will be for *National Family Week,* and the third will be honoring *National Homeschooling Education.*  Do a thumbnail sketch for each design (A).  Then, draw your best design in the large figure box (B).  Color when finished.

**A. Thumbnail Sketches**

**B.**

# Lesson #200: *Starting a Stamp Collection*

This page will be for beginning your own stamp collection. As you receive mail, start peeling the stamps off the envelopes, and gluing or taping them below. Next to each stamp, draw its design with colored pencils, using as much detail as possible. Sharpen your pencils!

## My Stamp Collection

# Lesson #201: *Charting a Course*

When I was a young boy, I had a large collection of baseball cards. I wanted to keep them, but never did. I also wanted to bury some coins, a few nickels, pennies, and dimes. I did not do that either. I often regret that I did not bury a treasure. By now, it would be worth a lot of money, and it would be fun to dig it up. For this assignment, put together a little treasure and find a place to bury it. Make a map to show where it is hidden. Draw a rough draft for your map below. Be creative with it! What is the date? How many steps from each marker to the treasure? Is there anything that you want to say on the map? Do you want to put your directions in some sort of code, perhaps writing backwards? Draw some landmarks on your map. You may want to tone your paper with a light brown pencil, and add the details with black and dark brown for a rustic effect.

**Map**

# Lesson #202:  *Seeing Spectrum Colors*

**Science:**  *A knowledge of general laws obtained through testing by scientific means.*

Today we will study spectrum colors, or the colors of a rainbow produced when a ray of light passes through a transparent prism.  In figure box B, copy the spectrum colors.  Start by drawing a three-dimensional prism (A), with light passing through, and the spectrum of colors it produces.  Use your ruler and a light blue colored pencil.  Color when finished.

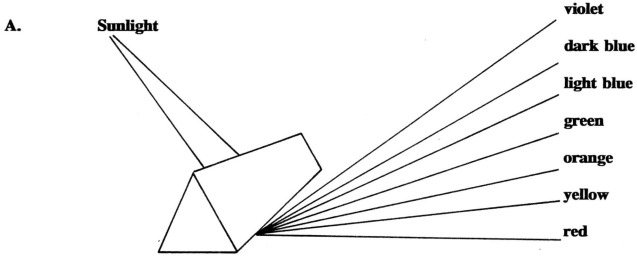

**A.**  Sunlight

violet

dark blue

light blue

green

orange

yellow

red

**B.**

**Pointer:**  You may want to remember spectrum colors the next time you color or paint a rainbow.

*"The fruit of the Spirit is love, joy, peace, patience, kindness, goodness, faithfulness, gentleness, and self-control."*

Galatians 5:22-23

## Lesson #203: *Nutrition*

**Nutrition:** *The process of nourishing the body.*

A very important part of our education is learning about *nutrition*. We should learn how to lead a healthy and happy life by eating the right foods. For this assignment, fill the two figure boxes below with foods. In A, draw and color foods that are not good for you, and in B, draw and color foods that are healthy for the body. List 10 of each of the foods underneath your drawings. Finally, draw and color some happy fruit in C, such as smiling grapes, cheerful cherries, happy apples, etc.

**A. Foods that are bad for you.**          **B. Foods that are good for you.**

**Unhealthy Foods:**          **Healthy Foods:**

_____          _____
_____          _____
_____          _____
_____          _____
_____          _____
_____          _____
_____          _____
_____          _____
_____          _____
_____          _____

**C.**

# Lesson #204: *God's Little Acre Health Food Restaurant*

Let's pretend you are going to open a health food restaurant. Do a drawing of the restaurant in figure box A, and letter *God's Little Acre* on a sign above it. Are there any signs in the windows? Is there a front porch or outdoor cafe? Does it have nice landscaping with trees and shrubbery? Color it in when finished. Next, create a menu on the bottom of the page (B). Letter all of the specials for the day and list the price for each item. Finally, draw and color some nice designs to go around the pages of your new menu.

**A.**

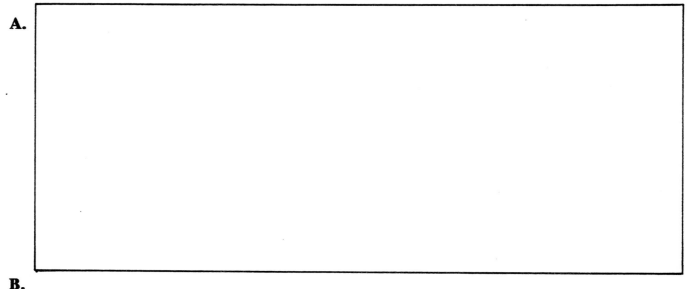

**B.**

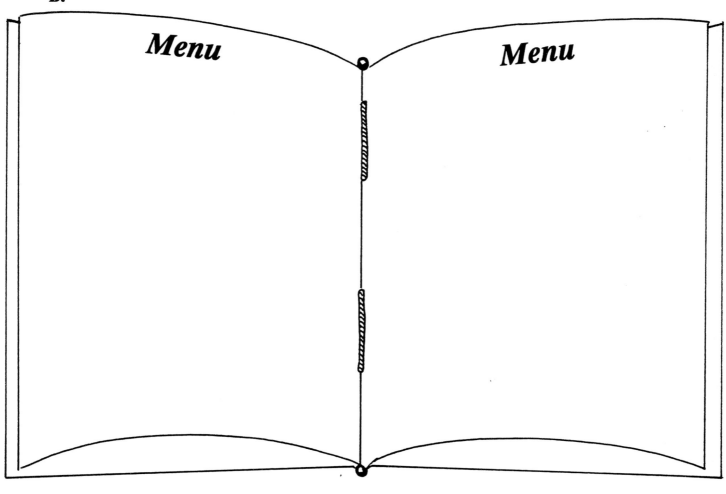

# Lesson #205: *The Greatest Man of the 20th Century*

Who would you choose as the greatest person of the 20th century? When I had to do a report in college, my choice was Dr. Albert Sweitzer. Do you know who Dr. Sweitzer was and what made him great? Do a 150 to 200 word report on Dr. Sweitzer below. Draw his portrait and draw a picture of some event during his lifetime. After reading about his life, do you agree that he was one of the greatest men of the century?

**Dr. Albert Sweitzer**

# Lesson #206: *Inventions*

Leonardo Da Vinci observed birds in flight during the 15th century and believed that man could also fly. He invented a flying machine and stated that if it was well made, and was turned rapidly, then it would climb to the sky (A). Below are two of his studies. Design a flying machine in figure box B, and explain how it functions.

**A.**

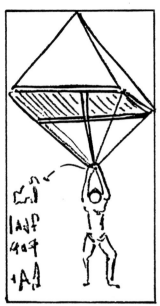

**B. Flying Invention**

**Operating Instructions**

# Lesson #207:  *A Renaissance Man*

Do you know what a Renaissance man is?  It is someone like Leonardo Da Vinci, who has a wide range of interests and is an expert in several areas.  Being a Renaissance man is being *well-rounded*.  That is why it is important to have a balanced education in writing, penmanship, history, language, science, art, and even athletics.  Music appreciation is also an integral part of being well-rounded.

Today, you will have a creative assignment.  Find a selection of classical music you like, close your eyes, and listen to it.  What do you see?  Are the colors warm or cool?  Is it something abstract?  Draw a picture below while listening to classical music.  If you find this too difficult, simply listen to the music and begin drawing and coloring anything you like.  You may want to do a contour drawing, allowing your pencil to flow with the music (A).  Finally, write the title of the music and the name of the composer, along with a description of what you see in the music (B).

A.

B.

**Title:** _____  **Composer:** _____

**Description:**

_____

_____

_____

# Lesson #208: *Illustrating a Children's Story*

## Composition: *The act of arranging in an artistic form.*

For this assignment, you are going to write and illustrate a children's story. First, write the basic story line below. Include such words in your story as: sunshine, mountains, umbrella, rabbit, running brook, songbird, or be totally creative! Do some thumbnail sketches below, to help form ideas about your characters, their personalities, and the setting in which your story takes place.

When you have formulated the story and all the characters, proceed to place illustrations in the figure boxes on the next page. Write a segment for each page of your story on the lines below the squares. To do a larger storybook, you may want to use white poster board for your cover and pages. Simply cut the poster board into even sizes, draw the illustration, and write your story below each picture. You may decide to use a computer for your lettering. To bind your text, use a hole punch, and make two or three holes along the left side. Tie the binding together with string or ribbon.

**Main Characters.......   Other Characters.......   Settings.......**

Story Line.........

**Pointer:** When doing a great deal of artwork on the same topic, repeating the same characters and settings over and over again, it may be a good idea to trace. To trace onto poster board, do your drawing first on regular paper, then rub pencil lead over the entire back of the drawing. This will create a carbon. Place your drawing on the poster board, and outline everything with a pencil. Lift your drawing, and there will be a light imprint on the poster board for you to work with. Making a carbon will save a lot of time and work.

# Lesson #209: *Keeping a Journal - A Day in the Life of* _____.

It's journal time!  Are there any observations that you have made during the studies in this chapter, or any interesting things that you have drawn?  This page could be a summation of all you have learned or observed, or simply some of your thoughts.  Do not forget to do some drawings along with your writing.

---

**Date:** _____

_____
_____
_____
_____
_____
_____
_____
_____
_____
_____
_____
_____
_____
_____
_____
_____
_____
_____

Name: _____     Date: _____

## Lesson #210:  *Academia Examination*

I.  **Select the correct word, and place it in appropriate blank (5 points each):**

botany          zoology          entomology          astronomy
history         science          anatomy             numismatics
nutrition       composition      philatelist

1. _____ is the study of objects and matter outside the earth's atmosphere.

2. The process of nourishing the body is called _____.

3. _____ is a record of significant events.

4. A branch of zoology that deals with the study of insects is _____.

5. _____ is a branch of biology dealing with plant life.

6. A person who collects or studies stamps is called a _____.

7. _____ is the act of arranging into an artistic form.

8. The study of the structural makeup of the human body is called _____.

9. _____ is the science of animal life.

10. The study of the world and its phenomena is called _____.

11. _____ is the study or collection of coins and paper money.


II.  **True or False.  Place a T or F next to each statement. (3 points each):**
   1. Over 95 percent of all living creatures are invertebrates.
   2. A Renaissance man dresses up in a lot of frivolous costumes.
   3. A horse's bones have many of the same names as a human's bones.
   4. A philatelist is a person who studies coins, tokens, and paper money.
   5. The mature standing human figure is six head lengths tall.
   6. A zoologist studies plant life.
   7. Invertebrates are members of the insect family.
   8. Hellenistic art is another name for Greek art.
   9. Egyptian art is similar to Impressionism.
   10. Michelangelo and Leonardo da Vinci were both artists during the Renaissance.

III. **Essay.  (15 points)**  On a separate sheet of paper, write a 100 word report comparing the artwork of the Impressionists with the artwork from the Renaissance.  Name some of the artists, and tell what you like about each era, comparing the works.  What is the difference in styles and in philosophy?

**(Answers on page 310)**

# Painting

*"I want to recapture the freshness of vision which is characteristic of extreme youth when all the world is new."*
**Henri Matisse**

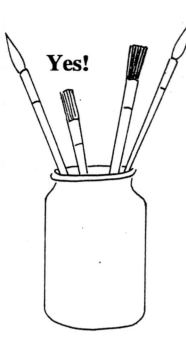

**Yes!**

# Beginning Painting

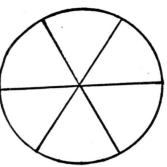

Painting is enjoyable and exciting. Everyone loves to paint and experiment with color. It is a wonderful way to spend your time and a real challenge to develop the creative talents which God has given you. Remember, painting is a learned discipline. Anyone can learn how to paint!

First and foremost, the student should learn to take care of his art materials and work area. The number one problem with painting is that it can be messy; so messy that it prevents many parents from wanting their children to pursue this course in art. However, it does not have to be a messy program. Listed below are a few painting pointers and some basic rules to assist in keeping a tidy area and making painting a joy in the home.

**Pointer #1:** *Never lay your brush down!* Most students become preoccupied with their artwork, and place their brushes on the palette or on the table. Inevitably, the brush rolls into the paint, which then covers the handle. As the student picks up the brush again, their hand becomes covered with paint. Eventually, while preoccupied with their painting, and unaware of the mess, the student will wipe their hands on their clothes and the paint continues to smear. The solution is to never lay your brushes down. Store them hairs up in a sturdy jar to keep them contained. The paint will stay on the tips of the brushes and not on your clothes, the floor, or the table.

**Brush Container**　　**Palette**

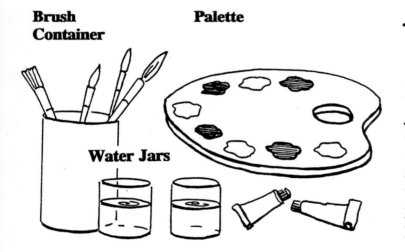

**Water Jars**

**Pointer #2:** *Protect and organize your painting area.* Place newspapers on the table before beginning, and situate everything in a convenient place. If you are right-handed, place your palette to the upper right at just enough distance to keep your arm from smearing the paint (see page 281).

Place two jars or small containers above and to the center of your painting. Use these as water containers. One jar is for cleaning brushes with paint on them, and the other is for adding clean water to paint to make it spread farther. Knocking the water containers over can occur more easily if the water cups are paper or plastic. Remember, select solid jars for holding water and place them at arms length. Also, situate a sturdy jar to the upper left of your painting to hold your brushes when they are not in use. Keeping everything in the upper left and upper right, will give you more room and help avoid accidents that may occur with quick movements. When brushes are contained with hairs up, there will be little mess.

**Pointer #3:** *When mixing colors, always start with the lighter color and add a touch of the darker color to it.* For instance, if you want to mix blue and yellow to make green, take a   little blue and mix it with the yellow. If that is not enough blue, mix a little more. But remember, always mix the darker color into the lighter one. If you mix the lighter color into the darker one, you will have to keep adding and adding until you have a big muddy pile and you will have wasted a lot of paint. When squeezing paint out of the tubes onto your palette, start with only a medium amount of paint (see below). Too much paint will be a waste. Also, keep your paint puddles clean throughout your painting. When mixing colors, pull a little of one color out of the puddle. Then clean your brush in the dirty water container and wipe it with a paper towel or rag before continuing. Next, pull a little of the other color from the other puddle. Never put a brush with one color on it into a puddle of another color. If you want to add just a touch of water to your paints to make the colors more fluid, use your clean water container.

clean
water

dirty
water

start with
medium amount
of paint

light color

dark color

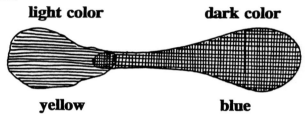

yellow

blue

**Pointer #4:** *Wear your painting clothes.* Never wear nice clothes when painting because there is always the possibility of an accident.

**Pointer #5:** *Hold your brush near the end of the handle.* Beginning students have a tendency to hold their brushes tightly and near the hairs, thinking this will give them more control. On the contrary, students have more control when holding brushes farther back on the handle. This also gives students a more relaxed sense, a freer motion with the brush, and a certain joy in painting.

**Pointer #6:** *Apply light colors to your painting first, then add dark colors.* It is more difficult to add a lighter color over a darker one, than to add a darker color over a lighter one. For instance, imagine you are painting a green field. You may want to color the field yellow, so it will be filled with sunlight. Then, add a thin layer of green over the yellow. This will make your green a much warmer and brighter color. Do not be too heavy with your dark colors; just add a little and spread it around, then add a little more, and so on. You can always add more, but you can not add less.

**Pointer #7:** *Clean your area when finished.* Leave your art area as clean and neat after you have finished as before you started. Clean your brushes and store them hairs up. Place your painting in a secure place until it dries. Throw away or store the newspapers and old paint in your work area until next time. If you are using acrylic paints, you can store them in the freezer and use them again. Clean your water jars and wash your hands.

# Materials

Below is a list of materials that you will need in order to start painting. This list is meant to be both practical and efficient.

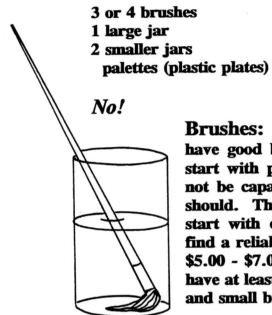

*No!*

3 or 4 brushes
1 large jar
2 smaller jars
  palettes (plastic plates)

acrylic paints
4 - 22" x 28" sheets of white poster board
rags or paper towels
painting clothes or smock

small  medium  large

**Brushes:** It is important in painting to have good brushes. Too many students start with poor quality brushes and will not be capable of painting the way they should. This does not mean you have to start with expensive brushes. You can find a reliable set of three brushes in the $5.00 - $7.00 range. The student should have at least 3 brushes: a large, medium, and small brush.

Never leave your brushes in water! Brush hairs are glued in place and leaving them in water may cause the hairs to fall out. Also, leaving your brushes in water will cause the hairs to bend, and many times they will not return to their normal position.

**Poster Board:** Canvas is a good surface for acrylic paint; however, we will start with poster board because it is more practical. You may obtain sheets of 22" x 28" white poster board at local stores. Cut it into smaller sections to paint on. In the beginning, smaller surfaces are better because you will save on paints. Also, when doing smaller paintings, you will notice all your brush strokes and will come to a quicker understanding of what you are learning. Finally, try painting on different colors of poster board!

**Jars:** As mentioned, a large jar is good to use for storing brushes, and two smaller jars are good for holding water, one for dirty water and one for clean water.

**Rags or Paper Towels:** These are needed to wipe your brushes after they have been cleaned in water. Your brushes should always be clean. When wiping paint from a brush, be careful not to get the paint off the rag onto your hands.

**Acrylic Paints:** Acrylic paints are a good introduction to painting. They are a bridge between tempera paints and oils, they are relatively inexpensive, they can be painted with either thick or thin applications, they offer bright and bold colors, and they clean up with water if taken care of immediately. We recommend the Accent Blending acrylic paints in 2 oz. containers. This is a good introductory set for learning blending, mixing, and color theory.

# Lesson #211:  Before Beginning to Paint

Much of what we will learn in painting is going to be like a scientist in a lab.  We are going to take different colors and see how they react when mixed with other colors.  On the bottom of the paint card, you will notice a simple code for color abbreviations.  R is red, Y is yellow, B is blue, Gr is green, Or is orange, V is violet, Br is brown, W is white, and Blk is black.  These codes will assist you in your scientific research.

## Setting Up

Let's prepare our area as mentioned in Pointer #2 in the introduction of this chapter.  Make sure to place newspapers down before your begin.  If you are right-handed, place your rags and palette to the right.  This will give you easy access when you need them.  Your two water containers go to the top, and a little to the right, closer to your painting hand.  Finally, place a container to the upper left to hold your brushes.  Check below (A) to see how to set up if you are left-handed or right-handed.

### A.  Right-Handed    Use This Amount of Color    Left-Handed

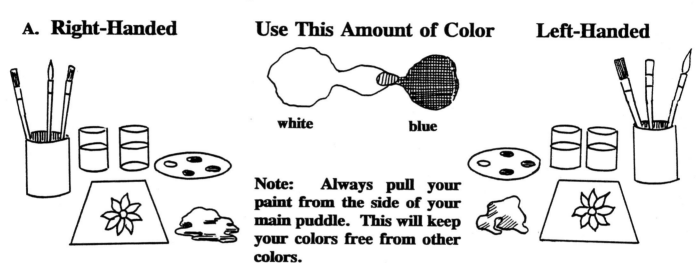

white                blue

**Note:  Always pull your paint from the side of your main puddle.  This will keep your colors free from other colors.**

Using a plastic plate, pour out four small puddles of color:  yellow, red, blue, and white.  If you are using containers of paint, make sure to shake them before pouring.  It is good to start with about the size of a dime for the primary colors, and the size of a quarter for white, since you will be using more white than the other colors.  When painting, make sure to clean your brush in between colors.  Dip and clean it in the water container that you will use for cleaning brushes.  Clean the brush well and wipe it dry with your rag.  It is good to work with the same color as much as possible.  This will save time and paint.  For instance, if you are painting a yellow banana, you may want to leave the yellow on your brush even when you are painting an orange, because you will need the yellow for the orange.  Remember, *always pull the colors from the sides of the puddles.*  This will keep your main puddle clean.

### B. *Yes!    No!*

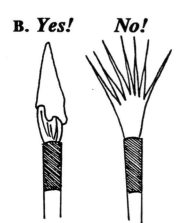

Note: Do not *scrub paint* with your brush!  Scrub painting occurs when you do not put enough paint on your brush and therefore have to scrub it on.  Look at the two brushes to the left (B).  You will be able to tell if you are scrub painting by the hairs of your brush.  If they are all separated and scraggly, then you do not have enough paint on your brush.  Always paint with a *loaded brush*, that is, a brush with a lot of paint on it.

# Lesson #212: *The Color Wheel*

We will start our painting program with the *color wheel*. Take *Paint Card #1* and place it in front of you. There are really several parts to this assignment: coloring the color wheel, mixing colors, blending colors, and painting a sky. First, let's paint the color wheel in the top left corner. Using your medium size brush, dip it in yellow and paint the yellow pie section on your color wheel. Take your time and make sure to stay within the lines. Learn to paint with *control*. When you have finished, paint the two circles marked "Y (yellow)." Before cleaning your brush, mix a little yellow with white and also paint the circle "Y/W."

Next, paint the red pie section. Remember, take your time and paint with control, staying within the lines. Then, paint the circle "R (red)" below the two yellow circles. Before cleaning your brush, mix a little red with white and paint the circle "R/W."

Next, mix a little red into yellow. Remember, *always start with the lighter color, and add just a touch of the darker color to it*. Start with yellow and add a touch of red to make a nice orange. If it is not dark enough, add a touch more red. Paint the pie section between the yellow and red with this orange. While you are still working with orange, paint the top circle to the left under *Mixing Colors*. Then, take out a little of pure yellow, add a touch of your orange, and paint the circle directly under the orange circle a *yellow/orange*. To orange, add a small touch of red, and paint the bottom circle in the first row a *red/orange*. Clean your brush well before moving to the next color.

Dip your clean brush in blue and paint the blue pie section. Then, pull out some white, and add just a touch of blue to it. This should be a light blue. Paint the bottom right circle "B/W." Now, let's see if you can make a very light blue. To white, add only a very small touch of the light blue you just made. Paint the sky above the *horizon line* in the figure box with this very light blue.

For violet, pull out red (the lighter color), and add a touch of blue (the darker color) to it. *Add a little white to your violet*; this will give you a lighter color. Paint the pie section between the red and blue with your violet and then paint the middle circle of the top row under *Mixing Colors* with this color. In the circle beneath the one just painted, make another violet by adding more red and paint it a *red/violet*. Add more blue to your violet and paint the bottom circle a *blue/violet*. Before cleaning your brush, paint the water (below the horizon line) in the figure box a blue/violet. Use short horizontal strokes to paint your water, leaving some white areas in between your strokes to give your water some sparkle.

## Paint Card #1: *Color Wheel*

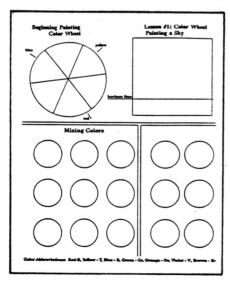

Last of all, start with yellow (the lighter color) and add a touch of blue (the darker color) to make a green. Paint the top pie section green, and then paint the last circle in the top row under *Mixing Colors* green. To yellow, add a little of this green, and paint the circle under the green circle a *yellow/green*. To green, add a little blue and paint the last circle a *blue/green*. When your paints have dried, you may want to try placing a *thin, light layer* of another color over the six circles of color to the right, to see how it changes them. Keep this second layer of paint thin so you can see the bottom layer under it.

# Lesson #213: *Color Chart*

Now, let's make a *large* color chart. Take a piece of white, 22" x 28" poster board, and draw your diagram (A). First, use a round object, like a small plate or a large jar lid, to draw a circle for your color wheel in the upper left corner. Then, using a ruler, divide the circle into twelve equal pie sections. This will be your color wheel. Notice that it is different than the color wheel on *Paint Card #1* because it consists of the primary colors, the secondary colors, and the *tertiary colors*.

## A. Color Chart

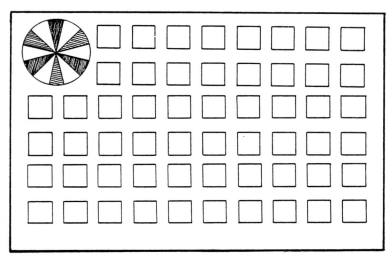

After drawing your color wheel on the poster board, measure out a series of small squares approximately 1" each in rows going all the way across and down the entire surface. Leave about 1/2" space underneath each row. Take your time and make a pleasing color chart that you will be able to appreciate and use for years to come.

After you have finished designing your chart, paint the color wheel. First, paint the primary colors in every fourth section of your color wheel: yellow, skip three spaces, red, skip three spaces, and then blue (B). Next, paint in the secondary colors, skipping a space between each of the primary colors. For example, yellow, skip a space, orange, skip a space, red (C). The tertiary colors are in between the primary and secondary colors: yellow/orange would go between yellow and orange, red/orange would go between red and orange, red/violet would go between red and violet, and so forth. With each secondary and tertiary color that you make, paint one of the squares on your color chart with that same color. Underneath each color square, print the colors you used to make that color. Start with the color you used most, and then the next color, and then the color you used least. For instance, if you made a violet, you may want to print R/B/W, meaning that you used more red, some blue, and a little white.

You may continue to mix and paint colors for your color chart, but do not paint in all the squares because you are going to learn more about combining colors as we progress through this chapter. However, you can at least mix the colors that you have learned so far. Remember, underneath each color, print the colors that you used to make that color.

## B. Primary Colors

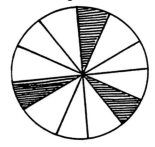

yellow
red
blue

orange
violet
green

## C. Secondary Colors

# Lesson #214: *Complementary Colors*

**Paint Card #2**

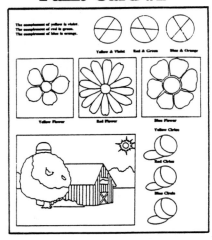

As we learned in Lesson #6, *complementary colors* are colors that are opposite each other on the color wheel. Take a look at the color wheel you painted on Paint Card #1. The complement of red is green, which is directly across from it. The complement of yellow is violet, and the complement of blue is orange. Complementary colors are used:

*1.  For shading.*
*2.  For painting a background.*
*3.  To darken or dull a color.*

Most beginning students use black or dark brown for coloring their shaded areas. However, let's say that you want to shade part of a banana. If you blend a *touch* of violet (the complement of yellow) into the yellow while it is still wet, it will give you a nice color for a shaded area. Likewise, if you want to paint a background and do not know what color to use, generally speaking, a complementary color is a good choice. For example, if you painted an apple, you may want to paint a green background behind your subject matter. Finally, if you want to darken or dull a color, try adding just a touch of its complement. When mixing complements, *only use a touch of the complementary color.* If you use any more, it may overpower the other color.

Place *Paint Card #2* in front of you. First, paint the yellow pie shape on the top of the card. While you still have yellow on your brush, paint the first flower yellow, as well as the entire circle and its shadow under *Yellow Circle*. While the circle is still wet, take only a tiny *touch* of violet and blend it into the shaded side and shadow of the circle. If you used too much, add a little yellow over it. This should give you a nice shaded area.

Next, take your violet paint, and paint the other pie shape in the first color wheel on the top of the card. Make sure you *add white to your violet to make it lighter.* Before painting the background of the flower, make it much lighter by adding a touch of violet to white. *Background colors should be light and not overwhelm the subject matter in the foreground.* Also, paint the silo and roof on the barn violet.

Paint the pie shape in the second color wheel red, as well as the red flower, the barn, and the middle circle and its cast shadow under Red Circle. While the barn and circle are still wet, add a touch of green to the shaded side of each. Remember, *only add a touch of the complement.* You are making a dull red. If it is too green, add a little more red to it. Paint the complementary pie section green and the trees around the barn. While the large tree is still wet, add a *touch* of red to the shaded side. You are making a dull green. Paint the distant trees and the bush with the same dull green.

Next, mix a light blue by adding a little blue to white. Paint one of the pie shapes in the last color wheel, the blue flower, and the blue circle and its cast shadow. Then, paint your sky with even a lighter blue. Remember, skies are generally very light in color.

While the blue circle is still wet, add a *touch* of orange to the shaded side and blend it in. To finish, paint the hay in the barn a dull yellow. Can you mix a nice color for the tree trunk, barn door, corner of the roof, and the opening behind the hay? Finally, add your new colors to the color chart from Lesson #213.

# Lesson #215: *Mixing Colors*
## Paint Card #3: *Mixing Colors*

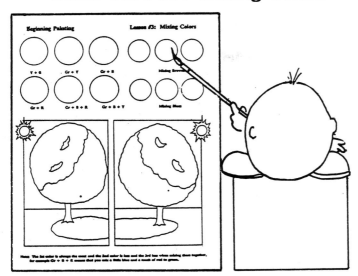

Place *Paint Card #3* in front of you. Today we are going to practice mixing more colors. In the first circle above *Mixing Blues*, mix a little blue into white. Then in the second circle, make a lighter blue by mixing a little less blue into white. Finally, in the third circle, make the lightest blue you can, making it almost white. Then take this very light blue, and paint the skies behind the two trees on the bottom of the card.

## Points to Remember:

1. *Always start with the lighter color, and add just a touch of the darker color to it.*
2. *Skies are generally lighter in tone than anything else in your picture.*

Next, mix some greens in the six larger circles. In the first one, mix yellow and blue to make green. To yellow, add just a little of this green, and paint the second circle a bright yellow/green. *A bright yellow/green is a color that you will find outdoors when the sun is shining on green vegetation!* Paint the part of each tree and all the grass that is in sunlight with this bright yellow/green.

In the third circle, mix green and blue to make a dark green. After you have painted the circle with this dark green, paint the shaded side of each tree and the area of grass under the trees that is in the shadow. Also, paint the little spots that are on the light side of the trees.

Next, mix a yellow/green, like in the first two circles. Add a *touch* of red, the complement of green, to dull the color. Remember, *only add a little of the complement*. Then, paint the circle "Gr + R" with this dull green color.

In circle "Gr + B + R," add some blue and a touch more red to make a darker, duller green. Finally, in circle "Gr + B + Y," take a touch of this dull green, add it to yellow, and paint the last circle. You have just made a wide assortment of greens. If you want to experiment with other varieties, try adding white to green.

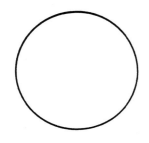

Let's make a brown for the tree trunk. In the first circle on the top row of *"Mixing Browns,"* mix yellow plus some red and only a *touch* of blue or green. Then, in the second circle, take a touch of this brown, and add it to yellow to make a lighter brown. In the third circle, add a little of the darker brown to white, to make a lighter brown. Select your favorite brown from these, and paint the tree trunks. Finally, paint the two suns yellow. Place the new colors on your color chart from Lesson #213.

# Lesson #216: *Warm & Cool Colors*

We have learned that the warm colors are red, yellow, and orange, and the cool colors are blue, violet, and green. Let's experiment with warm and cool colors, and see if we can create some beautiful butterflies.

Place Paint Card #4 in front of you. First, color the three geometric shapes in the upper left (the rectangle, triangle, and circle) with warm colors: red, yellow, and orange. Then paint the next series of geometric shapes with the same warm colors, but see if you can make each of them lighter. Remember, red, plus a little yellow and white, will give you a lighter red. White added to yellow (W/Y), and orange (W/O), will also make them whiter. Remember, paint with as much of the same color as possible. For instance, if you have just painted the triangle yellow, you may want to paint the wing of the butterfly with the same color. This will save you from cleaning the brush after each use and will save on time and paint.

Paint the top butterfly with warm colors. First, paint the entire butterfly with a thin layer of yellow paint by adding a drop of water to your paint puddle. You should still be able to see the pattern and details underneath the color. Then, start painting the designs on the butterfly with various mixtures of warm colors. You may want to make some parts a pink, and others yellow/orange or red/orange. Be creative with your colors! Start with a medium size brush, and as you begin to place some of the smaller details in, go to your smaller brush.

Next, paint the three geometric shapes directly under *"Cool Colors."* Paint the rectangle blue, the triangle violet, and the circle green. Then paint the bottom row of geometric colors the same three colors, but this time lighten each one of them by adding white.

Paint the butterfly on the bottom of the card with a combination of cool colors. Start by painting it a very thin violet, so the patterns and details under the color can be seen. Then, add a variety of light, cool colors to all the details and patterns.

## Paint Card #4: *Warm & Cool Colors*

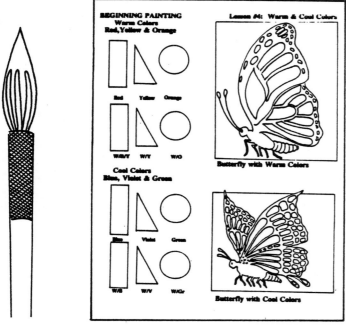

What color do you want to paint the backgrounds? You can use complementary colors by painting the background of the yellow butterfly with very light violet, and the background of the violet butterfly a very light yellow. Or, you can use a light warm background, like a light orange for the yellow butterfly. A light cool background for the violet butterfly would be a light blue. Finally, do the eyes and antennas. Take an extra fine black marker, and go over some of the lines you may have lost when painting, like the long antenna.

**Pointer:** One way to paint with *control* is to turn your picture around either sideways or upside down. This will give your hand and brush better angles when trying to paint corners or lines.

# Lesson #217: *Impressionism*

## Paint Card #5

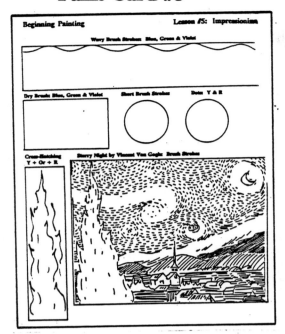

*Impressionism* is a style of painting in which the artist is more concerned with color and brush strokes than with realism. Some of the great Impressionists were Claude Monet, Vincent Van Gogh, and Pissarro. Go to the library, and see the vivid colors and brush strokes they used in their paintings.

For today's assignment, place *Paint Card #5* in front of you. Mix some cool colors like light violet, light blue, and light green, using a lot of white in each. Then, taking one color at a time, dip your brush into a lot of paint and pull it across the long figure box on the top of the paint card. Make each brush stroke long and wavy, not stopping from beginning to end. If you start to run out of paint, twirl the brush in your fingers to use the paint on the other side of the hairs. Make long, wavy strokes with light blue, light violet, and light green, keeping them close together.

Take these same three colors, and practice circular brush strokes in the circle in the middle of the paint card. Make short circular strokes with your brush, going around and around. (Notice the circular strokes below.)

In the next circle, place some short vertical blue/violet strokes. A short vertical stroke goes up and down. Add some red/violet strokes in between the blue/violet strokes, filling the entire circle with short vertical strokes. Do not let any white show between the strokes.

Next, make a field of grass by using *pointillism*. Pointillism is the use of dots. Mix some greens, and using a medium size brush, fill the *Field of Grass* figure box with an assortment of green dots. Then, mix a lighter green by adding green to yellow, and place this color in between the other green dots. Mix a darker blue/green, and add this color in between the other dots of colors. Then mix some violet, and place some of this color in between the greens. Finally, mix some red with white and a touch of yellow, and place those dots throughout, covering the entire figure box with dots of color. What do you think? Does it look like a field of flowers?

Look at the swirling tree in the long figure box on the bottom of the paint card. It is similar to the tree that Vincent Van Gogh painted in *Starry Night*. Mix a green and paint short wavy vertical strokes, showing the shape of the tree. Then, mix a lighter green, and add more short wavy vertical strokes. Mix a dark green, and fill in any open areas. Finally, mix a light violet, and add some of these strokes to give it a little more color.

**Pointillism**

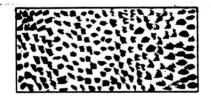

**Circular Brush Strokes**

**Short Vertical Strokes**

**Wavy Strokes**

For the last part of this lesson, paint the picture on the bottom of the paint card of *Starry Night* by Vincent Van Gogh. First, mix a violet and paint short strokes across the sky following the patterns. Then, mix a dark blue and fill in some of the areas with this color. Add a red/violet with short brush strokes. Finally, add a lighter blue, filling the sky with cool colors. Mix a yellow and white, and paint some of the open areas inside the circles and moon with more short strokes, filling the sky with light.

For the land, start with a dark blue/green and paint the distant hills, distant trees, and the land with short brush strokes. Paint the large tree in the foreground with short, wavy strokes. Add to the hills, trees, and land a lighter green, but not too light because it is night-time. Finally, add a deep red/violet throughout the landscape.

Paint the roofs of the buildings with a deep red. It could be the same red/violet that you already used. For the sides of the buildings, use a blue/violet and a light blue for the church steeple.

When painting, remember:

1. *Always mix at least two colors together.*
2. *Land is darker than sky.*
3. *Use a medium brush when painting impressionistically.*

## Lesson #218: *Your Signature*

Signing your name to a painting is a very important part of the picture. Many beginning artists simply take a large brush and paint big dark letters across the bottom. This is not what you are supposed to do. When signing your name, use a very fine brush and mix a color that compliments some of the colors in your picture. You may want to sign *"Starry Night"* with a light blue/violet or red/violet over the dark green grass. The best place to sign your name is in the bottom right corner. It should be a stylized signature; one you design to be both simple and pleasing to the eye. Notice below how Albrecht Durer, Claude Monet, and Vincent Van Gogh signed their names.

Look at the way I sign *"Stebbing."* It took several days of experimenting with my name to come up with this design, or logo, for my artistic signature. On the bottom of the page, practice your artistic signature. Then return to all your completed paint cards, and sign your name with a pleasing, artistic signature.

**Practice your artistic signature here**

**Albrecht Durer**

**Vincent Van Gogh**

**Claude Monet**

**Stebbing**

288

# Lesson #219: *Painting Fruit/Color Upon Color*

So far we have been painting very thick, or *opaque*. When you paint opaque, you can not see through the colors. However, when you paint thin, or *transparent*, you can see the colors underneath. For today's assignment, we are going to paint with very thin layers of color by adding water, so that our colors will be transparent.

## Paint Card #6: *Painting Fruit*

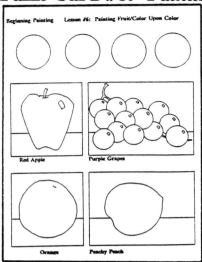

Place *Paint Card #6* in front of you. First, paint the first two circles on the top of the card yellow. Paint the third circle orange, and the fourth circle red. Then, take a thin layer of red, mixed with water, and paint over the first yellow circle. This should create an orange color as the thin transparent red will allow the yellow to show through to make the orange. In the second circle, place a thin layer of blue over the yellow. This should create a nice transparent green. In the third circle, place a thin layer of purple over the orange, creating a warm brown. In the last circle, place a thin layer of blue over the red, to create a violet. If your paint is too watery and begins to *puddle up*, wipe your brush dry, and *lift* some of the wet paint off the surface.

Paint the apple with a thin layer of orange. Do not paint over the little window in the apple or the grapes. This is a *highlight*, and will be left white. Then paint a transparent red over it. Leave the right side of the apple more orange, as it will be the side which the light is shining on. Take a little touch of blue, and blend it into the left, or shaded side of the apple, to give a darker red.

Paint the grapes with a light layer of red mixed with a little water. Then, add a thin layer of blue over them, making sure not to cover your little windows, or highlights. Paint a little more blue with water on the left side of the grapes and leave the right side more red, showing a light side and a shaded side.

Next, paint the orange and peach yellow. Then take a thin red and paint over the orange. While the paint is still wet, see if you can dot the surface of the orange with a clean brush to show *texture* on the orange. Experiment with white, yellow, and red to make a peach color. These colors will not be as transparent as the others, but thicker to show the texture of the peach.

For the background of the fruit use *complementary colors*. Remember, complementary colors can be a good choice when selecting a color for a background. For the red apple, mix a very bright green with a lot of yellow and water, and paint a thin background behind it. Then, for the violet grapes, mix a light yellow with water and paint a thin background. For the orange and peach, paint a very light blue background, since blue is the complement of orange. However, behind the orange, paint a thin blue background. Behind the peach, paint a light blue background by mixing a little blue with a lot of white.

Last, paint the table underneath the fruit with brown. Make a nice brown by mixing any two of the secondary colors: orange and violet, violet and green, or green and orange. You can make your browns lighter by adding yellow or white to them. Finally, make a dark brown by adding a little more red and blue to it, and paint the stems of the apple and grapes with this color. Do not forget to sign your painting with a nice, light color.

# Lesson #220: *Painting a Landscape*

A *landscape* is a picture representing a view of natural inland scenery, like mountains, hills, valleys, and lakes. When painting a landscape, there are several things you should know:

*1. The sky is lighter than the colors on the land.*
*2. Most landscapes have a foreground, middle ground, and background.*
*3. Colors in the background are lighter and there is no detail.*
*4. Colors in the foreground are brighter and there is more detail.*

Take out *Paint Card #7* and place it in front of you. We are going to paint the landscape on the bottom of the card. First, make a light blue by mixing a touch of blue to white and paint the sky. Then, add a touch of red to the light blue, to make a very light violet. Paint the top circle under *"Violets"* with this color, and then paint the distant mountains a light violet. Add some blue and red to this color and make a darker violet. Paint the other circle under *"Violets"* with this color along with the lake in the landscape. Make sure not to paint the little sailboat.

## Paint Card #7: *Landscape*

Next, mix a light green by adding a touch of blue to yellow. Paint the distant trees on the other side of the lake, the field beneath the hill, and the right side of the large tree in the foreground with this color. Make a lighter green by adding a little more yellow, and paint the grass on the upper hill with this color as well as the three little blotches on the shaded side of the large tree. Then, mix a darker green, by adding more blue to the green, and paint the three small trees near the lake, the shaded side of the large tree, the cast shadow of the tree (except on the shaded part of the road), and the cast shadow of the fence on the grass. Using your small brush, paint the little blotches on the light side of the large tree with this deep green as well as the stems and leaves of the three flowers.

Make a brown by mixing yellow, red, and a touch of blue. Paint the top circle under *"Browns and Blacks"* with this color, as well as the shaded side of the trunk of the large tree, and the sides of the picket fence. Then, make a lighter brown by adding either yellow or white to the brown, and paint the bottom circle under *"Browns and Blacks"* with this color, as well as the light side of the tree trunk and the front parts of the fence.

Make a pink by adding a touch of red to white, and paint the top circle under *"Pinks"*. Then, add a little yellow to pink for the bottom circle. Select either one of these colors and paint your road. For the shaded part of the road add a touch of blue to the pink and paint in the area. Finally, color the three flowers in the foreground with yellow and red mixed together. What do you think of your painting? How do you like the purple mountains, pink road, and browns you made? Do not forget to sign your painting with a nice artistic signature in a light color.

**A.**

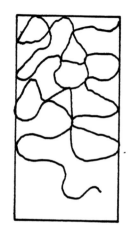

# Lesson #221: *Monochromatic Colors*

*Monochromatic* means one color. Learning to do a painting in tones of one color will teach you much about that color and how the absence of other colors can actually make color. *"Less is more"* is a good statement. Today, we will do a monochromatic painting in blues. Place *Paint Card #8* in front of you. First, take your pencil, and draw a design using contour line in the long figure box to the upper right on the card. Leave the shapes fairly large, so you can paint in each of them (A). Remember, a contour drawing is one continuous line.

Take blue straight from the container and paint the first circle on the top of the card. We will use this to compare the other blues we make. Blue, like most other colors, is too bright, or intense, straight out of the tube. That is why colors need to be mixed with other colors. Add a touch of blue to white to make a very light blue and paint: one of the circles, a few of the patterns in the contour drawing, several parts of the teapot that are going to be light, and the sky outside the windowpanes. Notice the cast shadows on the counter made by the teapot and window panes, which tells the direction the light is coming from. Therefore, the shaded side of your teapot will be on the left. Make the different areas on the teapot light or dark with a variety of blues. Next, make a black, or very dark blue, by adding red to blue until it is as dark as you can make it, and then add a *touch* of yellow. If you add too much yellow, add some more red and blue. This should give you a deep rich, black. Paint one of the circles on the top of the card and then paint the little opening inside the spout on the teapot. Mix some of this black into white to make a light blue/gray. Add a little blue, and paint another circle. Notice this is a completely different blue than the blue straight out of the tube. Paint more patterns in your contour drawing and add this new tone of blue to your color chart.

## Paint Card #8: *Monochromatic Colors*

Beginning Painting    Lesson #8: Monochromatic Colors

Blue

Blue Period

See if you can make enough blues to paint the nine circles. Your black and white mixtures will be a good base to produce more variations of blue. Paint the remainder of your contour drawing and complete the picture of the teapot. Leave the window pane, and the light areas on the counter around the teapot, white. White areas will give your painting life. Also, try to have lighter areas against darker areas. Sometimes if your blues are the same tone of color, the areas will blend together. Try to create *contrast* by having a difference between light and dark tones. Do you know any other ways of making blues? How about adding a touch of orange (the complement) to some of the blues. How do you like your monochromatic painting? Many artists have done a series of paintings like this. Have you noticed that painting takes thinking?

291

# Lesson #222: *Analogous Colors*

*Analogous colors* are any three colors that are next to each other on the color wheel. When using analogous colors in your paintings, you will create a sense of harmony. Place *Paint Card #9* in front of you. Notice that the color wheel has twelve pie sections: the primary colors (yellow, red, and blue), the secondary colors (orange, violet, and green), and the tertiary colors (yellow/orange, red/orange, red/violet, blue/violet, blue/green, and yellow/green).

Let's paint the color wheel starting with yellow and work our way around it clockwise. First, paint the top pie section yellow, as well as the first musical note, and the breast and wing of the bird on the bottom left. Remember, *paint with control*, keeping the paint within the guidelines. Make the color orange, and paint the third pie section, the second musical note, the head of the bird on the bottom left, and the beaks and feet of both birds.

Note: As you continue to mix colors and paint, select any three colors *next to each other* on the color wheel and paint the circles on the upper right of the card. Then, select another three colors next to each other, and paint the circles below them. Also, paint the word *"BIRDS"* with colors that are next to each other, i.e. yellow, yellow/orange, orange, red/orange, red, red/violet. Do not forget to paint each musical note in the same order as you paint each pie section on the color wheel. Finally, paint the colors on the birds as it states. For the darker areas of the bird on the left, use a red/violet, and for the darker areas for the bird on the right, use a blue/violet.

## Paint Card #9: *Analogous Colors*

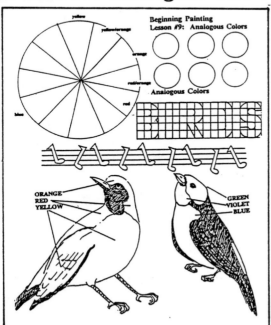

Adding orange to yellow will make a yellow/orange for the second pie section. Adding a little red to your orange will make a red/orange to paint the fourth pie section. Mix a violet with red and blue, add some white to lighten it up, then skip a space and paint the seventh pie section. Then, add some red to make a red/violet and paint the sixth pie section. Add some blue to it to make a blue/violet and paint the eighth pie section. Mix some blue into green and paint the tenth pie section a blue/green. Finally, add a touch of green to yellow to make a bright yellow/green and paint the last pie section. Now you have a beautiful color wheel! You can use this as a reference for complementary colors or to select colors for an analogous painting.

Did you paint all the circles, complete the word *"BIRDS"*, the musical notes, and the birds on the bottom of the card? How do you like using analogous colors? You may want to take some small pieces of white poster board and do several small paintings using various selections of analogous colors.

# Lesson #223: *Painting Colorful Pictures*

Let's have some fun and paint four colorful little pictures. Place *Paint Card #10* in front of you. Generally speaking, the first thing you should paint is the background. One reason we do this is because it is easier to paint over something than to go around it. For instance, suppose you were painting a tree in winter. It is much easier to paint the sky first, and then paint the limbs and branches over it, rather than to paint the tree first, and have to paint the sky around each and every branch. Therefore, we will paint our backgrounds first. Mix a blue/green and paint the background behind the parrot and the tropical fish. Then mix a very light blue and paint the sky behind the flamingo and the porpoise. Finally, mix a darker blue/green and paint the water underneath the porpoise. (Do not paint the splash; leaving it white is probably the best choice.) Make sure to mix enough of each color. One of the major problems with beginning students is that they run out of a color and then do not know how to mix it again. However, part of your education is to experiment and learn how to mix the colors you desire.

Next, mix a yellow/orange, and paint every other stripe on the tropical fish, the sun behind the flamingo, and the feet, beak, and eye of the parrot. Paint the breast and head of the parrot with a warm red/orange. Look at the color wheel you created in the last lesson and select some nice colors to paint each row of feathers on the parrot: one row blue, another violet, another green, another yellow, etc.

## Paint Card #10: *Painting Colorful Pictures*

Beginning Painting     Lesson #10: Creating Colorful Paintings

Make a dark blue or black by mixing blue and red together until it is as dark as you can make it and then add a touch of yellow to make it even darker. Paint the lower beak of the parrot with this color and the triangle on the upper beak. Paint every other stripe on the tropical fish, the tip of the flamingo's beak, and the underbelly of the porpoise. Take your smallest brush and paint a black speck, or dot, in the center of the parrot's and flamingo's eyes.

Next, mix a little red into white to make pink. Add a touch of yellow to this to make a warmer pink and then paint the flamingo with this color. Make a brown from this pink by adding some more red, yellow, and a touch of blue. When you have made a nice brown, paint the branch that the parrot is perched on.

Finally, paint the rest of the porpoise by making one or two nice blues for his back, fins, and nose. (Look at the blues you used in your monochromatic painting of the teapot and select several of them.) However, when painting the remainder of the porpoise, leave the reflections white that are on his back and fin.

# Lesson #224:  *Painting Fish with Tones*

Let's paint some more fish!  Place *Paint Card #11* in front of you.  For today's assignment, you are going to paint a *Mako Shark* and an *Atlantic Pompano*.  Just as Lesson #221, you are going to paint with *monochromatic* colors.  However, let's give the background of the picture a nice color by painting it a light blue/green.  Pull out a lot of yellow and white and mix a little blue into it.  Take your time and paint around the two fish, painting with control.

Then, make some blues and paint in the circles above the fish on the paint card.  Start by making a dark blue/black.  The shark's upper back, fins, and tail are a very dark blue, and his middle portions are a middle blue tone.  Mix a little of this dark color into white to make a blue/gray, and then use this to mix a variety of other blues.  Paint the shark with at least three different tones of blue.  Leave the highlight on his back white (or paint it a very light blue).  His underbelly is also a very light blue.

For the Atlantic Pompano, add a little blue/green to his fins.  Make it a different blue/green than the water.  Paint the rest of his body with a series of lighter blues.  The Pompano fish is lighter in tone.  Remember, mix your colors in the circles above the fish before beginning.  Finally, paint the eyes of both fish with a deep orange.

## Paint Card #11:  *Painting Fish with Tones*

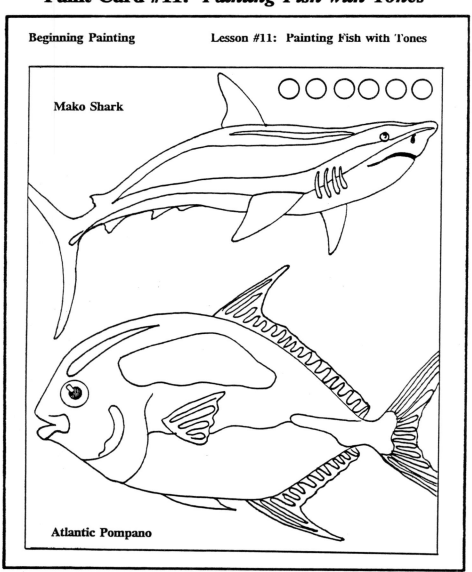

Beginning Painting                    Lesson #11:  Painting Fish with Tones

Mako Shark

Atlantic Pompano

# Lesson #225: *Painting Brown Boots*

Today, let's make some nice browns and paint the boots on *Paint Card #12*. There are many ways to make brown. Most beginning students make browns without even knowing it. Brown is a mixture of the other colors and there are a wide assortment of browns that you can make. Browns have many names: burnt umber, raw umber, burnt sienna, raw sienna, etc. Another name for browns is *earth colors*.

Notice that the boots were drawn with contour line - one continuous line going in and out, over and under. This style of drawing can create some interesting patterns for painting. Try making contour drawings of different objects or do a copy of the boots. When doing paintings from contour drawings, make sure that all the areas you create are fairly large, making then easy for painting.

violet      orange

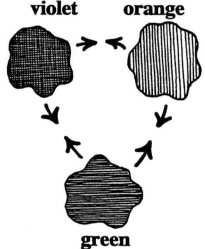

green

To make some earth colors, prepare a puddle of each of the three secondary colors. Mix a puddle of orange, a puddle of violet, and a puddle of green. One way of creating browns is by mixing two secondary colors together. First, mix violet and green together to make a brown. This will be a rather dark brown and will be good to paint inside the top of each boot, the little shoestring holes, and a couple of other areas on each boot. (With each color you mix, paint one of the small boots on the top of your paint card.) Before moving to the next color, add some white to your brown and create a lighter brown. Paint another one of the small boots on the top, and some more areas in the larger boots.

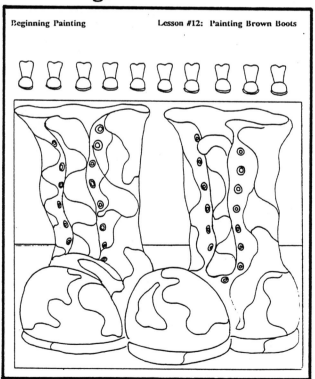

Beginning Painting      Lesson #12: Painting Brown Boots

**Paint Card #12:** *Brown Boots*

Next, mix green and orange together to make a lighter brown. Paint one of the smaller boots on the top of the card and then some of the areas on the two larger boots. Add some white to this brown, paint another small boot and some more areas on the larger boots. Then, mix orange and violet to create another brown. Paint one of the small boots on the top of the card, and some other areas on the larger boots. Add some white to this color and paint another small boot and other areas on your boots.

Finally, mix a brown by adding a touch of red to yellow and then a touch of blue or green. (Adding too much blue or green will make the brown turn greenish.) When you have made a nice brown, paint in one of small boots and add some more color to your larger boots. Add white to this brown and do the same. Try adding a little more red to your brown to make it reddish or a little more yellow to make it yellowish. Add all these colors to your boots. When you are finished, select two nice colors to color the background and the floor.

# Lesson #226:  *Depth with Warm & Cool Colors*

Did you know that some colors advance and other colors recede, or go back in the distance?  Colors like red, orange, and yellow advance.  Whereas, colors like blue, violet, and green go back in the distance.  Another way of putting it is that *warm colors advance and cool colors recede.*

For this assignment, place *Paint Card #13* in front of you.  Look at your color chart and decide what colors are warm and what colors are cool.  A color must be either warm or cool.  Then try to show depth in this picture, by painting the objects in front with warm colors.  All the objects in the background, or behind the other objects, should be painted with cool colors, as well as the distant background. Be creative in your painting with your selection of warm and cool colors!

Before beginning, make sure to test your colors by painting the small geometric shapes on the top of the card.  Sign your painting when finished.

# Lesson #227: *Painting Flesh Tones*

Place *Paint Card #14* in front of you. For this assignment, we are going to make flesh tones, or skin colors. All flesh tones, whether they are yellow, red, black, or white have a basic orange undertone. So, orange is the color you should start with in creating skin colors.

First, add a touch of red to yellow to make an orange. Add a touch of this orange to white and you have made a delightful flesh tone. Notice this is a very soft and subtle orange. The key to making a good flesh tone is to keep it *light*. When you have made your light flesh tone, color in one of the circles on the paint card and all the areas that are in light. Use the sun and arrow as a light source to show which side of your subject matter is going to be the lightest. Paint the light side of the figure, finger, and head. The fingernail will be an even lighter color, made by adding a touch more white to this color.

Mix a darker flesh tone by adding a touch more red and yellow to your flesh color. This is a truer orange color. Whenever you paint something, you will have a light side, a dark side, and a middle tone. The area in the middle, between the light and dark sides, will have the most true color in it. For example, if you were painting an apple, the most red would be in the middle area. Paint another one of the circles with this richer flesh tone and then paint the middle areas of the figure, finger, and head.

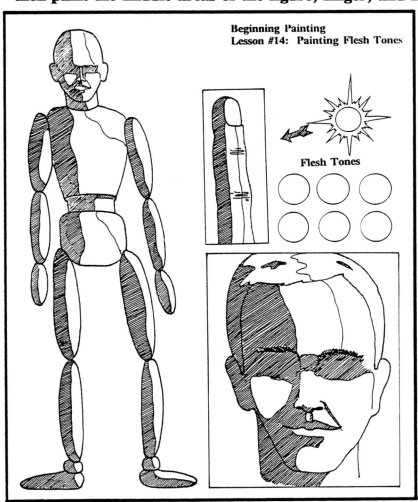

Finally, mix a darker color for the shaded parts. (Notice these areas have been shaded with line to assist you.) No details have been placed in the face. We are not going to concern ourselves with details at this time, but more with molding our subject matter with different tones of color. For this darker tone, add some blue or violet to your flesh color. This may seem awkward at first, but the more you paint like this, the more you will understand that areas in shade are painted with cool colors. Paint one of the circles and all the areas in shade. For the hair, mix a nice brown, making it lighter or darker by adding various combinations of white or red.

**Paint Card #14:** *Painting Flesh Tones*

# Lesson #228: *Reds & Greens*

Place *Paint Card #15* in front of you. Today you are going to paint a red apple and a green tree. Do you remember how to make a light red? First, add a touch of white to red and paint the first square. Add a touch of yellow to red and paint the second square. Notice that neither one of these colors makes a light red. Mix a light red by adding a touch of yellow and white to red and paint the third square and the light side of the apple. (This will be the right side with the little window, or highlight on it.) Do not paint over the highlight. Next, mix the middle tone for the apple. This will be in the area between the light side and the shaded side. The middle tone is the part of the apple that will have the most true color, or the richest red. However, do not use the red straight out of the container because it will be too bright or intense. Add just a little yellow and white to break down the color, but keep it much richer than the light side of the apple. For the shaded side of the apple, add a touch of blue to red. Do not add too much blue or it will turn muddy or violet. When you have mixed a deep, dark red, paint another square on the top of the card and then the shaded (left) side of the apple. Do you remember what the complement of red is? It is green. If you add a little touch of green to the red you made for the middle tone, you will make a dull red. Mix this color, and paint the next square. Add some white and yellow to it to lighten it up and paint the next square. Finally, add a touch of blue to make it darker, and paint the last square.

## Paint Card #15: *Reds & Greens*

Let's now make a light green. First mix a touch of blue into yellow, and paint the first square on the second row, the middle area of the tree, and the background trees. Then, add a little of this green to yellow and paint the second square, the light side of the tree (right), the grass around the tree (Do not paint the grass in the shaded area under the tree.), and the background behind the apple. (Remember, green is the complement of red, and can make a nice background color.) Make a slightly darker green by adding a touch more blue to it and paint the next square. Add a touch of red, the complement, to this green to dull it down and paint in another square. Finally, add a touch of blue to this dull green, paint another square, the shaded side of the tree, and the shade underneath.

In the third row of squares, see how many blues you can make. You can mix a blue with a touch of its complement, orange. You can add a touch of red to it to make it darker, and you can add different amounts of white to it to make it lighter. Then make the lightest blue you can and paint the sky behind the tree. In the last row, make a series of browns (refer to *Paint Card #12*), and select your nicest browns to paint the apple stem and tree trunk.

Finally, paint the little objects under the squares by *dip painting*. Dip painting is done by dipping your brush into three or four different colors, and painting with this combination. Do not go back and forth with your brush, but allow the colors to stay just the way they are when they come off your brush. Use your smallest brush for this exercise.

# Lesson #229: *Light & Shade*

Place *Paint Card #16* in front of you. Today you are going to paint light and shade, just like you did with flesh tones on *Paint Card #14*. The top row will be painted with red tones from light to dark; the middle row will be painted with a variety of blues; and the bottom row will be painted with green tones.

Do you remember how we made a red lighter? Add a little yellow and white to it. Remember, if you add just white to red, it will turn pink. And if you add just yellow to red, it will turn orange. Mix a light red, notice where the light is coming from, and paint the light side of the pyramid, can, and box. Paint the open lid of the can and box with this light color also. The middle tone will be the most red in color. Remember, the middle tone will be the truest (most red) color. For the inside of the opened can and box, and the left side of the can, add a touch of blue to your red to make it deeper and darker.

Paint the objects in the middle row blue. The light side will be a very light blue, made by mixing a touch of blue to white. The middle tone will be a medium, truer blue. (Add a touch of white to this middle tone, so it will not be too dark.) Finally, for the deep, dark areas inside the can and box, and the left side of the can, mix some red with blue to make a deeper, darker color.

The bottom row of objects will be painted with green. First, make a medium green by adding blue to yellow. Paint the middle of the pyramid, can, and box with this green. The light side of each object will be painted a very light green by adding just a touch of green to white. Make sure this green is very light. Finally, paint the inside of the can and box, and the left side of the can, with a very dark blue/green by adding more blue to your medium green.

## Paint Card #16: *Light & Shade*

# Lesson #230: *Painting Pastel Colors*

For our last paint card assignment, place *Paint Card #17* in front of you. Today you are going to paint some pastel flowers and green leaves. *Pastel colors* are colors that are light and colorful like pink, violet, and light blue. Evening skies are often filled with pastel colors. These are delightful colors to paint with and can create some colorful pictures.

See if you can make a nice pink, violet, light blue, and cream color. (Refer to your color chart for these colors.) Experiment with each color in the flowers on the top of the paint card before painting the flowers in the picture. Paint the center of the flowers with a light yellow/orange.

Drawing and painting leaves has always been a problem for most beginning students. First of all, you do not need to place a lot of details in your leaves. Look at the leaves behind the flowers. These were created by using one long contour line. Contour drawings are great for making compositions for painting. You may want to practice drawing leaves like this before beginning.

Do not paint all the leaves the same green. *Be colorful with your greens!* Mix a wide assortment of greens to use in your paintings. You can make a light green by adding yellow, a dark green by adding blue, a duller green by adding its complement - red, and you can change the tone by adding white. On the bottom of the paint card, mix at least six different greens and paint the leaves. Then, paint all the shapes behind the flowers with an assortment of lively greens.

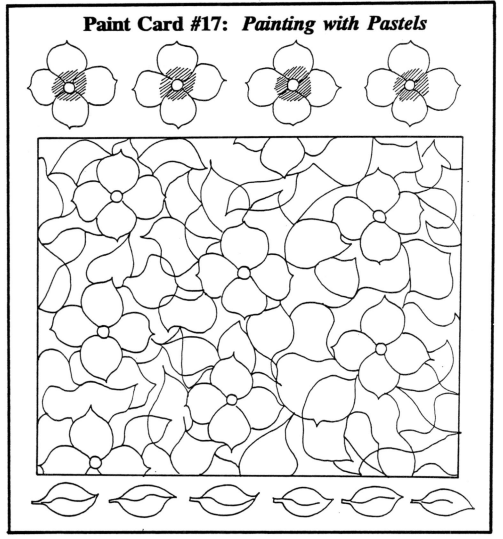

**Paint Card #17:** *Painting with Pastels*

# Painting on Poster Board

Poster board is a practical surface to paint on with acrylic paints. It is inexpensive and holds paint fairly well. An entire sheet of white poster board measures 22" x 28". However, it is more practical when cut into smaller sections. Cut some sheets to measure 11" x 14", and some to 5 1/2" x 7". For beginning painting, the smaller the better. It will really save on paint. Learning different techniques and experimenting with color and brush strokes does not need to be done on large surfaces.

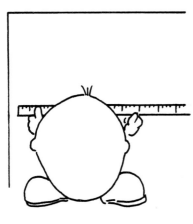

If you do not make parallel guidelines, your lines will be on a slant. Do you know how to draw a straight line that is equidistant from the top of the paper to the bottom? First, take a 22" x 28" sheet of poster board, and place it in front of you horizontally. With a ruler, measure down halfway, or 11" from the top right side and place a dot. Measure down the same 11" on the left side and place another dot (A). Connect the two dots with a yardstick, and you have a perfectly divided sheet of paper.

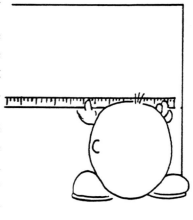

Take your ruler and measure 14" in from the top right side and place a dot. This will be the center of the poster board. Measure another 14" from the bottom right and place another dot. Connect the two and your poster board will be divided into even quarters (B). Cut the poster board and save the four 11" x 14" sheets for future painting exercises.

Now, place one 11" x 14" sheet horizontally and divide it in half. Measure 5 1/2" down from the top right corner and place a dot. Mark the same 5 1/2" down from the top left and place a dot. Connect with a straight line. Then, measure 7" in from the top right and 7" from the bottom right, and place dots. Connect the dots, and your poster board will be divided into four equal sections of 5 1/2" by 7" (C). Cut and save for future painting assignments.

A.
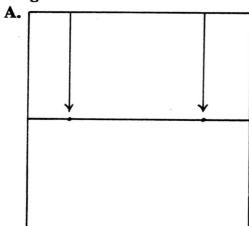

B.
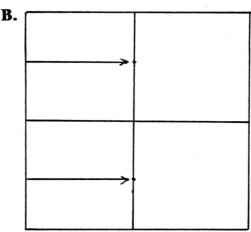

C.
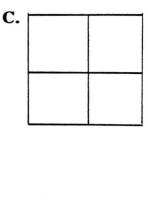

**Pointer:** You may want to cut some at 5 1/2" x 14", and then fold in half to 5 1/2" x 7". This size should fit into the standard card envelope. This is an excellent size for making greeting cards!

## Lesson #231: *Coloring Cartoon Characters*

A.

There are many styles of painting. We have gone over several methods and techniques. Today we are going to paint flat. Most of the time I do not recommend a *flat* approach, but sometimes it can be beneficial. Many illustrations that you see in the comic section of the newspaper are done with flat and bold colors. It is a very simple, basic approach to painting.

To the left is a simple cartoon figure (A). The shapes are very basic. It's quite easy to color in the shapes with flat colors. Draw a cartoon character in figure box B. Keep the design large and simple. You may want to copy a cartoon character from a book or comic section. When you have it just the way you want it, copy your character over again on one of your 11" x 14" poster board sections and paint it with bright and lively colors.

B.

*"As water reflects a face, so a man's heart reflects the man."* **Proverbs 27:19**

## Lesson #232: *Contour Design Painting*

Let's do a painting that is simple and basic, like stained glass. Marc Chagall did some colorful paintings this way. George Rouault was another painter who broke everything down into the simplest components. You may want to go to the library and look at some of their artwork.

Do a contour drawing for this assignment. First, find a story or picture from the Bible that you like. Use one of your 11" x 14" poster boards and do your drawing with one continuous line. Allow the pencil to go over and under other lines, not lifting it from the paper the entire time. Practice your drawing on a piece of paper before doing your finished assignment on the poster board.

Notice the nice patterns you are creating. As different as these patterns may look, you will still be able to see the images that you had in your mind or that you had copied from a picture. When you have finished, turn to *Paint Card #9: Analogous Colors*, and select four colors that are next to each other on the color wheel to paint your picture with. Or, select some creative colors from your color chart to color your picture with.

## Lesson #233:  *Painting a Greeting Card*

For this assignment, you are going to paint a greeting card.  Take one of your 5 1/2" x 14" pieces of poster board, and fold it in half to 5 1/2" x 7".  *Score* your fold by pressing a ruler firmly along the crease from one side to the other.

Select a work by one of the Impressionists to copy.  Find a picture that is relatively simple and colorful.  You may want to look at works by Monet, Pissarro, or Van Gogh.  Draw the picture in the figure box below before beginning on your card.  Be colorful with your picture.  Practice *"dip painting,"* and be an impressionist!

# Independent Studies

Now that you have finished the chapter on painting, what else would you like to paint? Remember, whatever you decide to paint, try to use color theory in mixing, blending, and applying colors. Before doing a painting, it is also good to do a little drawing of it with colored pencils to make sure you have everything just the way you like. Listed below are some assignments that you may want to paint as independent studies.

**Lesson # 234:** *Sunrises & Sunsets* Cut two pieces of white poster board to a size of 11" x 14", and paint a sunrise on one and a sunset on the other. You can go outside and paint from life, or copy from pictures. Look at skies painted by William Turner.

**Lesson #235:** *Painting a Still Life* Paint a still life of fruit with analogous colors. Use fruit that are similar in color, like plums and purple grapes, or peaches and oranges, or limes and green grapes. Use a sheet of 5 1/2" x 7" white poster board.

**Lesson #236:** *Pots & Pans* Find some pots and pans that have the same basic color and set them up in a pleasing composition. Your shadow box would be good for this. Do a drawing of your composition first, and then do your painting on an 11" x 14" piece of white poster board.

**Lesson #237:** *Green Bottles* Collect several green bottles and place them in a pleasing composition. Do your painting on a sheet of 11" x 14" white poster board. Can you mix a variety of greens? Do not forget to use the complementary color. What color will you background be?

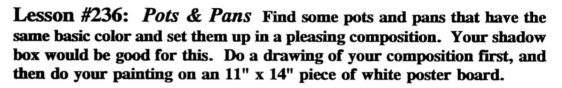

**Lesson #238:** *Stories from the Bible* Select some stories from the Bible to paint. Do a thorough drawing before beginning. You may want to find Biblical illustrations and paintings to copy from. Research Carl Bloch and Rembrandt van Rijn.

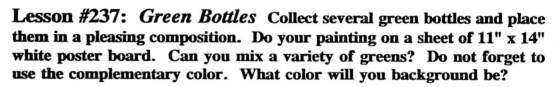

**Lesson #239:** *A Farm Scene* Paint a farm scene. If there is not one nearby, you may want to look in a magazine. *Country Magazine* or *Creation Magazine* usually have some beautiful farm scenes to copy.

**Lesson #240:** *A Winter Scene* Find a winter scene to paint. You may want to copy from a picture or photograph. The important thing is to see other colors in snow besides white. Try placing a very light blue or violet in some of the shaded areas and a light touch of pink in other areas. Lightly draw in your composition with a colored pencil.

**Lesson #241:** *A Colorful Clown* Find a picture of a colorful clown and paint it on a sheet of 11" x 14" poster board.

### Lesson #242: *Painting Flowers*

Do a painting of flowers. You may want to draw your picture with contour line to keep it simple. Use a light colored pencil, and draw your picture on 5 1/2" x 7" poster board before beginning. Try colored poster board. Make sure to mix a variety of greens for the leaves and stems. Use your color chart to select nice, colorful colors.

### Lesson #243: *Springtime*

Find a picture of springtime and do a painting of it on a sheet of 5 1/2" x 11" light blue poster board. Before beginning, lightly draw in everything with a colored pencil. Check your color chart for some nice, light pastel colors.

### Lesson #244: *Painting a Self-Portrait*

Do a self-portrait on a sheet of 5 1/2" x 11" brown or other colored poster board. Look in a mirror to do your portrait and place a good light on your face to create a light side and a shaded side. Lightly draw your portrait first.

### Lesson #245: *A Tree with Many Greens*

Go outside and paint a tree. If it is not summertime, paint a tree by copying from a picture in a magazine. Do your painting on 5 1/2" x 11" poster board and use a variety of greens in painting the leaves.

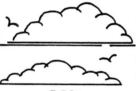

### Lesson #246: *Painting Clouds*

Go outside and paint some clouds on a piece of 11" x 14" blue poster board. Try to see the light side and the shaded sides of the clouds and paint more colors than just white in your clouds.

### Lesson #247: *Painting from Memory*

Find something that you want to paint. You may want to do a study of objects on a shelf of your kitchen cabinet, or what is outside the window, or a plant. Do a painting of it without looking at the subject you are painting. Painting from memory will allow you to be more creative!

### Lesson #248: *Tropical Fish*

Take a large sheet of white or blue poster board and draw large and small tropical fish on it. Then, paint them with lively, tropical colors.

### Lesson #249: *Contour Drawing & Painting*

On a sheet of 11" x 14" poster board, do a contour drawing of a subject of your choice, making sure that your drawing is one continuous line. Then, select colors from your color chart to color the different areas.

### Lesson #250: *Copy the Masters*

Find a reproduction of a painting by George Rouault and copy it on a 5 1/2" x 7" sheet of white poster board. Also, copy a picture of Edgar Degas' ballerinas on another sheet of poster board. Select colors from your color chart.

**Lesson #251:** *Painting Peaches* Set three peaches in front of you. Use your shadow box if possible and place colored paper under them for a nice backdrop. Paint them large on a sheet of 11" x 14" poster board.

**Lesson #252:** *Painting Onions* Place several onions on some brown paper. A paper bag will be fine. Shine a light on them and draw them large on a sheet of 11" x 14" white poster board. Do you see other colors in the onions?

**Lesson #253:** *Colorful Birds* Find four pictures of colorful birds, and draw each on a sheet of 5 1/2" x 7" white poster board. You may want to try using different colored poster board to paint them on or even to make colorful greeting cards with your pictures. Make sure to draw large.

**Lesson #254:** *Three Ties* Find three colorful neckties and place them in a pleasing composition. Draw them on a sheet of 11" x 14" white poster board and then color the patterns and designs with bright and lively colors!

**Lesson #255:** *Zoo Animals* Select some zoo animals from pictures: a zebra, giraffe, tiger, etc., and draw them on 5 1/2" x 7" sheets of white poster board. Then, color them with colors that match their true colors.

**Lesson #256:** *Colorful Rocks* Find three small rocks or stones and place them in front of you. Select some nice colored paper to put behind and under them and draw them large on a sheet of 5 1/2" x 7" poster board. How many colors do you see in the stones besides black, brown, and grey? See if you can make them colorful.

**Lesson #257:** *Painting to Classical Music* Select some classical music to listen to. Close your eyes and see what you imagine. What colors do you see? What type of feeling do you get from listening to the music? See if you can paint what you imagine from listening to the music. If nothing else, just paint nice colors to go along with the music.

**Lesson #258:** *Earth Colors* Earth colors are all the browns that you see in nature, such as trees, leaves, dirt, and stones. Go outside and find some bark and nuts from a tree. Place it in front of you, and see if you can paint it matching the exact browns that you see.

**Pointer:** Remember, paint on different colored poster board. You will have some wonderful results! Try brown, blue, red, orange, yellow, or green to paint on and see what you think.

*"Write them on the doorposts of your houses and on your gates."* Deuteronomy 6:9

## Lesson #259: *Keeping a Journal*

This will be your last journal entry in *Feed My Sheep*. Make it as interesting as possible! Practice penmanship and let your thoughts be creative. What about observations and revelations in your studies? What are you going to draw and discuss? The lines for you to write on are not included. See if you can lightly draw in your own guidelines or place a piece of lined paper underneath the page to write on. This will assist you in keeping your own journal.

# Lesson #260: *Painting Examination*

**I. True or False?** Place a "T" or "F" next to each number (3 points each).

1. Hold a brush as close to the hairs as possible when painting.
2. A palette is an apron used when painting.
3. Brushes should be placed on your palette when not in use.
4. Red, orange, and yellow are warm colors.
5. Secondary colors are green, violet, and blue.
6. Orange and yellow make red.
7. A monochromatic painting is done with red, orange, and yellow.
8. An analogous painting is done with any three colors that are next to each other on the color wheel.
9. Leave your brushes in water for a long period of time to remove the paint.
10. The best way to shade a color is by adding black.

**II. Fill in the blanks** (5 points each).

1. The three areas that make up a landscape are foreground, background, and

   _____.
2. A _____ color is good to use for dulling another color.
3. Red and _____, and a touch of blue make brown.
4. Red, blue, and _____ make black.
5. _____ and white make pink.

**III. Essay.** Who is your favorite artist. Discuss one of your favorite paintings by him or her and explain why (15 points).

_____

_____

_____

_____

_____

_____

**IV. Essay.** Suppose that you are going to do a painting of flowers. Explain three color theories that you will use in your painting (20 points).

_____

_____

_____

_____

_____

_____

**V. Essay.** Explain why you should not use black and brown in your paintings as a beginning artist and what colors you could use as a replacement for these (10 points).

_____

_____

_____

(Answers on page 310)

# Answers to Exams

## Lesson #23:
### Color Examination

I.
1. green
2. yellow
3. red
4. orange
5. violet
6. blue
7. blue
8. analogous
9. white
10. green
11. violet
12. orange
13. red, yellow, orange
14. blue, green, violet
15. black, brown

## Lesson #71:
### Drawing Examination

I.
1. E
2. Q
3. H
4. I
5. P
6. J
7. D
8. A
9. O
10. S
11. C
12. L
13. T
14. N
15. B
16. G
17. K
18. R
19. M
20. F

III.
1. F
2. T
3. T
4. T
5. F

II.
1. student's choice
2. values
3. line
4. horizontal
5. lines, lines

## Lesson #96:
### Rules & Measurements

I.
1. horizon line
2. vanishing point
3. eye level
4. two
5. two
6. depth
7. technical
8. guidelines

## Lesson #121
### Anatomy & Portraits

I.
1. 8
2. eye
3. pelvis
4. 5
5. nose
6. Leonardo Da Vinci
7. front, three-quarters & profile
8. self-portrait
9. Renaissance
10. portrait

II.
1. C
2. D
3. F
4. H
5. G
6. B
7. E
8. A
9. J
10. I

## Lesson #185:
### Art Appreciation

I.
1. G
2. H
3. D
4. J
5. A
6. B
7. C
8. E
9. F
10. I

II.
1. Raphael
2. Remington
3. Byzantine art
4. Hellenistic
5. student's choice

## Lesson #210:
### Academia

I.
1. astronomy
2. nutrition
3. history
4. entomology
5. botany
6. philatelist
7. composition
8. anatomy
9. zoology
10. science
11. numismatics

II.
1. T
2. F
3. T
4. F
5. F
6. F
7. F
8. T
9. F
10. T

## Lesson #260:
### Painting

I.
1. F
2. F
3. F
4. T
5. F
6. F
7. F
8. T
9. F
10. F

II.
1. middle ground
2. complementary
3. yellow
4. green or yellow
5. red

*"May He give you the desires of your heart and make all your plans succeed."*

Psalm 20:4

**Dear Students,**

I hope you have enjoyed *Feed My Sheep,* and have learned about art through a wide range of subjects. My wife and I would love to hear from you. Maybe you would like to give us your comments on the book, or tell us about lessons that you really liked or had difficulty with, or send us copies of your artwork. If nothing else, write us just to say, *"Hello."* Until we meet again, *"May the Lord bless you and keep you, and may His face shine upon you."*

In Christ,

*Stebbing*

**Barry F. Stebbing**
Box 48 Dept 18
MacFarlan, NC 28102

# Do You Have All Your All Materials?

Do you need any of the recommended art supplies to complete your art lessons? *How Great Thou ART Publications* has everything needed for each and every lesson from *Baby Lambs Book of ART* all the way up to *God & the History of Art.* These art materials are the supplies that Barry Stebbing specifically recommends for the various courses and curriculum, selecting the best quality at the most reasonable price. For example, the Prismacolor pencils made by Berol are ideal for all the colored pencil exercises and the pure pigment blending paints are excellent for the painting assignments. Likewise, the watercolor markers, drawing pencils, and brushes have been well tested and approved. Give us a call today! The art materials will be sent out to you immediately and your student will then be ready to do his very best work! Ask about our *"bundle package"* special.

# Do You Need Extra Paint Cards?

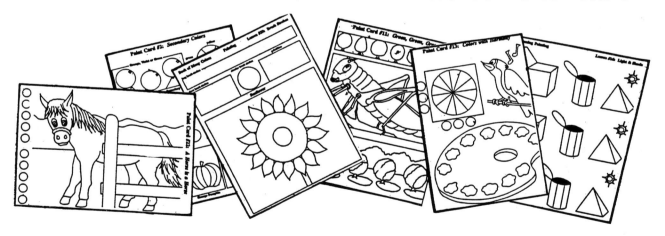

*Paint Cards* are 8 1/2" x 11" heavy, index stock cards used for the painting assignments in *I Can Do All Things, Feed My Sheep, God & the History of Art,* and *The Book of Many Colors.* Even though one set of paint cards is included with each of these texts, Barry Stebbing recommends one set per student. For extra sets of paint cards at a special price call our office today.

·····························································································

**How Great Thou ART Publications  1-800-982-DRAW**

e-mail: howgreat@vnet.net  Visit our gallery on the Web!: www.howgreatthouart.com

*Don't forget to ask for a free catalog!*

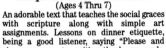
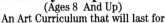